PELICAN BOOKS

A669

THE CHURCH OF ENGLAND

PAUL FERRIS

Paul Ferris was born in Swansea in 1929 and educated at Swansea Grammar School. He served for two years in the R.A.F. after the war, worked on an evening newspaper in Swansea, and came to London in 1953. He is a freelance writer but works in close association with the *Observer*, on which he spent six months as news editor in 1962. He has broadcast and written for magazines. He has written an inquiry into the City of London, *The City*, and has had three novels published, *A Changed Man* (1958), *Then We Fall* (1960), and *A Family Affair* (1963). Paul Ferris is married and has two children.

PAUL FERRIS

THE CHURCH OF ENGLAND

PENGUIN BOOKS

Penguin Books Ltd, Harmondsworth, Middlesex, England
Penguin Books Pty Ltd, Ringwood, Victoria, Australia

—

First published 1962
This revised edition published by Penguin Books 1964

—

Copyright © Paul Ferris, 1962, 1964

—

Made and printed in Great Britain
by Cox & Wyman Ltd
London, Fakenham, and Reading
Set in Monotype Bembo

CONTENTS

NOTE TO THIS EDITION

The original edition of this book, published in November 1962, was a few months too early for the explosion caused by the Bishop of Woolwich's paperback, Honest to God, *which came out in good time for Easter 1963. Before* Honest to God *one could smell the fuses burning, but the precise location and extent of the forthcoming blast were uncertain. By Whitsun 1963, a clergyman who, a few years ago, had published a book criticizing the Church of England, was writing to me – a little sourly, I thought – that 'for radical treatment of the religious situation, the Bishop of Woolwich seems to have beaten us both'. He certainly had.*

Other fuses are burning; other explosions are in prospect. The present edition of this book includes a little of the smoke.

I would like to thank the clergymen
who helped me when I was gathering material
for this book, and read some of the chapters; my
wife, for her research; and
John Silverlight and Ivan Yates, who
gave valuable advice.

CHAPTER ONE

A VIEW OF THE CHURCH

ALTHOUGH the Church of England's history is strewn with dismal predictions that have been proved wrong, it's hard for an outsider to avoid the conclusion that something has it by the throat. For the moment, the attack is being contained. The Church is so large and old, it presents so many faces and operates at so many levels – moral, social, spiritual, mystical – that assaults on (or by) one part of it are easily dealt with by the others. There are convenient words to dismiss heresies and deviations; 'pelagianism' or 'antinomianism' rest like poultices on the sore spots. There are convenient categories in which to put clergymen with uncomfortable ideas – those who say, as some are now beginning to say in loud and tactless voices, that the Church must consider everything and insist on very little. They can be written off as academics: not for them the hurly-burly of a tough parish in Bradford or Bristol, but cool cloisters and dangerous books by foreign theologians, from which they raise their heads only to appear on television – egged on by producers to compete with Evensong by broadcasting ruderies about the Church. Or they can be scooped up in a phrase – 'the Cambridge school of theologians', or, better still, 'South Bank Religion', meaning religion as practised in the Diocese of Southwark, which extends over South London from the River Thames.

But the innovators arouse more than gestures of annoyance and contempt. One sign of anxiety among those in the Church who oppose the 'new theology' is that, while the innovators are dismissed as a hapless minority who know no better, they are also taken seriously as the harbingers of moral ruin. When the Profumo scandal came to light in June 1963, the *Church Times*, the leading Anglican newspaper in Britain, carried letters and comments that linked, in unequivocal terms, sexual immorality and the wicked liberalism of the 'new theologians'. It may be that these were the views of another hapless minority. But it was a vocal minority, and represented an important stream of thought within the Church.

Some of the events that led up to this situation are traced in more detail in Chapter 11. A Cambridge clergyman, H. A. Williams, the Dean of Chapel of Trinity College, was an early spokesman, with television broadcasts in 1960 and 1961 in which he questioned the historical detail of the Resurrection, and suggested that fornication is not always and inevitably wrong. *Soundings*, a collection of 'Essays Concerning Christian Understanding', was published in September 1962, edited by Dr Alec Vidler, Dean of King's College, Cambridge, and caused a modest stir. Some of the eleven essays were too abstruse to make an impact outside narrow circles, and perhaps the two that received most of the popular attention were those by Vidler himself and H. A. Williams. Vidler wrote about the Church of England's possible development as a Church unencumbered by too much formal religion. Williams, who is keenly interested in psychology and analysis, wrote about 'the effect of self-awareness upon our understanding of morality'. He was roundly attacked by many Christians, and he was widely supposed to have said, once again, that fornication didn't matter. What he did say was that to exploit another person or oneself was wrong: promiscuous love-making might mean exploitation in most cases, but where it didn't, there was no sin.

But the crucial book was the Bishop of Woolwich's *Honest to God*. This little paperback of 141 pages, published on 19

March 1963, has become the theological best-seller of all time. It was preceded by a potted version of the Bishop's thesis in the *Observer*, headed 'Our Image of God Must Go'. This phrase didn't occur in the article. But on page 124 of the book, the bishop says that 'we have to be prepared for *everything* to go into the melting-pot – even our most cherished religious categories and moral absolutes. And the first thing we must be ready to let go is our image of God himself.' *Honest to God* derives from other books by other theologians, but it was the first voice from a high place within the Church of England that seemed to be casting doubt on large areas of traditional Christian faith, or at least on many ingredients of that faith. 'God', in these terms, emerged as a kind of synonym for 'reality': no more.

The Bishop's views were soon being quoted out of context – but this, after all, is the way in which most people receive radical ideas. The Church of England has become aware of powerful threats to its peace of mind and perhaps to the structure of its beliefs. Confusion over what, exactly, the Church of England *does* believe has been delighting cynics and worrying Christians with a conscience for many years – perhaps for centuries. But there has never been such a confrontation as the one that has been dragged into the open by *Honest to God*.

At least the Church of England is an appropriate place for this to be happening. Among the Church's clergy, let alone its laymen, there are wide differences of opinion on doctrine, and no central authority exists to make theological statements *ex cathedra*; it's a long way from the Roman Catholic situation. The theoretical position was set out in the thirty-nine Articles of Religion, drawn up about 1562 to define doctrine for the newly-formed Church after it had broken with the Pope. They are unequivocal statements. Article 4, 'Of the Resurrection of Christ', says: 'Christ did truly rise again from death, and took again his body, with flesh, bones, and all things appertaining to the perfection of Man's nature; wherewith he ascended into Heaven, and there sitteth, until he return to judge all Men at the last day.'

Before a man is ordained, and again each time he goes to work in a parish, as vicar or curate, he must give 'general assent' to the Articles. Some clergymen say they should be taken literally – this view is heard most often from Low churchmen, the Evangelicals, since the Articles were drawn up at the height of Protestantism after the Reformation. High churchmen, the Anglo-Catholics, object to this Protestant bias; they might, for instance, dispute the statement in Article 28 that belief in Transubstantiation, the changing of the substance of the bread and wine at Holy Communion into the flesh and blood of Christ, is 'repugnant to the plain words of Scripture'. Dr J. I. Packer, a Low Church theologian, who pleads for their absolute acceptance, writes ominously that 'No Christian society can nourish itself on the poisonous diet of double-talk and double-think'. But many clergymen seem to find it a nourishing diet, and go on conveniently half-believing in the Articles. The rare public protests catch the headlines. One unusual clergyman, the Rev. John Pearce-Higgins, who went from a London suburb to a post at Southwark Cathedral in 1963, made a protest before the bishop in the cathedral, and set off a round of attacks and counter-attacks. But to amend the Articles would be a huge and dangerous task; the sophisticated view is that it would also be an unnecessary one, since the Articles have never been indispensable to Anglicanism. And so the Church continues, in theory, to subscribe to them, and to everything in its Book of Common Prayer, including such statements as the one in the Athanasian Creed that those outside the Faith shall 'perish everlastingly'.

Everlasting damnation is far removed from the Christianity

of Williams, Vidler, Robinson, and the rest; it also goes against the grain for more orthodox churchmen. The head of the Church, the Archbishop of Canterbury, can say, and Dr Ramsey, the present Archbishop, has said, that he personally expects to meet atheists in Heaven. 'I expect to meet some present-day atheists there,' he said in an interview with the *Daily Mail* in 1961. At first a number of clergymen suggested privately that the Archbishop was misquoted – there is no end to the possibilities of misquotation over theology. When it was established that the Archbishop did say it,* many clergymen accepted the statement as a decently liberal sentiment. The *Church Times* remarked that it was 'perhaps hardly calculated to encourage parish priests in their endeavours to convince unbelievers of the utter necessity of saving faith in Christ'. Dr Packer said in the *Church of England Newspaper* that the Archbishop was wrong, suggesting that to entertain the idea of the salvation of atheists was 'false charity, the sort of kindness that kills'. Plaintive letters appeared from churchpeople, lay and clergy, who asked what they were supposed to be doing if anyone could be saved. A man at the Church Society, a doctrinaire organization, said to me sharply: 'The atheist doesn't have to face Dr Ramsey, he has to face God', and the *Church Gazette*, the society's journal, was soon rebuking the Archbishop with a text from St John, 'He that believeth not is

* Lambeth Palace agreed on the phone that the Archbishop had used the words, but said the article gave a 'necessarily much shortened account'. An expanded version, as given by the Archbishop's secretary in a letter, was: 'The Archbishop believes, of course, that those who reject belief in God are in great spiritual peril since salvation is through the atoning work of Our Lord. On the other hand he believes that we are taught by Our Lord's parable of the sheep and the goats that some who have had no chance of knowing Our Lord in this life may yet receive an eternal reward through having unconsciously ministered to Him.'

condemned already'. The row, such as it was, soon subsided – the only part of it that most people saw was the original remark in the *Daily Mail* – and things went on as before.

Whether an atheist can enter Heaven may be a difficult question, but nothing like so difficult as the question of what the phrase 'Heaven' is supposed to convey. A middle-aged clergyman who has lost his faith (but continues to preach and administer the Sacraments 'out of nostalgia'; there are a few like him) suggested that it was all very well to say that the old ideas of Heaven and Hell were unsophisticated and could safely be treated as mythology. His father, he said, was also a parson. 'Inside his church was a little door for the Devil to leave by as the congregation entered – that was what people *believed*. Heaven and Hell were as real to them as the floor and ceiling are to us. To talk glibly about "imagery" is trying to get out of an awkward spot.'

Many of the faithful say flatly that the Virgin Birth and Resurrection are facts, that they must be believed in literally, that it's folly to try to make faith easy for outsiders, that Christianity is 'a mystery religion, the prerogative of initiates, and the Church is not an inclusive, but an exclusive society' – this was a writer in *Prism*, a magazine run by a High-Church ginger group.

Going from one clergyman to another, it's sometimes hard to believe they inhabit the same Church; 'diversity' becomes contradiction. The Rev. Nick Earle is a young teacher of mathematics and an open-air preacher at Tower Hill, in London, who wrote a Penguin Special called *What's Wrong with the Church?* He had Firsts in mathematics and theology at Cambridge, and, though he would probably resent the description, is a rising young intellectual; his book is informed and radical (though not in the sense of *Honest to God*) and some ecclesiastical reviewers criticized it for being immoderate. Earle said, in conversation, that 'While I think one can leave the Virgin Birth on one side in the main argument, with the Resurrection one cannot. It's a fact, it's unique, and there's no possibility of comparing it with anything. I decline to entertain any epithets to the word "fact": this is Resurrection fact'. Earle takes his stand on the Bible: life and one's senses prove nothing. 'I can show someone a sunset, he can show me a cancerous bone. There simply is no evidence for the existence of Jesus Christ except in the person of Jesus Christ.'

Another young Church intellectual, the Rev. David Edwards, born in 1929 – Earle was born in 1926 – took a First in modern history at Oxford, and has been a Fellow of All Souls, the first to be ordained for nearly half a century. Edwards, too, has written a well-reviewed though politer book about the Church, *Not Angels but Anglicans*. He is managing editor of the S.C.M. (Student Christian Movement) Press, which published *Honest to God*. Edwards's personal views on the Resurrection, again in conversation, were as follows:

In late Victorian times the question of whether Jesus rose from the dead was a fascinating one – you couldn't carry on believing in God if you didn't believe it. But in the twentieth century the general religious certainties have crumbled away, and we've realized that to believe in Christ as the Lord is the main thing. The historical question of whether he rose from the dead doesn't matter in comparison. I think he did, but that's not the centre. The suggestion that he did doesn't make sense unless you have a tremendous belief in him. An existential commitment to Christ as Lord is what matters.

Edwards, like the Bishop of Woolwich, would find himself agreeing with much of what the German theologian, Rudolf Bultmann, says about the need to 'demythologize' the Gospel, separating the hard core of what is relevant to Christian life today from the ancient and mythical view of things.

'Bultmann says the Virgin Birth and the Resurrection are myth. The thing to do is to concentrate on what the myth is intended to express.' For Edwards, the debate has moved on from the simple question of 'true or false?' that still concerns most people – a greater number, perhaps, than he would be willing to concede. But he agrees that 'a lot of the clergy, and most churchgoers, would say that without the Resurrection, there's nothing'.

Any two clergymen are likely to disagree on, say, the probability of direct divine intervention in everyday life. Some will say that one can hardly expect to comprehend the divine plan, and see God's hand in trivial matters. Some will use euphemisms like 'a continuing interest'. Some will accept it without reservation, like the parson who said his college principal, dying of cancer, was saved by prayer, or the friar who said he received his call to the religious life as a result of seeing T. S. Eliot's *The Cocktail Party*. Soon after, his parish priest sent him to see the Anglican Benedictines at Nashdom Abbey. 'When I got there, one of the brothers was writing a thesis on Eliot's work – what my Communist uncle would call coincidence, but what I see as a definite calling to me by God.' A vicar's wife recalled how she and her husband had been praying for the financial needs of the parish. 'Not long after this the archdeacon came and told us he'd got some money to spend,' she said cheerfully. 'It's not often God answers prayers in this way – one's astonished, though one shouldn't be.'

Such beliefs coexist uneasily with sophisticated talk of 'demythologizing' and books like *Honest to God*. Only an idiosyncratic church with its roots in the obstinacies of the English temperament could survive the tensions. 'The Anglican theological position,' a clergyman reminded me, 'has been to secure general agreement on primary matters

16

and to let the rest go by private assent. Elizabeth I's statement about not making windows into men's souls is a good
one.'

The Church's diversity is what its clergy like, most of all, to
impress upon outsiders (in the uproar over the 'new theology', the merits and demerits of being 'comprehensive' have
been sharply canvassed. Those who are radically inclined
suggest that here is the great opportunity for Anglicanism to
justify its freedom; the conservatives say crossly that toleration
is all very well, but this is going too far). The Church presents
the paradox of an institution 'by law established', with the
Sovereign as its 'supreme governor', that owes much of its
strength to the fact that it has always been carefully and un-
institutionally vague about matters that might blow it apart.
Even the phrase 'by law established' appears to have no legal
authority, and the exact relationship of Sovereign to Church
is even more difficult to define than the relationship of Sovereign to State. The Church has two kinds of central government – the Convocations of Canterbury and York and the
Church Assembly, which includes a secretariat on Civil Service lines at Church House, Westminster. But authority is dis-
persed and hard to isolate; the most centralized function is that
of the Church Commissioners, a part-clergy, part-lay body
that controls the bulk of the Church's capital.

The alternative to vagueness and looseness is to be an
authoritarian Church, which is the Roman Catholic solution;
Anglicans usually regard this with distaste. The parson's freehold gives the occupant of the vicarage or rectory (vicar and
rector are now the same thing) a legal title to his house and
garden, as well as to the churchyard and perhaps to other
land – his 'glebe', on which he can farm, or even operate a
coal mine should there happen to be one there already. It gives
him security, encourages him to speak his mind, and helps

THE CHURCH OF ENGLAND

maintain the anti-authoritarian tradition of which it is itself a part.

Christians like to give precise definitions of the Church, though the definitions are usually meant for those who are in it. 'The true image of the Church's function in society is that of a beacon light set on a hill, throwing its beams for all to see so that none can say where the light ends and darkness begins,' wrote Leslie Hunter, the former Bishop of Sheffield. 'People must realize that the Church is not merely the parson,' the Bishop of Southwark, Mervyn Stockwood, told the *Daily Mail*. 'It is Christians living in a community and penetrating society at every level.' Dr Wand, a former Bishop of London, said it was 'not a very hazardous conclusion to draw, and may even be regarded as inescapable, that the Church is intended to be, and actually is, an anticipation of Heaven here upon earth.'

Perhaps the definition most often heard, and one that's especially popular with young and authoritarian clergymen, is that the Church is an organization for worship: not a bureau for furthering sound morals or a pressure-group for better behaviour, but the place men arrive at in order to worship God. It is, they will point out, the definition of the nineteenth of the Church's thirty-nine Articles: 'The visible Church of Christ is a congregation of faithful men, in the which the pure Word of God is preached, and the Sacraments be duly ministered. . . .' While numbers of clergymen are anxious to prove – whether by protesting against the Bomb or opening coffee bars – how relevant they are, others make a virtue of being irrelevant in the eyes of pagans. Nick Earle wrote in *What's Wrong with the Church?* that 'What the world calls the irrelevance of the Church is its essential characteristic' – Earle's phrase for it was 'otherworldly quality'. The test of any ecclesiastical organization, said Earle, is 'the extent to

18

which it affords Almighty God the opportunity of proving the power – not of a general and well-meaning beneficence – but of his own particular kind of love'.

The outsider who asks about the Church is told that he can't understand it unless he's inside it, even, sometimes, that it's impertinent of him to try. A Durham clergyman, asked about the strategy, or lack of it, of English parishes, said it was 'very easy to start worrying about whether we've got the right technique or whether there may be some method or vision which so far has escaped us. Behind it all lies the uneasy feeling that we ought to be "successful". Once we start worrying about that, we are sure to be less than faithful'. Ask innocently about 'reputations' in the Church, and whether they are more easily made in town or country parishes, and among the more worldly replies will be a sprinkling of tart remarks: 'I'm not interested in reputations' (a Lincolnshire town clergyman) and 'Clergy aren't ordained to make reputations, but to serve the Church where they are needed' (an Anglican monk). The clergyman who has lost his faith, quoted earlier, said the trouble was that once the secularist became a believer, the reasons for his disbelief ceased to mean anything: 'Ideas are tamed when they're taken into the Church.' But he was a believer who had become a secularist, and the reverse process had been at work.

Outsiders rarely bother to define the Church of England, and when they do it usually pains the churchman, because it must (he thinks) be wrong. The popular image of the Church has some sour ingredients. The scowling clergyman in the newspaper picture-strip says things like 'I'll deal with her when she returns' and 'I absolutely forbid you to go on with this nonsense, and that's an end of it' – this was in the *Daily Mail*'s 'Carol Day' serial, and made a man at the Church Information Office angry. 'Typical Curate Style' is sufficient as a stage-comedian's instruction, with a peppering of 'deah Vicars' and 'Ah, yesses!' in the script. The up-to-the-minute clergyman may find himself lampooned just as drastically, as in Michael Frayn's account in the *Guardian* of 'St Vitus's Yuthe Klub at East Screwe, where the Reverend Al Parsons officiates. The Reverend Al not only wears drainpipes and winkle-pickers, but also plays chicken on his autocycle, smashes the juke-box at dances, and is regularly caught writing "damn" and "bottom" on the lavatory wall'. There is also the friendly, middle-class joke, often found in *Punch*, where it's somehow clear that the clergyman in the picture is meant to be an Anglican. Mahood's drawing of a clergyman at breakfast, rebuking his wife for burning the toast, is typical: 'Dash it, Emily, that's the third time this week I've had to retract grace.' From the upper-middle-class standpoint, the Church is often mildly amusing – Established, 'one of us', doing a grand job, and able to take a joke at its own expense. The twenty-six (of forty-three) diocesan bishops who have *ex officio* seats in the House of Lords make few speeches there these days, and are heard in strength only on such topics as capital punishment. But the Lords are quick to spot an ecclesiastical joke. When they were discussing how to make motorways safer, the Bishop of Leicester asked that 'As an alternative to the crash barrier will the Government consider the excavation of a continuous trench or pit, thereby limiting the disastrous consequences to the vehicle leaving its course?' This was followed by:

LORD CHESHAM (Parliamentary Secretary, Ministry of Transport): It is usually considered to be the business of the Church to save us from the pit. (Laughter.) The trouble is there would not be room for this on the central reserve.

Whatever the churchman's definition, when the outsider

thinks of 'the Church' he probably thinks of bishops, clergy, and a network of buildings. He thinks of an organization. Merfyn Turner, the welfare worker, wrote in *Safe Lodging* of how men in gaol will join the Christian Scientists or the Society of Friends because word goes round that members get cash on discharge. But 'Anglicanism, associated as it is with Authority, is accepted as part of the régime. It gives no hope of reward'. The lower down the social scale, the more people seem to regard the Church as an instrument of Them; this loss of contact has been the theme of many anxious books by churchmen, though no one is ever sure what outsiders do think about the Church. Richard Hoggart in *The Uses of Literacy* (published in 1957) says he finds no conscious anti-clericalism among the working-class; people are 'faintly cynical' towards the parson, who is 'in with the bosses'; and 'In so far as they think of Christianity, they think of it as a system of ethics'. In Tom Harrisson's *Britain Revisited* (1961), Hoggart's accuracy in reporting what people say, when asked what they understand by religion ('doing good', 'being kind', etc.), is queried, and remarks such as 'I do go to church, and I feel better for it – well, I suppose it's hope' are quoted instead. But, agreeing with Hoggart, Harrison finds that 'No real scorn or dislike of religion is openly expressed, and very seldom privately'. A few years before, however, in *English Life and Leisure* (1951), Seebohm Rowntree and G. R. Lavers had found 'so widespread a dislike of the ministers of religion of the Anglican and Free Churches that it can only be described as anti-clericalism'. The sociologist Bryan Wilson, writing in the *Twentieth Century* in 1961, talks about the 'dramatic change' in the status of the priest or minister: 'He has rapidly passed from being the intellectual doyen of society to being a member of the profession with the lowest specialist educational demands . . . The [low] level of clerical stipends and ministerial salaries is a reflection of the changing evaluation of their role – and God's role – in our society.'

Parsons, however evaluated, are not common in modern British fiction. One writer who has pleased many churchmen with her picture of a parish priest is Margery Allingham, whose Canon Avril is vague, happy, and devout, his virtues unimpaired by the times. In *The Tiger in the Smoke* (published in 1952) the canon speculates painlessly:

What is the soul? When I was a child I thought it was a little ghostly bean, kidney-shaped, I don't know why. Now I think of it as the man I am with when I am alone. I don't think either definition would satisfy the theologians.

The canon is a kindly old gentleman, impossible to shock with sin because of his inner calm. A grittier kind of parson was described in *The Humbler Creation* (1959) by another woman novelist, Pamela Hansford Johnson (wife of Sir Charles Snow), in the shape of the Rev. Maurice Fisher, who, like Canon Avril, has a London parish, but who suffers sexual temptations like the next man. Fisher casts a cold eye on such things as the 'religious pidgin-English' of impromptu prayers, and missionaries:

He had never been sure, in the unanalyzed caves of his mind, of the value of the mission field. Today, in a world alternately crawling with fright and making Zulu noises of optimism, it seemed more vain than ever.

As a result of this novel, Lady Snow (who is a Christian) was invited by two archdeacons to talk to a week-end conference of newly ordained clergymen. She says that she 'found far more sympathy for the book among the older men, and senior men, than among the younger and junior ones. Some of the younger ones found it hard to believe that if my parson were in a proper state of grace, temptation could even exist; I said it could, and it did, and if it existed and became too strong the results would generally be found in the yellower Press'.

What novelists and journalists, and peers and average men, think of Church and clergy is a matter of concern for churchmen; yet in the long run the Church says that none of it matters. Herbert Butterfield in *Christianity and History* talks about 'thousands and thousands of priests and ministers' preaching the Gospel week by week – 'a phenomenon calculated greatly to alter the quality of life and the very texture of human history; and it has been the standing work of the Church throughout the ages'. Heretics and radicals come and go; the work continues. The trouble is that the work is seen to be done on a diminished scale. English parsons now preach the Gospel to a shrunken audience. No one has figures for churchgoing. The last and only 'Census of Religious Worship in England and Wales' was made by the Government in 1851, when, on Sunday 30 March, with a total population of 17,927,609, the heads of 10,419,380 worshippers were counted – though this included many double and treble attendances, so that the checkers estimated a total of 7,261,032 individual attenders. The Church of England took more than half, with an estimated 3,773,474 attenders, or slightly above one in five of the population. Even then the 'absolutely insignificant' proportion of working-class people in urban congregations was being commented on. The middle classes, said the report, were becoming more religious, and with the upper classes, 'a regular church-attendance is now ranked among the recognized proprieties of life'. But the 'labouring classes' stayed away – because, suggested the report, they disliked the class distinctions maintained in churches, they suspected the motives of paid clergymen, and they lived in poverty, whose 'fearful, never ceasing eloquence' was too much for the 'intermittent voice of Christianity' (nowadays the eloquence of prosperity gets the blame). By 1851, England was already divided. In the new, raw town of Sheffield, with a population of 135,000, the Church of England had 14,800 attendances. In the mellower atmosphere of Bristol, with 2,000 more inhabitants, attendances came to 34,600.

In *English Life and Leisure* Rowntree and Lavers compared churchgoing figures at York over half a century, and showed that in 1901 Anglican attendances at all services were more than one in seven of the population, and by 1948 about one in twenty-one. What has remained more constant has been the hard core of Christians. *Facts and Figures about the Church of England*, an occasional publication by a central Statistical Unit, which since 1959 has given the Church its first sets of accurate and exhaustive information, shows that in 1901 the number of people taking Holy Communion on Easter Day – an obligatory act for Christians – was ninety-four per 1,000 of the population aged fifteen and over. After 1915 the rate fell below ninety (except for 1925), below eighty in the second half of the 1930s, and now seems to be hovering in the low sixties. This decline of thirty per cent in Easter communicants is far smaller than the decline in general churchgoing.

Facts and Figures shows how the influence of the Church varies from place to place. Every inhabitant of England, whether he likes it or not, is a parishioner, and in the absence of evidence to the contrary is assumed to be a member of the Church of England. In Hereford – a rural diocese frequently quoted in Church statistics because of its high ratio of clergy to inhabitants and its general statistical godliness – nearly three-quarters of the children are baptized. Lincoln and Worcester are close behind. But in London and Liverpool fewer than half the children are baptized by the Church. Over the whole country, sixty-seven per cent of the population have been so baptized, and are Church members of a kind. If Confirmation is taken as indicating membership, the figure is twenty-four per cent. If the Church's Electoral Roll (which is open to those who are baptized and take the trouble to apply), seven per cent. Easter Communicants are six per cent of the population. Within this six per cent is the still smaller number who go to church regularly. None of these degrees of membership has much legal standing. In the index to Halsbury's *Ecclesiastical Law* (Church Assembly edition, 1955, annotated 'For sale to the Bishops and Clergy of the Church of England only'), the entry against 'Church members' says only '*See* parishioners'. It is the parishioners, who are born and not made, whose rights and obligations are enumerated; church attendance, except for dissenters who go somewhere else, is still a duty; the law still presumes blanket coverage.

In one field, the public schools, 'blanket coverage' remains a fact. Here the Church has a privileged position, and large numbers of young men who are going to have power in politics, law, management, and teaching receive several years of compulsory attendance at chapel, once daily and sometimes twice on Sundays. Confirmation is 'the done thing'. The headmaster of one leading school said it was not his practice to take atheism seriously. He added, without irony, that he told boys there was such a thing as respect for other people's opinions; they had to read the lessons in chapel even if they were convinced of their own lack of belief. 'In the last resort,' he said, 'this is simply a question of good manners. If you don't believe, you can go! I'd rather not have that quoted.' Boys, masters, and masters' wives crowding into chapel on a Sunday evening make an impressive sight. Sermons vary from sharply intellectual pieces, usually by the chaplain or headmaster, to vapid storytelling, more often by visiting clergy, who are bemused by so many faces. Whether compulsory chapel embitters young agnostics, and how much of 'public school religion' is still composed of notions of fair play rather than specifically Christian teaching, are matters debated inside the schools themselves. But the conclusion is generally that the great public schools are Church foundations, that their house-masters (who are often jealous of their right to prepare for confirmation) and chaplains have a straightforward job to do: to leave a deposit in the mind. 'Although the ordinary boy doesn't feel that singing *Onward Christian Soldiers* helps him to be a Christian,' said a housemaster, 'the great central thing, that a man *ought* to be a Christian, does sink into his mind. He goes away on the whole thinking he ought to be a Christian, wanting to be one, and feeling slightly guilty if he stops being one altogether. Obviously we are an organization for the indoctrination of the Christian faith.'

In the colder world of the parishes, the Church has, in order to perform its central functions of baptism, confirmation, marriage, burial, and Communion, something over 12,000 plain clergymen at work as 'incumbents' – rectors and vicars, who have the 'living' – and their assistants, technically 'assistant curates' but invariably referred to as 'curates'. Another 1,000 or more clergymen work without livings, most of them attached to cathedrals, lecturing, teaching, or doing some kind of office work; a few work in factories or even practise psychiatry. The Services have 280 chaplains. 'Dignitaries' occupy another 850 parishes, and range from retired bishops to rural deans, who are ordinary and usually over-worked parish clergy with informal responsibilities for a number of parishes. Above the parochial rank and file the pyramid of authority narrows sharply, with 106 archdeacons – bishops' officers, at least two to each diocese, with heavy duties of inspection and consultation. Next come about forty suffragan bishops, responsible for specific areas within dioceses, and working under the forty-three full-blown diocesan bishops, who include the Archbishops of Canterbury and York. But each of the forty-three dioceses has its own pyramid and possesses considerable autonomy. Besides the working clergy there are the retired: 3,400 out of a total of 18,000, an enormous figure that troubles the Church. Most of the retired clergy are to be found in the South of England; in the diocese of Chichester, which includes salubrious resorts like Eastbourne and Worthing, close on half the clergymen are retired – while in the North a place like Bradford has just ten retired parsons out of 180 in the diocese.

*

It is the clergy of the Church of England, in England, that this book is chiefly concerned with: the bishops, bureaucrats, industrial chaplains, money-raisers, partisans, publicists, monks, theologians, teachers, and men in the parishes. What they must all care most about is God. What they must all be holy, intelligent, or astute enough to do is make the idea of God the most important thing in the life of a secularized community, preserving the mysteries of Christianity without being obscurantist and slamming the door on science and psychology. They are saddled or blessed (opinions vary, even among clergymen) with peculiar clothes, and archaic language and rituals that are, nevertheless, withdrawn only at the risk of being breezily, disastrously contemporary. The solemn procession of parishioners down the nave of a church at a Sunday-evening 'rhythm service' in a London suburb, carrying symbols of their work to offer at the altar – housewife in apron with cut loaf, typist with typewriter, man with golf clubs – may be involving people in the service, but the smirks from the choir and the uneasiness on the faces of some of the processors lessen the effect. The pop-song-type hymns sung by the boy with the electric guitar are professional and musically effective, but the young clergyman's commentary from the pulpit seems a little smooth: 'The rhythm and style is 1961, but the good news is everlasting – Christ has risen . . . God doesn't ask us to be respectable or clever, high-brow or low-brow. All he asks us is to be *honest* and admit we have failed and are sorry and are going to try again. Will you stand. . . .' The reluctance of clergymen to change any of the traditional titles, to call a rural dean a 'chairman', is understandable: in a modest questionnaire* answered by thirty parsons, twenty-four disagreed, most of them vehemently, that there were 'too many fancy names in the Anglican vocabulary' (and twenty-one of the thirty considered they had 'social standing' in the parish).

More important, parsons must have an attitude to such things as strikes, capital punishment, and nuclear weapons. A number are members of the Labour Party, and more would rank as sympathizers. A strong social conscience is at work in the Church, not necessarily looking for quick results. A clergyman concerned with social thinking, the Rev. John Rogan (see Chapter 7) said the 'classical Anglican situation' was that 'the

* The idea was to get a representative sample of clerical views by sending fourteen questions to 120 clergymen, chosen at random from *Crockford's Clerical Directory*. This proposal caused people who knew the clergy to laugh significantly when they heard of it. As it turned out, about a dozen of them had either died or couldn't be traced by the Post Office. (*Crockford's* incorporates a five-page list of clergy whose whereabouts aren't known.) Another seven wrote refusing to cooperate, usually through overwork or doubts about my competence. Thirty sent replies, a few monosyllabic but most of them gratifyingly meaty. The other seventy or so threw the questions away and put the enclosed stamp to better use. The questionnaire and a short analysis of the results are given as an Appendix.

Church is not an executive institution but the articulator of fundamental ideas'. The Church was not 'the imperious law-giver to an expectant world'; it made its contribution as one group among many, and in a specialized society, its role was to 'make men sensitive and equipped with some basic ideas which they alone can relate to the various degrees of life in which they live'. Meanwhile books, pamphlets, pressure-groups, and parish activities continue the Church's social functions in a society where prosperity complicates the simple doing of 'good works'.

Internal Church affairs take many clergymen's time and passion. Questions of 'party' – whether one should be 'High' or 'Low', wear vestments or go without, regard Communion as a sacrifice or an act of remembrance – aren't as explosive as they were fifty years ago, but several thousand parsons belong to one or other of the party organizations; a film made to show what happens in a country church has two versions: No. 1 in which the Anglo-Catholic vestments are worn, No. 2 with the clergyman wearing cassock and surplice, as approved by Low churchmen. The rewriting, after three and a half centuries, of Canon Law, the intimidating structure of ecclesiastical regulations, has been going on for years, to the accompaniment of hair-splitting, rancour from minorities who feel themselves under attack, and sarcasm from churchmen who question its value and think that for a body of men to sit discussing whether Canon B37 should allow the ashes of the dead to be scattered outside consecrated ground is a waste of everyone's time. Relations between Church and State, and the appointment of bishops, deans, and hundreds of parish clergy by the Crown, is another point of controversy.

But the bulk of the clergy, and of Church members generally, aren't especially interested in any of these things – party, Canon Law, Establishment. They cling to an awkward status in town or village. An archdeacon said: 'People want us to be spiritual *and* earthy – not little Mulrooneys come out of a seminary, nor boozers being all things to all men.' Most parsons just concentrate on the parishioners. A clergyman in a slum-clearance estate in a Yorkshire town, his parish made up entirely of council-house families, described his congregation and his work like this – an unsensational account of life in a community where the fires of Christianity have cooled:

As found in our newly built parish church at 9.30 a.m. on a Sunday morning (minus a few older men and women who will have been at 8.00 a.m.), the congregation will consist of about forty children of Sunday-school age, who prefer adult worship to Sunday-school, ages ten–twelve. There will be about another forty young teenagers confirmed during the previous two or three years, and a few casual boys and girls, who float in and out from week to week. The teenagers gradually thin out, as marriage and work and secular influences claim them, and there are only a handful in their twenties. Almost all the youngsters will be unaccompanied. Parents not usually interested.

The next significant group is in the thirty-five to forty-five age range, of those who are not tied by family cares, the children now being to some extent off their hands. These are people who are settling down in life and looking for the more enduring realities. But it is not a very large group. Beyond this there is a sprinkling of old people, the old-stagers who have kept the flag flying throughout the years; there are few of them. We should expect to have between seventy-five and ninety-five communicants, and another forty–fifty not yet confirmed, either children or newly attracted adults.

The impression of visiting clergy is of vitality and vigour and yet of devotion. The service lasts about one hour and a quarter, long by present-day standards, but they endure (rather than enjoy) my preaching. The singing is strong, and we keep the pace up, though with primitive organ-playing. But I note the underlying instability of the many who manage to keep up their good intentions for a few weeks or months, and then fall back into the old ways. It is such an effort for many of them to keep anything up for long, whether at home, at work, or at church.

Women greatly outnumber men, only partly because of shift-work. Most men wouldn't be seen dead in church, and many of the women have to face a lot of criticism from their neighbours. Seeing them at the altar-rail, one is touched and humbled by their devotion, and by what their worship means to them – I am speaking of the adults in general. Among the teenagers, there are fewer boys than girls, but not so few as among the adults. I find them a fine lot, and receptive.

A typical Evensong congregation will consist of about six old people, about twelve of the devout, who have come to the morning service, a dozen or more of the keener teenagers coming for the second time, and a sprinkling of others, who make up the odds and ends of our congregation, totalling about forty people.

This would describe typical congregations on an average Sunday. On festivals and important days, the numbers of communicants increase by about twenty-five per cent, but not Evensong numbers. Not much to show after six years' hard labour, but numbers increase about five or ten per cent each year. It is only a tiny fraction in a parish of 12,000 though we have contacts with a far larger number. The movement of population does not help us, as the better families whom we try to make leaders tend to leave the parish, their places being taken by slum-clearance families. Our young people have to find houses elsewhere once they marry. So by and large we consider this as a mission parish and plan it accordingly. It is exciting and challenging, but immensely hard going.

An interesting sideline on the financial as opposed to the social status of this parish is that the church people, whether of the 'respectable' or 'slummy' background, are likely to be poorer than those outside the church. Parishioners who really set out to make money leave the church, and church people will often refuse extra paid work in order to continue with their church life. This is true despite the low wages general here.

Not all parsons care as much as this one. A director of one of the professional fund-raising companies that have been at work in parishes in recent years, who is a Christian himself, made this assessment: 'Forty per cent of parishes have got a good incumbent who's alive and kicking. A further thirty per cent are capable of making big improvements when they get down to it, and thirty per cent are difficult parishes for us, needing a lot of help because they haven't got good incumbents.' He added that this wasn't a judgement of their money-raising ability, but of their overall competence.

How, though, does one judge whether a parson is 'competent'? How does the parson know it himself? If congregations were at the 1851 level, it would be possible, though not necessarily correct, to measure success by the number of churchgoers; as it is, head-counting is generally frowned on and treated as typical journalistic misunderstanding of the situation, though few clergymen avoid talking (as the housing-estate parson quoted above) about their work in terms of quantity. If it were only a question of diminished congregations, parsons might continue to minister to the faithful with as much zeal as before – this, indeed, is what happens in many, if not most, cases. But doubt and uncertainty are in the air.

Sermons, and letters from clergymen in the Church Press, show understandable uneasiness and even bitterness at the 'new theology'. The destructive content of the ideas is easy to grasp: there is no Being in the sky, the historical stories are bleached of certainty, there is no pocket-sized moral code to measure behaviour. But what goes in their place? We must accept responsibility: we must not exploit: we must fall back, in the Bishop of Woolwich's words, on the 'reliability of an utterly personal Love'. But how does a vicar instruct children, and plain-thinking members of the Mothers' Union, and old men with fading minds? For the moment, he takes most of his comfort from the past; and so the Church of England seems full of ideas that are waiting to be accepted or refuted.

To an outsider it seems unbearably poised. In Christendom generally (of which the Anglican Communion throughout the world represents perhaps five per cent) there is a feeling that time is short. In the words of Dr S. H. Miller, Dean of Harvard Divinity School, in a much-quoted address to theological students at Princeton in 1961:

Only one kind of religion counts today, and that is the kind which is radical enough to engage in this world's basic troubles. If it cannot do that, then it can do nothing which merits our concern or the world's respect. Religion which is interested only in itself, in its prestige and success, in its institutions and ecclesiastical niceties, is worse than vanity; it is essentially incestuous. Religion reveals itself in struggling to reveal the meaning of the world.

But time, say many clergymen, has been short before. And the Church of England's machinery and individuals continue to work, with varying degrees of efficiency, in the framework of a large and seemingly permanent institution. Like most institutions, it stubbornly presents its two aspects – one to those inside, the other to those outside. I am, of course, an outsider.

CHAPTER TWO

HOW TO BE A CLERGYMAN

THE chapel of Oak Hill Theological College, in pleasant wooded countryside to the north of London, is as contemporary as a post-war classroom. The wood is pale, the windows tall, the heating efficient. For decoration there is a blue tapestry, with crowns, behind the wooden Communion Table, and a single spray of flowers. It has a little of the anonymity of a crematorium chapel. The lack of ornaments is intentional. Oak Hill, founded in 1932, is a 'party' college, owing its allegiance to the Low, or, as it prefers to be called, the Evangelical tradition. Within this tradition it represents the Conservative wing, which includes those who still believe that the Bible, back to Adam and Eve, is the literal reporting of history. Few of them would be 'literalists' in this way; but for everyone at Oak Hill, the Bible is especially important. Here, salvation is a personal, emotional matter; the significant thing is not what is seen outside but what is felt inside; Christianity should look in to a man's heart, not out to ornaments and ceremonies. At a college like Oak Hill, everyone has his 'personal testimony', which he will give at the least provocation, describing how a man, a book or a random thought began a process that (in most accounts) passes through a stage of prolonged prayer, kneeling on a hard floor, before the truth of Christ became apparent. Once saved ('born again'), the unsaved become a company of the blind. Atheists don't enter Heaven here; a student will shake his head and declare: 'There are two classes of people – the wise and the foolish, the insiders and the outsiders. I believe that everyone knows there's a God. Some people move from that to believing there isn't. That's what an atheist is, and I shan't meet that man in Heaven. If there's a possibility, then I'm wasting my time.'

Most of the sixty or seventy insiders in residence at Oak Hill will mellow after a few years in parishes; but, having come here because this offered them the type of Christianity they wanted, they will continue to bear the stamp of the college. For them, the chapel isn't a place of ornate ritual but a high-powered classroom in which the Bible is expounded and their anxieties are straightened out by detailed prayers.

Before breakfast on a Friday, the vice-principal took a service of worship and instruction. In the pews, individual flaps fold down to make a ledge for note-taking. The clergyman wore a black gown, with two white tabs, the 'preaching bands', at his throat. In the distance could be heard early commuters' trains. The text was from Mark, chapter 4, and the sermon concerned parables, and the insight they offer of the Kingdom of God. There was a lot of finger-waving, and the phrase 'Read, mark, learn, and inwardly digest' was used twice. Parables, said the preacher, are designed to test not the intelligence of the hearer but his moral responsiveness. Then followed an anecdote. He was at a boys' camp in the country-side, and the Bishop of Norwich had been visiting them one Saturday morning. The bishop was returning to Norwich, and suggested to the superintendent that he might take a couple of boys with him in his car to spend the afternoon in town. The superintendent got two buckets and walked slowly across the field. 'Most of the boys went on playing, but two of them came up to him and said, "Do you want some water, sir?" "Oh, no," he said, "but if you go and brush your hair you can go to Norwich for the afternoon."' There were appreciative smiles and chuckles from the students. 'Well,' said the preacher, smiling himself, 'that's what it says here:

35

God is the rewarder of those who respond. You can be deliberately blind, like those boys who didn't see. Jesus avoids giving a compelling manifestation of himself – the kingdom of Heaven holds men at arm's length.'

The preaching had authority; self-consciousness is nowhere apparent at Oak Hill, and the following morning the chapel was filled for a prayer meeting, at which students stood up as they felt inclined, and asked for prayers on everyday matters: for a nurse taking her exams; thanks for a wife recovering from illness; for a forthcoming visit to a town in a 'low moral condition', where five students were going, two to testify and three to sing; thanks for a service the previous week, after which 'a lady and two boys took booklets'; for the inmates of a remand home – 'advance them and really sort them out for the Lord'.

Most students, or 'ordinands', spend two years at Oak Hill. As at all the twenty-six theological colleges in England, there is a concentrated course in Church history, Christian doctrine and worship, and Bible study, which includes a paper in Greek; at the end of it comes the General Ordination Examination, sometimes referred to as 'God's Own Examination', which is academically the equivalent of a pass degree at Oxford or Cambridge. Graduates, of whom there are not many at Oak Hill, find this easy; to others it may be a trial. Few fail to pass in the end, though sometimes it means several attempts. The papers go to examiners, usually parish clergymen with a special knowledge of the subject, who are paid £5 for setting a paper and two shillings a script for marking; as long as they are not heretical, the ordinand's personal views are of no significance, provided he shows he realizes that other views are possible.

Oak Hill doesn't go in for the intellectual gymnastics, at times verging on agnosticism, found at some colleges. Nor is there much doubt, as there is in widening theological circles, that the Bible is reporting historical fact. An Old Testament class began at 9.25 a.m., after a short prayer by the lecturer – an elderly clergyman in dark grey suit, standing by the blackboard – who went on to talk quickly and firmly about the military successes of Joshua, detailing the tribal dispositions, and pointing out how recent excavations were throwing light on the events described. '*And he burnt Hazor with fire*', the lecturer read, adding: 'Hazor's been excavated recently and found to be quite a large and well-fortified city.' It had been suggested, he said, that Joshua's history was exaggerated, and that the account was a summary of many campaigns. He didn't agree; critics who felt that Israel was unlikely to have been a coherent nation as early as this were making a purely subjective judgement. He talked about Martin Noth, a German theologian, who took an unliteral view of much of the Old Testament. 'Concerning the Exodus from Egypt, he thinks there was some marine disaster – some Egyptian chariots fell into the sea, or something.' The class laughed. 'There was someone called Moses, but no one knows what he did.' There was more laughter. 'I'm giving an extreme view. He's got his followers, and it's brilliantly worked out. You'll find a copy in the library.'

A similar briskness marked a lecture on homiletics, or the art of preaching, by the Principal, the Rev. Maurice Wood, who was a Commando in the war, and holds the D.S.C. A long-chinned, vigorous man in middle age, he leaned on a desk and talked easily, suggesting that the opposite of dullness isn't slang, that 'the pulpit demands a certain sense of occasion', that the congregation is 'not listening to the words of the minister but the ministry of the word'. Preaching was more than words: it was to be possessed by the Holy Spirit. In a matter-of-fact voice he went on: 'Let us remember that we're marked men on the Devil's list. God can use us to bring people to Jesus . . . and for that very reason the powers of evil would like to do all they can to stop our ministry being effective. Those who stand near the captain are targets for the archer's arrows. The ministry is dangerous.'

Wood makes it sound a fact; the Devil is not a convenient bit of mythology in his life. One of the strong men in the Conservative Evangelical wing, he went to Oak Hill after being Vicar of Islington, in London, an important Evangelical parish. He lives with his wife and children in a roomy first-floor flat within the college; the bell-rope passes up through a hole in the hall carpet and into the roof above. On a wall of the flat is one of the framed texts of which Evangelicals are fond: 'It became known that He was in the home.' Another prominent mark of his churchmanship is the photograph of Billy Graham on his office desk downstairs, signed 'With affectionate regards, Billy' – many Anglican clergymen, particularly Anglo-Catholics, wince at the sight of those big lapels and blazing eyes, but to Evangelicals, Graham is a potent figure.

On the students' notice-board the earnestness was continued. An appeal for tinfoil had scribbled on it: 'This notice could have been written on half a sheet of this paper! Is this Steward-ship?' (Stewardship is a movement to encourage use of one's money, time, and possessions for the Church.) Someone had added: 'Then you could not have written this rude remark.' To one side had been pinned a typewritten extract from Bishop Stephen Neill's Pelican book, *Anglicanism* (1960), taken from a passage where he says that the Church of England, alone among the great Churches of Christendom, has 'never yet taken seriously the provision of adequate training for the ministry'. The extract read: 'Four centuries have passed since the accession of Queen Elizabeth; in all these years the problem has never been radically dealt with, and the ignorance of the average Anglican theological student today is the astonishment of his opposite number in every country on the continent of Europe.' No one had scribbled anything on this.

Neill's charge is heard throughout the Church, and scarcely a month goes by without some new (or old) accusation being made against theological colleges: their outlook is suburban, their facilities are inadequate or their atmosphere is too cloistered. All twenty-six are independent, run by governing bodies of varying distinction, and none of them existed before the nineteenth century. They were developed to give practical and devotional training to men who would, most of them, have been university graduates; they were never intended to be theological seminaries, often catering, nowadays, for ordinands who have come straight from grammar or secondary-modern schools, or, answering a call to the ministry in middle-age, from being Army officers or commercial travellers or works managers. According to Neill the Church hasn't enough scholars to staff the colleges. Many of them are short of money, and are helped by central Church grants. But whatever their defects, they are unlikely to be replaced by anything else for a long time to come. And any idea of a 'learned clergy' in the old sense has been abandoned.

Controlling things at the centre is an organization called the Central Advisory Council for the Ministry, usually abbreviated to 'CACTM' and pronounced 'Cacktum', which is one of the bodies through which the Church Assembly works. CACTM controls no colleges directly; plans for such a college, large and high-powered, were abandoned early in 1962, partly because of opposition from existing colleges. CACTM's function is to find men for ordination and advise on their training. It runs selection boards, sets examinations, and is the Church's general conscience, policy-maker, and watchdog over ordinands; its inspectors visit colleges every five years, to report on everything from teaching and administration to the food. The Council is headed by a bishop and is responsible to the diocesan bishops. (Bishops alone are able to ordain a man, and indeed, can ordain anyone they like without reference to CACTM or colleges – though this happens only rarely.) In the past it depended on the individual bishop. If he was easy-going and liked a man, a chat over a glass of sherry might be enough. If he was a scholar, he might look for scholarly ordinands. Although it's usual to deplore the old haphazardness, a certain nostalgia can be observed. 'In the old days,' said one of the staff at CACTM, 'you went cosily through the pattern of public school, university, and theological college, and you were nicely cooked by the time you were twenty-three.' In his country vicarage – near a university town so that he would have access to libraries – an examiner shook his head and said: 'Those of us who are scholastically inclined may deplore the fact that the clergy are not what they used to be, but ... there you are.' CACTM's method is still thought to have a touch of the sausage-machine about it.

Figures vary, but in a year there might be inquiries from 1,200 men. About three-quarters of these eventually present themselves at one of CACTM's weekly selection conferences, held at various centres, where they spend two or three days being looked at and interviewed by clergymen and laymen. The official line is that no one actually fails, but is sent away to be more effective as a layman than he would be as a clergyman; a blunter official at CACTM said: 'We get an awful lot of men we can see as curates but not running the show for themselves – *devout* young men. . . .' Of the 800 or 900 who attend selection conferences, just under three-quarters make the grade, though about 100 of these finally decide they were mistaken, and are never ordained. In the end some 600 men, or half the number who made some move towards entering the Church, are made deacon – the first stage, which lasts at least a year, before the deacon can become a full clergyman, entitled to celebrate Communion, marry, bless, and absolve from sin. Church administrators watch these figures like hawks, and when the number of ordinations went above 600 in the early 1960s, the first time since before the First World War, there was a feeling that a breakthrough had been achieved – an intake of between 600 and 700 a year is regarded as the minimum needed to replenish the ageing ranks of the clergy. About one ordinand in six is more than forty years old. Rather more than one in three will have been to a public school – the numbers here seem to be declining, an encouraging fact for those who condemn the middle-class nature of the clergy, though discouraging for public schools, which take such pains to maintain the old order. Even so, the public schools provide a large number of men for the Church. From figures supplied by the Headmasters' Conference, it appears (my calculation) that 20,000 boys leave public schools each year; the Ministry of Education shows 300,000 leaving State schools. The public schools, with about 300 CACTM candidates a year, are therefore offering one in seventy to the Church, while State schools, with 500 candidates, offer one in 600.

When the selectors – who never include a woman – have a man in front of them, it's not altogether clear what they look for; an official booklet, *Men for the Ministry*, speaks comprehensively of conviction, devotion, experience of the world, intellectual calibre, imaginative insight, Christian hope, and a realization of one's inadequacy. A bigoted man would be looked at closely. So would someone with five 'O' levels and nothing more. So would someone who, as reported by a

THE CHURCH OF ENGLAND

clergyman-selector in *Prism*, said he thought a priest was 'The highest form of humanity' ('It seemed to me,' added the selector, 'that man had been brainwashed'). What no one seems able to define is how the level of acceptance is decided. CACTM denies that any prearranged percentage is admitted; the fact that in ten years the percentage of men recommended by conferences has risen from sixty-one to the mid-seventies (with, since 1954, a variation that never exceeds more than a few per cent each year) is, said a man at CACTM, because the conferences are now in their stride, and weaker candidates are deterred by their dioceses, so that the quality of those attending is higher. No simple rules exist; presumably they never will. At Westcott House, a theological college at Cambridge, where most of the men are university graduates, and people have fewer preconceived ideas than at Oak Hill, one of the staff, who was a scientist as well as a clergyman, pointed to the complexity of motives:

Religion, as you're probably aware, is a very ambiguous thing. Religion may be a way of releasing one's power complexes: people may go into it because they want to release themselves. This is the negative side. The positive side is that God speaks to me, and how and where he does this involves a new way of seeing. . . . It is becoming a theological commonplace, and is certainly at Westcott House, that God and religion are two different things. God isn't simply religious aspirations – as far as we're dealing with religion we're dealing with dangerous stuff. . . . The Church is a horribly human institution, and the only justification for it is that occasionally God shines through and beyond the ghastly clothes and the rest of it, one discovers a love that surprises one – or what love is for.

Westcott House can't be pinned down as easily as Oak Hill. It is more sophisticated, and includes students who may be High, Low, or anywhere in between. You can meet fervent Evangelicals there, talking about a 'personal God', and you

42

can meet Anglo-Catholics with a mystical turn of phrase. But Westcott House is unlikely to produce extremists, as some of the 'party' colleges do; it exists for opposite reasons. It doesn't ram a particular kind of theology down the throats of its students, but lets them feel the draught of new ideas – a policy in accordance with the best Anglican tradition. The kind of clergyman who emerges from it has a head-start on the products of other colleges, should he have ambitions to be a bishop. According to figures published in a *Prism* pamphlet, twelve of the forty-three diocesan bishops who held office at the start of 1962 had been to Westcott House.

But Westcott, for all its diversity, has a strong ecclesiastical atmosphere. So, probably, do most of the colleges.* One that seems to lack it is Ripon Hall, at Oxford, an unusual college in a 'liberal' tradition – a tradition at present in eclipse in the Church – which invokes the 'modernist' doubts about Virgin Birth and Resurrection, radical enough in their day between the two world wars, but superseded now by harsher objections. A group of students at Ripon Hall agreed proudly that 'You won't get a line pushed at you here – it's left to the individual to work his own theology'. But another student thought this was dangerous. There is said to be no such thing as 'a Ripon Hall man' – it varies year by year. And, although the college would say that the suspicions are a thing of the past, there is sometimes a feeling in the Church that you must be a little careful of a place like this.

Whatever the students' views of the ministry, once they get to theological college they have to resign themselves to the syllabus of the General Ordination Examination. This, like the colleges, is always under attack. A former Regius Professor of Divinity at Oxford, Dr Hodgson, once said that able men

* I have been to four of the twenty-six: Westcott House, Oak Hill, Mirfield, and Ripon Hall.

despised it, and weak men had to cram. It has been widely criticized for dropping 'Christian Ethics' from its syllabus. This paper used to include such questions as 'What are the necessary characteristics of virtue?' and 'Are there any *industrial* occupations ethically incapable of being Christian vocations?' A widespread feeling exists that to attempt such questions is at least as important as to 'Discuss the significance of the tenses of a verb with particular reference to the present, imperfect, aorist, and perfect tenses' (paper in New Testament Greek, August 1961), or to 'Describe the forms taken by Egyptian monasticism' (Church History 1, August 1961). Christian Ethics was dropped because something had to go from an overloaded syllabus; it was often badly taught, it taxed the powers of weaker ordinands, and there was, and is, the hope that it can somehow be acquired in the parish. Another subject for which the G.O.E. finds no place is 'pastoralia' – how, apart from acts of worship, a clergyman should look after his parishioners. All colleges do something about this, and may include lectures by visiting psychiatrists and sociologists. A more modest type of advice is also given – for instance, to suggest that the raw young curate can write key sentences on a scrap of paper and tuck it under a wrist-watch. Maurice Wood at Oak Hill said that at his first baptism a curate was convinced he'd drop the baby, at his first wedding he was sure the ring would fall off the Prayer Book, and at his first funeral he was haunted by the thought of stepping backwards into the grave.

Behind the measurable, observable training at theological colleges are said to be fundamentals that matter more. A college may be deficient in learning, and chunks of its theology may be irrelevant to the modern world, but if it forms good habits of prayer and meditation, it will, say its apologists, have done the most important thing. An intensity is in the air.

Chapel is compulsory, though the amount of compulsion varies. Ordinands don't go out much. At a college like Oak Hill, a number of men will be married, and after their first year can sleep at home, as long as they don't mind being in college till 9.30 every evening, and back for chapel at 7.20 the next morning. At a college like Mirfield, run by the monks of the Community of the Resurrection, celibacy is more fashionable. Mirfield is High Church – at the other pole from Oak Hill. Even meals have a ceremonial aspect. At Oak Hill, they say a simple English grace before eating. At Ripon Hall they amble in and say grace to themselves, or not, as they feel inclined, at all meals except dinner. But at Mirfield no one enters the refectory till the college principal arrives; and grace is in Latin. Partly because of its general distinction, partly because one of its members, Father Huddleston, has opposed apartheid so fiercely in South Africa, the Community must be the best-known in the Church of England. Mirfield is a small town outside Huddersfield, and the Community, which adjoins the college, occupies what was once a millowner's property, on rising ground, with a view of railway lines, bare sweeps of grass, and distant chimneys. At Mirfield they have the knack, rarer among Anglicans than Roman Catholics, of combining the secular with the religious. Their worship is highly organized, there is much academic distinction, they are good at publicity; the letters 'C.R.' after a man's name keep cropping up not only in theological journals but in the *TV Times*, television having discovered that the religious communities have some telegenic personalities. They put out crisp pamphlets with titles like *Who Would Be a Priest!*, written in plain English, full of ingenious understatements, steering the difficult course between piety and heartiness. Whereas at an extreme Evangelical college, the agnostic is soon on edge, half afraid some ebullient student may start to accuse him of

45

something in a loud voice, at Mirfield coexistence is easy; the note of accusation is absent.

But men trained at Mirfield have a stamp of authority, a trace of asceticism. The atmosphere at the college is markedly unfeminine, though the days when girl-friends had to lurk in doorways in the town, and when (as a Mirfield man said), 'anyone who married was looked on as an unhappy sort of compromise', have gone. Still, Mirfield probably produces an unusually high proportion of clergymen – always called 'priests', just as at Oak Hill they would always be 'ministers' – who are going to remain unmarried; officially the Church recognizes no merit in celibacy, but one in seven of its incumbents is a bachelor.

At Mirfield the emphasis is on corporate prayer, on the value of the Sacraments, on ritual; there are vestments and candles and incense, and people believe firmly in the 'Real Presence' of Christ in the Communion bread and wine – that Christ is somehow present in the substance of the food (though without changing its physical texture and appearance) regardless of the faith of the individual communicant. One of the ancient Mirfield jokes concerns the ordinand, hitch-hiking near the college, who was given a lift by a local mill-owner. 'You can get in,' he said, 'but let me tell you something, your Community stands for the two things I hate most, Roman Catholicism and Communism' – the Christian Socialist movement was behind the founding of the Community in the 1890s, and its tradition of social action has been carried on by some remarkable men, of whom Huddleston is certainly one. Ordinands at Mirfield are nearly all graduates; the G.O.E. doesn't loom very large in their lives, and they have more time for other things. Ecclesiastical kite-fliers, missionary bishops on leave, and men with red-hot theories of how to evangelize England are always anxious to have a hearing at theological colleges, and Mirfield, where they can expect an intellectual audience, is bombarded with requests from speakers who would like to be fitted in. Mirfield men are worth getting at. Most of them turn into priests with a presence. Few are so innocent as to believe that what awaits them is (in the words of a *Prism* writer, giving a warning to ordinands), 'a world gone cross-eyed with telly and overtime', and that 'all they have to do is to go along, wave wands, be nice, swish round in a cassock and become a Labour member of the Borough Council'. 'They are,' said the wife of one, 'faithful men.'

This priest, ordained a few years, is in charge of a parish in a northern town. He follows a 'rule of life', a simple pattern of prayers and confession, and reports every quarter to one of the monks at Mirfield. Asked about divine intervention, he had no cosy answer, equating every piece of good luck with a benevolent act by God: 'The deeper his spiritual life, the greater his understanding that whatever happens is God's will – that it's all part of God's will.' He paused, then said: 'In a sense that's a letout.' He paused again. 'But if you're willing to see the will of God if someone gives a hundred pounds, you must be prepared to see it if some fool gets into the church one night and burns it down.' The tower of his church – an ugly pre-war brick building that might, in the dusk, be a cinema – is visible over a large distance, and it's one of his ambitions to have an illuminated cross there; he thought red neon would be nice.

At Westcott House – though here, too, they have an ascetic tradition – the spiritual rigours of Mirfield are regarded with a certain wry amusement. Because all varieties of churchman-ship and sophistication can be found at Westcott, if someone uses a phrase like 'the work of the Holy Spirit', someone else will tell him to stop expressing pious sentiments and explain what he means. A student who had been a book-keeper said privately that 'If I thought we could have the Christian ethic without the Christian religion, I'd go back to book-keeping'. This desperate heresy, which leaves out the essential faith in the Resurrection, would stop him becoming a priest. His brand of Christianity seemed interchangeable with the philosophy of a good-natured humanist; but presumably he would be able to satisfy the G.O.E. examiners without baring his soul. 'From what I've encountered of the Christian ethic,' he said, '– love one another as I've loved you, and follow this up with a sacrifice – it's the only one I could take fully as my own. Its best expression I feel to be what one knows of the life of Christ. Whether the Church carries on is the main thing. I don't think the Church is very much; but if it preserves something of the West that's important, then I'll back it.' He added that the reason some people at Westcott made you want to curl up – he was thinking of the steelworker's son who had kept rising at a discussion the previous evening to talk about being saved, and how one shouldn't worry if one was mocked – was that they were concerned so ostensibly with making a niche for themselves in Heaven. Another ordinand, talking in his room, making Nescafé on a gas ring, kept saying that the theological-college set-up was out of date. 'Why are we here?' he said angrily. 'They build up tensions, and bells ring, and we do things. It's two years, like National Service in the Army. That's significant. In the Army I'd have picked up a rifle and blown anyone's head off if they'd kept telling me to do things like they do here.'

Not long before, someone had gone too far even for Westcott House, and had had to leave. The coffee-maker said bitterly: 'He questioned everything. He wanted an irreligious religion, so they gave him the choice – spend a term at Mirfield, where they've got bells ringing all the time and you're inspecting your soul every minute: or go. So he went. He went to the bishop, but the bishop wouldn't ordain him until he'd made his peace with the principal.' The coffee-maker's friend kept saying the college had no option. But the other insisted it had been wrong. 'He thought we were a set of gentlemen out to please,' he said. 'He thought we were *squarsons*. He used to go on about awful phrases like "the spiritual life". And they gave him the boot.'

The hardest question of all to answer, at Westcott or any-where else, is *why* they chose the ministry. They felt it suited them : they felt they ought to : they had never thought of any-thing else : they had thought of it as a joke, and the conviction crept up on them later. 'I knew beyond any doubt that God was calling me – it shocked me,' said one man. The very word, 'call', has been debased into a convenient euphemism. An ordinand at Westcott House told the joke about the parson who was offered a pleasant living on the South Coast. He went into his study to pray, to see if he had a call; his wife went to pack. But is there sometimes a voice that speaks? Cosmo Lang, the Scottish minister's son who became Archbishop of Canter-bury, once talked of 'a masterful inward voice. "You are wanted. You are called. You must obey."' Many have clerical backgrounds, and so move naturally into the Church. F. A. Iremonger, in his life of Archbishop William Temple, says how 'It is a commonplace of ecclesiastical biography that many a future priest and bishop has begun to rehearse his part in childhood. Some have built little shrines in wood, some have indulged in premature mortification, others have col-lected their earliest congregations in the nursery'. Temple, a bishop's son, had 'his own robe-case, at the top of which was laid a carefully folded surplice and a diminutive mitre'. The school chapel is still an influence. Other boys begin by hero-worshipping a clergyman; monks, and priests with a touch of saintliness about them, influence many teenagers. Billy

Graham brings them in. Older men often seem to be moved by a world-weariness, by a slow awareness that the office desk or (more rarely) the shop floor has lost its satisfaction. Not all psychologists would claim to have the last word in examining the ordinand's motives – Christians among them simply include the subconscious in the divine scheme of things – but there is ground waiting to be explored there.

The ordinands themselves, for whom the decision is still new, tend to give long, imprecise answers. Clergymen in parishes, looking back on an old decision, have briefer phrases – 'Just felt used to it' – 'Inner urges' – 'I wanted to work for an extension of the Faith' – 'To serve the Lord Jesus' – 'There came a time when the religious aspect of life was all that seemed to matter'. They are answers that mean nothing or everything. It depends on your point of view.

CHAPTER THREE

A CASE OF PATRONAGE

ON a hill above the Portsmouth road at Guildford stands a cathedral built of red brick that has scarcely begun to weather. A new cathedral is an event, and when this one was consecrated in 1961, twenty-eight years after a cross was set up on Stag Hill to mark the intentions of the Guildford Diocesan Conference, it made news in the Press and on television. What was even better for the reporters, though worse for the Church, was the fact that for a month before the consecration, on Wednesday, 17 May, the cathedral and its office of dean had been at the centre of a violent controversy.

The dean of a cathedral is the head of the group of clergy, the chapter, who serve the cathedral and look after the building. He ranks next to a bishop, is entitled to a seat in the Lower House of Convocation – the ancient governing body of the Church – is referred to as 'Very Reverend', wears a silk hood, has a deanery to live in, and earns, since 1962, not less than £2,000 a year. Each of the forty-three English dioceses has its cathedral – some of them old and rare, like Salisbury and York, others less prepossessing, like Southwark and Sheffield, that were once parish churches, and have been re-styled cathedrals as new dioceses have been carved out of the old structure, to keep pace with population movements over the last hundred years. The head of a parish-church cathedral is a provost, whose rank is similar to that of a dean, and who in addition is the incumbent of the parish.

Guildford, for the first thirty-four years of its life as a diocese, was served by a parish-church cathedral, the Church of

Holy Trinity with St Mary and St Luke. A small diocese, it was detached from one end of Winchester (founded 676) in 1927, at the same time as Portsmouth was detached from the other, to make better provision for the people who were starting to fill the countryside south-west of London; it covers the prosperous commuter-land of west Surrey, where the towns are growing fast, and every country lane conceals a desirable residence for doctor, merchant, or stockbroker. After St Albans, which has a comparable position north of London, it has had the greatest population increase of any English diocese in the last thirty years; but a county as salubrious as Surrey has less difficulty than anywhere in the country in filling vacant livings, and clergy have kept up with population. The diocese has only two or three parishes without a clergyman, of nearly 1,000 so placed in England, and it has one clergyman for every 3,500 people – though this is rather below the national figure of one to 3,300, which reflects the situation in rural, depopulated dioceses such as Hereford, which has one clergyman to every 1,000. Guildford isn't a particularly rich diocese, but the parishes give proportionately more to missions, in England and overseas, than they do anywhere else. In only one or two dioceses do more parishes produce a regular magazine. Guildford has a healthy air; and for many years its churchmen talked about the new cathedral, raised money for it, and saw the brick walls rise slowly on the long spine of hill above the town, with the central tower built on the highest point – a brass stag, set in the floor, records the fact. They began to build in 1936, but the war stopped them, and for years after the war there was only the brick shell of the chancel, a gaunt landmark from the by-pass or the railway. People talked about the 'Guildford folly'. The Church of Holy Trinity went on serving as a cathedral, and provosts, who were also rectors of the parish, came and went; according to the *Guildford and Godalming Times*, the cathedral project broke two of them, and they were sick men when they left Guildford.

In 1952 a man called Walter Boulton, a middle-aged clergyman with a reputation for good preaching and outspoken manners, who had spent most of his ecclesiastical life in India, was invited to be Provost by the Bishop of Guildford, Henry Montgomery-Campbell, later Bishop of London. He was told not to worry about the cathedral but concentrate on the parish, but after a few months got impatient, went round telling people that the folly on Stag Hill had to be either blown up or finished, and began to pump life into the money-raising. The building was completed to the point where it was usable, and it was generally assumed that as soon as it was consecrated, Boulton would move from being Provost of the pro-Cathedral to Dean of the Cathedral proper. Boulton was well thought of. He was not conventional, but he was unconventional without being breezy or flippant, which is the easy way out for clergymen; he had qualities that some of his parishioners called saintliness – a concern for people, an impetuous adherence to principle, and the courage of his convictions. Once, in Calcutta, he so offended business men with a sermon at the cathedral, in which he said they were 'digging their own graves', that they organized a petition to try to have him stopped. Preaching at York Minster, he suggested that bishops should be chosen for spiritual and not administrative qualities. He used his pulpit to attack Guildford Urban District Council over housing. He was controversial but he was popular with churchpeople; while to those who didn't know the difference between a provost and an archdeacon, he was a man of admirable vigour. Boulton intended the cathedral to be a new kind of diocesan centre, responsible for such things as psychiatry and medicine, family welfare, and industrial relations. In the early months of 1961, as the time for the consecration approached, he continued to plan for his cathedral. Mrs Boulton was choosing curtains for the deanery and deciding where the telephones would go. Then rumours were heard in Guildford, Boulton was seen to be worried, and towards the end of April, with less than a month to go, the news came out that he was not to be made Dean. For a month or two, the 'Guildford affair' embarrassed the Church almost as much as the 'Balham affair', which resulted in the unfrocking of a vicar who slept with a parishioner, had embarrassed it earlier in the spring. In a way it was worse. Balham proved only that clergymen are human, and that the Church is peculiarly bad at keeping its scandals to itself. Guildford was seen by many as evidence of malice, bungling, and fundamental wrongness in the whole relationship of Church and State. Walter Boulton was found a living in north Rutland, and went off with his wife (a clergyman's daughter) and children to live in a rectory on the edge of a scarp, where the parting gift of friends and parishioners, cheques for £1,900, came in useful to heat and decorate the large old house; it wasn't, and isn't, exactly his element; asked 'Do you hunt?' by a neighbour he replied, 'Hunt what?' Boulton accepted it all with more charity and less appearance of being hurt than most people would manage; he implies that a country living is a good place to think from and write in. 'Guildford', though, will have an uncomfortable sound in the Church for some years to come. And it remains a useful piece of ammunition for those who want the Church to be disestablished – to be free of its connexions with the State.

Unlike provosts, deans are appointed by the Crown. The letter telling Boulton that he was not to be Dean arrived on 11 March, and came from a senior civil servant, the Treasury Secretary for Appointments, who advises the Prime Minister

on various posts, not all of them ecclesiastical; the theory is
that the Prime Minister advises the Sovereign, who makes the
final decision, but it's accepted that the effective advice is given
to the Appointments Secretary by bishops and interested laymen, and that the final tick on the sheet of paper is made by
the Prime Minister himself. There is some evidence, in the
case of Guildford, that the Queen knew nothing of the affair –
at least, that she had been given none of the details – until
someone from the Church who was pro-Boulton told her
about it. Whatever the exact sequence of events – later in the
chapter there is an attempt to unravel it – it was the Crown
that was in a position to make the legal offer of the Deanery of
Guildford.

The Sovereign has been 'supreme governor' of the Church
since the Reformation, but long before that, Kings of England
had been in conflict with Popes, influencing or controlling the
appointment of bishops. The result of this distant struggle for
power is that the State, in one form or another, now appoints
all bishops, all deans – but not provosts – some canons, and
more than 800 vicars and rectors. Periodically, and always
when trouble like Guildford blows up, there is an outcry about
these appointments. They are blasphemous, they are shameful,
they are a running sore, they put the hierarchy of the Church
in the hands of politicians who might be pagans. 'Congratulations as you go forward to your high office,' wrote the Rector
of Woodford, the Rev. Christopher Wansey, an inveterate
enemy of the system, in a satirical 'Letter to an unknown
bishop-to-be.' 'And congratulations, too, on keeping your
name on the files of the Prime Minister's Appointments
Secretary!' A counter-argument, often heard from Low
churchmen who fear a steady movement towards Rome, is
that so long as we have an Established Church, the very
conditions of the Establishment will preserve England from

Popery. John Cordle, Member of Parliament for Bourne-mouth East and Christchurch, and part-owner of the Evangelical *Church of England Newspaper*, said in a radio discussion that 'why I particularly applaud the Established Church as such [is that] it keeps England Protestant. The Queen is the supreme governor of the Church of England, by law established. And by the oath she took at the Coronation, she is bound to retain the Protestant heritage'. A further argument for Establishment is that the State chooses better men than the Church would be likely to – that Crown appointments, in fact, are the only ones where any kind of system operates.

This argument is heard among clergymen, but is given its full weight only by one of the State's practitioners – such as Brigadier Watkins, who looks after patronage for the Lord Chancellor. While bishops and deans are appointed by the Prime Minister, the 800-odd ordinary livings of which the Crown is patron are split up among Government departments. The Prime Minister has about 160, the Home Secretary and the Duchy of Lancaster have about forty each, the Duchy of Cornwall has twenty-six, the Admiralty has a few; and the Lord Chancellor has the biggest slice of all, between 500 and 600 livings. Apart from this Crown patronage, the supply of clergy for English parishes is largely in the hands of 6,000 or 7,000 individual private patrons, the individual bishops, other clergymen, and 'boards of patronage' in the dioceses – there are no rules, only a confused system with its roots in the past, sometimes the past of over 1,000 years ago. So the Lord Chancellor's office is one of the few places where an overall strategy can be pursued for the good of the Church.

Brigadier Watkins has firm features with clipped grey hair, and carries a monocle and watch with chain. An active churchman and a Justice of the Peace, he was a professional soldier before he joined the Lord Chancellor's staff, his last appointment being in the Military Secretary's branch at the War Office. His father was a parson. He is very conscientous, refusing to treat the job as a sinecure, and has devised a workmanlike system to put the right man in the right place: 'I want to go on the same principle as when I was at the War Office in their personnel branch. I have to know everything about a man before I put him in a parish, and I get confidential reports – testimonials aren't worth the paper they're written on.'

Watkins deploys his manpower from the third floor of a building in Dean's Yard, a quiet square at the back of Church House in Westminster, facing the walls of Westminster Abbey. A large map with coloured pins shows the Lord Chancellor's livings, which are especially thick down the eastern side of the country. In another room are carefully maintained files. The brigadier says that 'When a man comes into our orbit he gets a personal file, and this isn't destroyed till the day he dies'. Information has been going on record in the Lord Chancellor's office for a long time. Watkins has the original authority which decided how many of the Crown livings were to be handled by the Lord Chancellor: a copy of the *Liber Regis*, the King's Book, dated 1536, whose 1,391 pages list the annual income of livings at that time; those worth more than £20 went to the Prime Minister, those below to the Lord Chancellor. Watkins said:

The earliest churches, were built by lords of the manor, and having built them, they said, Dammit, we ought to be able to appoint our own parsons. They may have pinched bits of land from wrongdoers. Now, from the time of the Norman Conquest, the Kings of England wanted to fight the Pope – this is why they wanted the patronage. But they couldn't handle it themselves, so they left some of the better ones to the Lord High Steward – the present equivalent is the First Lord of the Treasury, the Prime Minister. The others went to the Lord High Chancellor of Britain, the Keeper of the King's Conscience.

The total number of livings administered by Watkins remains constant, though for the sake of convenience, 'we do some swaps with bishops to get blocks in the same place'.

The files themselves are elaborate. One thick book of cards lists the Chancellor's parishes, with size and type of population ('agricultural', 'shopkeepers', etc.), the incumbent's age and stipend, details of the parsonage house, and the churchmanship in detail – not simply 'Central', but 'Central plus'. The importance of the parish is indicated by a code: (1) is a 'top-notch parish' with a tradition to keep up, (2) is ordinary urban, (3) is ordinary rural. There are further sub-divions – (3a) would be a large rural centre, (3b) an ordinary country parish. And what is the point of this meticulous grading? 'What I am leading up to,' said Watkins, 'is measuring the calibre of the man to go there.' The personal files on individuals were not available, but another thick book of cards, said Watkins, gave details of clergymen who wanted to move – included here were many incumbents who were not at present in the Lord Chancellor's livings, but who wanted to be. Small coloured discs made for easy assessment. Red meant a man was already under the Lord Chancellor's patronage. Dark blue was a 'market-town type'. Green meant his name had been put forward by an M.P. – 'If that happens, the man must have a reason for doing it.' Yellow meant there was something special. Blue meant he was suitable for a canonry.

The object, explained Watkins, is to know the men and the parishes; and in five years he has been to all his parishes at least once. 'I want to prove to you,' he said, 'that Crown patronage is as well administered as any and a sight better than most. We're appointing leaders in the countryside – one form of leader – and fundamentally there's no difference between leaders of the Church, leaders in the Services, or leaders in industry. The first thing I said to myself was, I must fit square pegs to square holes, round pegs to round holes. So I said I must know everything about the parish first.' He was looking for personality. 'You can't expect the earth, because we're short of supply. But I'm an old soldier, and having wandered round the world for thirty-two years, I've got some idea of selecting leaders.'

He described how the selection process worked in a specific instance, when the important Cambridge church of Great St Mary's was due to become vacant in 1959, the vicar, Mervyn Stockwood, having been offered the bishopric of Southwark. Stockwood had been filling Great St Mary's with under-graduates on Sunday evenings, and there was a reputation to maintain. 'For such a case,' said Watkins, 'I've got a drill, a special drill. I must know everything about it.' He heard from the Archbishop. 'I went and stayed with Stockwood, dined with the churchwardens, had drinks with the Union, had quite a lot of the lads to lunch, and saw the object of the church was to draw the undergraduate. I was then able to write a letter to fourteen of the bishops, say what was needed here, and ask if they had anyone to suggest. When it's a case like this, I go off my register and go world-wide.' Thirty names were put forward, and Watkins enlisted the help of the then Principal of Westcott House, the Rev. K. M. Carey. The list was brought down to six, and the Lord Chancellor, the Archbishop of Canterbury, and the bishop of the diocese made the final choice among themselves; here, as in most cases, the selectors worked by convincing one another, though the last word remains with the Lord Chancellor.

No one could be more painstaking than Watkins. But anti-Establishment clergymen might object not merely because they dislike the idea of confidential reports and indestructible files, but because they might question the principles on which the office is run. The Crown's yardstick makes inevitable assumptions of status and orthodoxy. The man who would be a social embarrassment is out – Watkins was explicit: 'I've got to guard my boss, and the Queen, really, against putting in someone who's had a nervous breakdown, or perhaps someone who's had to divorce his wife and marry someone else. That's what I call a problem child, and I wouldn't ask the Queen to deal with that. Or again, someone with extreme churchmanship, someone who's almost a Roman -- we shouldn't have to deal with someone like that, it would be a monstrous thing.'

Much of the machinery involved in Establishment is quaint rather than anything else. Watkins looks after one twenty-fifth of the Church's parishes with great efficiency, and his methods are important. But all manner of survivals exist in the shape of dry fibres that bind Church to State – from the Ecclesiastical Household maintained by the Sovereign, down to the relations between local mayor and vicar, where (as Harrisson's *Britain Revisited* reports) the vicar says encouraging words about the mayor in the first sermon of a new year of office, the mayor has vicar and wife round for refreshments in the mayor's parlour, and a cordial understanding is arrived at for the mayoral year. At the mayor-and-vicar level, Establishment is a rather shadowy idea behind the relationship. With the Ecclesiastical Household, a precise protocol is being followed. The Clerk of the Closet, a retired bishop, and his deputy are in charge; among their responsibilities is the College of Chaplains, consisting of thirty-four clergymen, chosen partly with an eye to having most parts of England represented, who continue to do what they were doing already, their sole duty being to preach an annual sermon before the Sovereign. They are all sound, and frequently distinguished. The 1961 list included K. M. Carey, W. G. Fallows, the Principal of Ripon Hall, the theological college; P. T. B. ('Tubby') Clayton who founded Toc H; and eight holders of the Military Cross. The deputy Clerk is also sub-Dean of the Chapels Royal (the Bishop of London is Dean), and his work includes looking after a chapel at Buckingham Palace and two at St James's Palace. Three 'priests in ordinary' are employed, and three deputy priests.

Then there are the margins of Establishment which are sometimes made to appear central, to be an indispensable part of the system. A wedding at Westminster Abbey is lent official approval by the faded green-striped awning that comes out, the carpet on the ground, the couple of cathedral canons greeting guests, and the policemen standing about, watching the taxis and Bentleys come round Parliament Square and draw up at the pavement. Newspaper photographers like an Abbey wedding; or it might be a wedding at the Queen's Chapel of the Savoy, a curious survival off the Strand, on land once owned by the House of Lancaster. The Crown annexed it five and a half centuries ago, but the chapel is still administered through 'the Chancellor and Council of the Duchy'. The priest in charge (at present the Rev. Roger Roberts, editor of the *Church Times*) is responsible only to the Queen – no bishop has a say in it – and is known as the Queen's Chaplain of the Savoy. His income is a private matter between him and the Queen. Since 1937 it has been the chapel of the Royal Victorian Order, and members of the Order are sometimes married there; the Chaplain preaches there on a Sunday, at services which are normally open to anyone, though if he wished he could (unlike a clergyman at an ordinary church) exclude the public. The nearby Savoy Hotel looks on it as its unofficial chapel, and if a guest needed an Anglican priest, this is where they would ring for advice (Roman Catholic guests are sent to Corpus Christi in Maiden Lane, to the north of the Strand). Walter Boulton, when he had been refused the Deanery of Guildford and was marking time while the row went on, was told that the Duchy of Lancaster would 'consider' it if he was interested in the Savoy Chapel, then vacant; but he felt it was 'a bit Alice in Wonderland', and turned it down.

When it comes to the appointment of bishops, the picture is equally quaint; many also find it distasteful. Not only does the Crown make the appointment, but it does so under a procedure that maintains the fiction of free election by the cathedral chapter, although the chapter has no option but to choose the name submitted by the Crown. A statute of 1533 lays down the rigmarole. When a bishopric is vacant, dean and chapter are 'granted' a licence, the *congé d'élire*, to elect a new bishop, this licence being accompanied by a 'letter missive' which tells them who they have to elect. If they fail to do as they're told, they become liable to the penalties of *praemunire*, which, as the anti-Establishment school repeats with relish every time a bishop is being elected, could mean the loss of civil rights, forfeiture of lands, goods and chattels, and imprisonment during the King's pleasure. Chapters don't fail to elect; nor, after the election, do archbishops fail to consecrate. Some ecclesiastical writers like to point out that it is through consecration, not election, that bishops derive their spiritual authority; however, like the chapter, the archbishop is under orders, and is subject to *praemunire* should he refuse to consecrate.

Crown appointments were something of which Walter Boulton had often been critical, without, perhaps, ever supposing he would be involved in an appointments row himself. When he returned to England, and the small parish of Fleet, in Hampshire, in 1949, his reputation was mainly in India, and especially Calcutta, where his long, leathery, pleasantly lined face and thinning grey hair endeared him to many and were disliked by a few, who found him too uncompromising. He was more than three years at Fleet, and it was there that Mont-gomery-Campbell approached him to go to Guildford in 1952. Later Campbell left Guildford, and was succeeded as Bishop by Ivor Watkins, who had been with Boulton at Cuddesdon theological college, and so was an old acquaint-ance.

By this time, Boulton had decided that the idea of the parish-church cathedral, with responsibility for a parish around it, was wrong: he wanted a cathedral pure and simple, serving the diocese, working 'on the frontiers', not tied down by the need to administer a parish. At first he found little response from Watkins. The Bishop wanted a parish-church cathedral; and he indicated to more than one person that he disagreed strongly with the ideas of his Provost, and doubted if he was the person for the job. But as the money came in and the cathedral went ahead on Stag Hill, Boulton, helped by lawyers at Church House, drew up the Guildford Cathedral Measure for the approval, first, of the Church Assembly, and then of Parliament. The lawyers pointed out that if he were content with a parish-church cathedral, he would automatic-ally become Provost of the new one as soon as it replaced Holy Trinity. But Boulton's plan required a 'cathedral peculiar', without a parish, which meant appointing a dean instead of a provost. The lawyers said this was a tricky point, since it meant that Boulton would have to resign as Provost before he could be appointed Dean. One suggestion put forward was to have the appointment of Dean in the hands of the Bishop, but the Crown refused to consider this. So the lawyers told Boulton that there would be a period immediately after his resignation when the Crown could appoint whom it liked. To this, perhaps unwisely, Boulton had two replies. The first was that he believed in the scheme and was prepared to take the risk; the second was that in any case it had been a gruelling job, and he was proposing to resign after the new cathedral was on its feet; the second reply was remembered, and, later on, whispered as one of the reasons for passing him over.

The Guildford Cathedral Measure became law in March 1959. The cathedral should have been consecrated the following year, but the building programme was behind schedule, and the date was put back to May 1961. About a year before this, the Bishop of Guildford had swung towards Boulton's way of thinking; he seems to have been a good, steady, not particularly outstanding man, with reservations about Boulton's ideas that continued after he had given his formal approval. But he had certainly made up his mind. One day towards the end of October 1960 he and Boulton were discussing the cathedral, and Watkins said: 'You will be carrying on, won't you?' Boulton felt it necessary to ask once again: 'Will you back my ideas?' Watkins said Yes, emphatically. But two days later he had a thrombosis and died, thus making it possible for the anti-Boulton group to shake their heads sadly and say: 'If only Ivor had been alive, he'd have taken Walter aside and handled the matter at diocesan level – you see, Ivor told him long before this that he wasn't going to be Dean.' Since Watkins is dead, no one can prove who said what; but the anti-Boultoners' version is implausible if only because the whole idea of the cathedral, as foreshadowed in the Guildford Cathedral Measure, was Boulton's, and Watkins, hesitantly at first and then with more warmth, had endorsed it. A seedy aspect of the Guildford affair was the way improbable remarks were attributed to the dead bishop. However, when he died it seemed no more than inconvenient.

'If Ivor had been quicker in making up his mind,' said Boulton, 'I'd have got round the diocese expounding my ideas of a cathedral. But until I was sure of him this was obviously impossible. I called a meeting of the cathedral chapter and said: "We're in an awful quandary. I was thinking of going round the diocese, but now what is one to do?" They said: "We think you ought to do it." So I did – and I was delighted by the way it was received and the enthusiasm it created.'

The following month, Boulton had a visit from the Secretary for Appointments, David Stephens, a civil servant of charming manners whose post is a more senior counterpart of Brigadier Watkins's – Stephens ceased to fill it later in 1961, and went to a post at the House of Lords. The Appointments Secretary advises the Prime Minister on the selection of regius professors, lords lieutenants, and museum trustees, but the controversial part of his work is helping to find bishops and deans. He works as Watkins does, writing letters marked *Private and Confidential*, visiting clergymen and important laymen, treading the soft grass of cathedral closes and the soft carpets of good clubs, accumulating information about candidates for the hierarchy. The Appointments Secretary follows the Civil Service principle that once a decision is made it becomes impossible to keep it a secret, so the thing to do is to leave decisions as late as possible. Boulton said (to me) that when Stephens visited Guildford towards the end of November 1960, it was to discuss finding a new Bishop of Guildford, not appointing the Dean. But as he was leaving after lunch, Stephens said: 'Well, Provost, what about the deanery?' Boulton murmured that this was a Crown appointment. Pressed as to how he felt, he said: 'I was thinking of getting out, but the late bishop and the chapter have urged me to get the thing started and carry on, say, for three or four years.' Ah,

c

said Stephens, the Crown couldn't consider temporary arrangements. So Boulton said: 'Then let's cut out the temporary and get it started.' Stephens returned to London, Boulton wrote to confirm that he thought his name should go forward, and no more was heard till the following year.

Shortly after Stephen's visit, though, the Provost was involved in another of the little disagreements that have cropped up through his career, when a red paper-backed book he had written, called *Marriage*, was published by the Mothers' Union. Boulton had not been over-keen when the Mothers' Union asked him, a year or two before, to write the book. He was busy, and before starting it, took pains to ensure that they would want to publish what he would want to write. For the Mothers' Union has uncompromising views on divorce. At Mary Sumner House, the headquarters in Westminster, where parties of women from the provinces troop round the offices, women officials in sensible costumes tell inquirers that 'the Mothers' Union has stood in its whole eighty years for the family, based on marriage as a permanent relationship'. There are 11,000 branches in Britain, with nearly half a million members, who, as an official said with a sweet smile, 'range from the dimmest of mums up to the professional woman'. Most parishes have a Mothers' Union branch; the vicar can close it if he wishes, but this rarely happens, and if it does, the members can affiliate to the diocesan or the central organization. The official object of the Mothers' Union is to 'strengthen, to safeguard, and promote Christian family life', and it does this chiefly by, as the phrase goes, the 'witness', that is, the good example, of its members. It issues posters, like the one entitled 'The Church's Home Guard', showing husband, wife, and four children sitting idyllically under a tree, with a church across the meadows. Divorce, to the Mothers' Union, is unthinkable for true Christians. It was founded in 1876, after the first Matrimonial Causes Bill had made divorce generally available, and no woman who has been divorced, whether or not she was the guilty party, may be a member. For years, when divorce was comparatively rare, this was an unexceptionable condition – so much so that, as the Mothers' Union points out rather plaintively, it's only in recent years that the original aims have been rediscovered. Instead of being seen as a jolly gathering of churchwomen, usually the middle-aged and older women, in the parish, headed by the vicar's wife and able to make its presence felt by the weight of its approval or disapproval, it now insists how specialized it is: a society to 'emphasize the lifelong nature of marriage'. Inevitably the Mothers' Union has a dated air,* and seems on the defensive. Bishops are no longer so ready to spring to its aid, and like most organizations with unsensational aims, it receives a bad Press because when nothing is going wrong there is nothing to report. Now and then vicars quarrel with branches and it gets into the papers – there was the North Country parish where in 1961 the vicar discovered he had 200 Mothers' Union members, of whom only a few, he said, were regular churchgoers; some hadn't been confirmed; no more than forty attended the monthly Communion service for members. The vicar's attempts to change this state of affairs led to disagreements, he dismissed the committee, the branch

* Even friendly references in parish magazines may have an edge. One diocesan news sheet, inserted in a number of magazines, couldn't resist remarking on the 'useful advice to M.U. banner parties at the Festival Services, recommending them to wear gloves, not to carry bags, but "walk slowly in step and in line, with shoulders touching and hands clasped", and not to wear veils over their hats. Next year, for a change, why not wear the veils over the banners, and carry hats, with heads touching and bags clasped? Or banners over the hats, with bags touching and heads clasped? Excuse our glove'.

complained to the parochial church council, and the P.C.C. took sides with the women and told the vicar that unless he reinstated the committee, the council's contribution to his stipend – between £4 and £5 a week – would be withheld. The vicar held out, they stopped the contribution and his telephone expenses, and the bishop had to come to the rescue with a grant from diocesan funds. 'On looking back,' the vicar said later (in a letter to me), 'it seems to me to be quite appalling that any Christian body should use financial blackmail of its priest to get its way, that a body of professing Christian women should calmly contemplate depriving a married man with a child of financial support to force him to do something that according to the constitution of the organization accepted by all of them is a matter entirely within his discretion.' Other vicars have been known to complain of 'dictatorial women' and 'pharisaism', and the joke that the 'Mothers' Union runs the Church' is, according to the clergyman who had the quarrel, 'a joke with more than a grain of truth in it'.

The commonest criticism of the M.U. is that it is harsher towards divorcees than is the Church itself. The Church has decided, by Act of Convocation, that the marriage service should be denied to a divorced person whose partner is still living. The State has never been asked to endorse this, and would certainly have refused if it had been asked. All the State says is that Anglican clergymen are under no obligation to marry a divorced person whose partner is still living. So the Convocation ruling is morally but not legally binding, and clergymen can marry divorcees if they wish – though few of them do. A divorced churchman may still take Communion, as long as he remains unmarried. But once he (or she) re-marries, he is, according to the strictest Church view, living in sin, because the Church's law doesn't recognize divorce in the modern sense of the word;* he will be virtually excommunicated (though there is no formal process) and refused Communion.

However, Convocation has also decided that if the bishop thinks it advisable, and no offence will be caused to the Church, he can let divorcees who have remarried take Communion. This is a modest concession to reality; and it is just such a concession which is said to be lacking from the Mother's Union, where a childless wife or even a spinster may join, but never a woman, however innocent, who has been divorced – let alone one who has remarried.

Endless controversy surrounds the matter. One month the Bishop of Bedford will write to the magazine *Theology* that, kind and holy as divorcees may be, 'as witnesses to the permanence of the marriage relationship, they are a dead loss. In exactly the same way the members of the M.U. would be a dead loss as witnesses to the power and beauty of virginity'. Next month the Bishop of Worcester and his wife write a joint letter to say the Mothers' Union attitude is a 'tragedy', and call for a 'more Christian spirit'. The Church wants to condemn divorce, yet has to coexist with a State which accepts divorce as a fact of life. One solution would be to follow the Roman Catholics: refuse to recognize divorce in the modern sense, but leave a loop-hole by declaring that for certain reasons, a marriage may have been null and void from the start.

This was the suggestion that Walter Boulton put forward in

* The Church's authority is the Canon Law of 1604, which dealt only with divorce *a thoro et mensa* (separation) and nullity; there wasn't, and still isn't in Canon Law, such a thing as the dissolution of a valid marriage. Thus the fully married person who has a divorce and then marries again is committing perpetual adultery as far as many churchmen are concerned.

the last few pages of his book for the Mothers' Union, *Marriage*, which caused the row at the end of 1960. After saying that Christians who had gone into marriage knowing what it meant could never be divorced in the Church's eyes, Boulton wrote of 'the very different situation if there was no preparation before marriage, and no discussion and clear agreement between the parties as to what their marriage meant'. Because the State now permitted divorce, argued Boulton, it meant that either or both the parties to a marriage might go into it honestly intending it to be a 'terminable contract', not a lifelong union. To deal with such cases he quoted a suggestion by the Bishop of Exeter, Dr Mortimer, who is a distinguished theologian, that the Church should set up 'marriage courts' to decide on the validity of marriages where there was any doubt about the intentions of man or wife. The Mothers' Union saw the manuscript, an official visited Guildford to discuss details, Boulton was offered a fee, which he declined, and the book was published. It was promptly attacked in a review in the *Church Times*, whose reviewer said it tried to establish a 'novel doctrine' of marriage which could 'only create dreadful confusion in the minds of any young couples who read it'. English law, it added, knew one kind of marriage, not two. A fortnight later, without reference to Boulton, the book, which had then sold 300 copies, was withdrawn by the Mothers' Union; the first the Provost heard of it was a phone call from a reporter, asking for his comments. The central secretary of the Mothers' Union was quoted in the papers as saying: 'The book was withdrawn because of criticism, and because, if it does give the impression that there are two types of marriage, it is contrary to the principles of the Mothers' Union. The Mothers' Union is absolutely solid on its views on marriage.' What happened, apparently, was that the *Church Times* review upset some branch officials of the Mothers'

Union, who referred it to the wife of the then Archbishop of Canterbury, Mrs Fisher, who was one of the M.U. vice-presidents, who referred it to her husband. They got cold feet at Mary Sumner House, and the book was withdrawn. In the meantime, the Mothers' Union had sent it to an 'eminent theologian', who seems to have replied that the book was clearly an attack on the Church's policy, that it was in advance of its times, but that for his part he largely agreed with the Provost – which was not surprising, since the eminent theologian was the Bishop of Exeter, whose ideas on marriage courts were quoted on page 100 as a central part of Boulton's argument. But the Bishop had been writing in a different context – a re-edition (1959) of Lacey's *Marriage in Church and State*, which was unlikely to be read by many members of the Mothers' Union. Boulton had made the point in a popular booklet, price three shillings. He had also – though this was not the Mothers' Union objection – raised issues affecting Establishment, since the idea of a State Church pronouncing on the validity of marriages, through the medium of special courts, would be distasteful to the State. A Jesuit writing in the Roman Catholics' *Catholic Herald* was quick to see this: 'Obviously the idea of Church marriage courts would involve a break with the State and an end of Establishment'. Boulton had been a little bold. He had not applied those brakes and euphemisms which provosts should apply, particularly if they wish to continue to rise. Everyone, including Boulton himself, denies that the row over *Marriage* was the reason for what happened later; but it was fairly obviously an example of the *kind* of reason that influenced the Prime Minister.

Boulton, and most of Guildford's churchpeople, went on expecting him to be appointed Dean until well into 1961. The Archbishop of Canterbury sent for him in February to discuss the consecration of the cathedral, due in May. He asked about the deanery, and Boulton replied: 'I propose to resign and the Crown will make the appointment.' The appointment of the Very Rev. George Reindorp, the Provost of Southwark, to be the new Bishop of Guildford had been announced the previous month, and he was made Bishop on 25 March. By this time the rumours about Boulton were abroad. On 11 March, in fact, he had received a letter from Stephens, the Appointments Secretary, telling him that the Prime Minister was unable to nominate him for the deanery, and offering the City of London church of St Mary Aldermary. Boulton consulted the canons who made up the chapter of the cathedral; they had taken it for granted that the Provost would be appointed, and they now felt insulted. They telephoned to Whitehall immediately, but were told they were wasting their time. So they advised Boulton to go to London.

At this meeting with Stephens, as at all the meetings that followed in the spring, nothing happened to change events. Boulton said he wasn't grinding a personal axe, that he probably *was* the worst person for the job, but that the people most concerned with the appointment, the cathedral chapter, hadn't been consulted. According to Boulton, 'Stephens said that one of the canons did write to him, but he was only an honorary canon. I said, "My dear Stephens, the honorary canons are going to *be* the governing body".' They had a brief and unprofitable exchange about Boulton's present position, which, said the Provost, was safeguarded by the existing regulations: nothing could be done about appointing a Dean until the Provost had resigned, and no one could force the Provost to go if he wanted to stay. Back in Guildford, some members of the chapter proposed that the old, parish-church constitution be left in force, and that Boulton, remaining Provost, should transfer from the old cathedral to the new. But this would have created an intolerable situation, and in the third week of

April it was announced that Boulton had resigned as Provost and Rector, the resignation to take effect from 18 May, the day after the cathedral's consecration. 'Diocese shocked by "sacking" of Provost', said the *Guildford and Godalming Times*. 'Humiliating experience after planning Cathedral's work.' People who had never read Trollope began to say it was like something out of *Barchester Towers*, and the machinery of local protest moved into action. The parochial church council, equally unconsulted, sent a deputation to the Archbishop of Canterbury, which returned without satisfaction; one of its members told the Press that 'there are certain limits below which the name of justice has a hollow ring'. This man, a senior B.B.C. official, had been a civil servant in India when Boulton was there, when 'Walter Boulton was a myth. The Governor used to say: "We must get Boulton up".' Of Boulton's particular gift, as shown in Guildford, he says that 'I think it's the word love, if you're going to talk straight. If there were a prize for discovering what his weaknesses are, the P.C.C. would win it on all counts. Impetuosity – no respecter of persons. But he was violently liked at all levels.' People in Guildford used, and use, phrases like 'He threw a light on things' and 'I was caught by him'. So there was much anger and sympathy. The discovery of a technical flaw in his resignation as Rector meant that while ceasing to be Provost, he could continue in the parish until he was offered a reasonable living elsewhere; his income as Provost and Rector had been £1,500 a year, and the church council agreed to make up his income as Rector alone – which would have been £340 – to £1,000, to pay him £150 expenses, and to let him have the rectory rent and rates free; with three children away at school, he wasn't in a position to take a severe cut in his stipend.

The Archbishop of Canterbury drafted a letter to send to anyone who wrote to him about the affair. It began:

I know well that Mr Boulton's ministry as pastor has been blessed by successful achievement. There is no doubt that in Guildford, as elsewhere, he has been an inspiring, loving, and successful pastor and leader. The deanery of Guildford will provide great pastoral opportunities, but other gifts, too, are needed for the whole range of demands which are presented by a new cathedral. It is no criticism whatsoever of Mr Boulton's ministry that the Crown's advisers should have come to the conclusion that they must look elsewhere for a dean.

But the general opinion in the Press, both Church and secular, seemed to be that if it was no criticism of Boulton it was certainly criticism of the Crown, which not only failed to recognize merit, but let the Provost, the chapter, the parish, and most of the diocese imagine the deanery was his, then snatched it away at the last minute. 'It is a situation which is manifestly unfair to Mr Boulton,' wrote the *Evening Standard*, 'but one which is likely to be repeated so long as the Church of England remains as much a nationalized society as the Coal Board.' The *Church Times* moved from 'sympathy and surprise' to the suspicion that 'there has been a serious miscarriage of justice'. The *Church of England Newspaper* (although, as a minor pillar of the Evangelical wing, it is strongly in favour of keeping the Establishment) said: 'It looks like a clear case of dirty work at the cross-roads. The night was dark, the victim was alone, the temptation was irresistible. The uproar, however, has been more than the assailant expected.' In Guildford, where the temperature was higher still, letters to newspapers spoke of 'public scandal', 'base ingratitude', 'spiritual McCarthyism' and 'Star Chamber' (though not everyone was on the Provost's side. Writing about a petition to the Queen that was organized by Boulton's supporters, and that, naturally, got no farther than the Prime Minister, the editor of the *Surrey Advertiser* said that 'The height of absurdity was reached. . . . The idea that the casual public were better qualified to judge the merits of an appointment than the Crown's advisers . . . makes nonsense of democracy'). In one London journal, some pointed remarks by a Boulton sympathizer nearly led to a libel action (not by Boulton) that would have delighted the Press if it had ever come to court. And under the surface, speculation and denigration flourished. While the Provost was being offered a selection of livings, and while the Press was saying how good a pastor he was, the whispers could be heard. The *Daily Telegraph* columnist, Peterborough, printed a friendly paragraph saying that 'Mr Boulton has spent twenty years of his life in India, where his selflessness was a byword. During the grievous famine there in 1943, while he was Canon of Calcutta, he sold his car in order to buy rice for Indians.' This would seem a reasonable piece of evidence for selflessness; but the same story was told to me by an anti-Boulton parson, who, after insisting that Boulton had known all along that he wasn't to be made Dean, said it was a 'story with classic ingredients – injustice to the clergy, the archbishop in his palace, etcetera. It was easy enough for Boulton to run a parish church, full of retired colonels who were devoted to him. A cathedral was a different matter. As for India, Boulton sold his car, apparently, to feed the poor. The result was that the man was totally unable to do his job properly for the next four years.' They were artful sneers. As for the mechanics, as opposed to the ethics, of the affair, the most reasonable excuse was that the absence of a Bishop of Guildford – from Watkins's death in October 1960 until Reindorp's installation in March 1961 – immobilized the machine, since Boulton's resignation as Provost had to be made to the bishop; until Reindorp's installation was near, then, it was impractical to tell Boulton, since he couldn't resign until there was a bishop to accept the resignation.

Attempts to have the appointment discussed officially failed. The Rev. Christopher Wansey, twisting the thorn in his elders' flesh, stood up at the Convocation of Canterbury and drew attention to the 'peculiar ecclesiastical death of one of her most respected members, the Provost of Guildford'. The Archbishop, Dr Fisher, who never had time for interruptions when he was in the chair, told Wansey to sit down, and refused to allow any discussion. The Provost of Southwell tried an oblique approach in the Church Assembly. He gave notice to the chairman of the Church's Legal Board of an interesting question:

If the Crown, through its advisers, takes action in connexion with the Established Church, which, because of its outward appearance of injustice, evokes criticism, what course is open to a member of the Church who seeks information whereby such criticism might be allayed?

But the Provost was ruled out of order, and his question was never put.

Boulton preached his last sermon as Provost on Sunday, 14 May. The church was full and the Provost was outspoken. 'Self-interest,' he said, 'steps in when a pronouncement may precipitate a crisis and the Church as an organization may suffer. So diplomacy displaces prophecy and administrative skill ignores truth. Word goes round – silence the protest, stop the arguments, close the ranks – and the Church is saved. But it is saving its body at the expense of its soul.' The next day it was announced that the Bishop Suffragan of Pontefract, the Rt Rev. G. W. Clarkson, had been appointed Dean of Guildford; asked how he felt about filling the position, Clarkson replied: 'The Lord will lead us all together.' On the Wednesday the cathedral was consecrated, and Boulton, his face expressionless, carried out his duties as Provost for the last time; some of those who watched it on television thought he was nervous; it was also observed, for what it was worth, that when he bowed to the Queen, she appeared to turn aside. The congregation included the Duke of Edinburgh, Princess Margaret, Mr Antony Armstrong-Jones, the Archbishops of Canterbury and Wales, twenty-three bishops, and sixteen deans and provosts.

The row lasted beyond the consecration. In June the Bishop of Leicester, R. R. Williams, was deploring 'hasty and ill-considered comment' on the matter, and the fact that 'the last weeks of Archbishop Fisher's Primacy have been clouded by an unhappy controversy'. Williams criticized our 'inquisitive society', and made the curious suggestion that there was a place for 'the occasional decision which is unexplained and confidently left in the hands of those to whom history and tradition have committed it'. Early in July Wansey made his way to Guildford parish church, where Boulton was still the incumbent, and preached at evensong about the 'solemn nonsense' of Crown appointments. 'At a time when new life is surging through the veins of the Church of England,' he said, 'safe men are being appointed as bishops and fire-extinguishers as deans. Today, when a man is appointed bishop, he goes not into the van of the Church's life, but as it were into the guard's van, where the brakes are.' The following week it was announced that Boulton would be leaving Guildford in August, having accepted the country livings of Market Overton with Thistleton: in the gift of the Bishop of Peterborough, financially among the best parishes in the diocese, miles and miles from anywhere.

The noise faded, except in Guildford, where Boulton's friends failed to find a site for an outdoor gathering to present the ex-Provost with a cheque. To use the Castle Grounds, they were told, would 'create a dangerous precedent', while the grounds of a grammar school were not available because the governors sought an assurance that no official reference would be made to the controversy. Eventually the gathering was held at Holy Trinity Hall, where Boulton was handed a cheque.

'One's vocation in this case,' he said to me at Market Overton, 'is, to put it bluntly, to be a guinea-pig.' Others, too, think the Guildford affair may have scratched the surface of some people's acquiescence in the system. Crown appointments were under review within six months (though there have been too many such reviews for anyone to be more than lukewarm about it). Meanwhile Walter Boulton has become a country parson again, with time to read and write. He has two churches and a few hundred people to look after. During term-time the rectory has too many rooms, but at holidays there are three children to help fill them. Sometimes there will be visits from his married daughters and their husbands. Boulton is an entertaining, companionable man, grave but not pious. Since the day they decided not to make him Dean, he has become a symbol of bad management and a piece of evidence for disestablishment. All this is arguable; a disestablished Church might make more mistakes than an established one; perhaps it is true that he would have been a poor administrator. But it *looked* wrong. Who were the anti-Boulton people and why were they anti? Was it true, as one of the rumours said, that Boulton's name had gone forward to the Prime Minister, only to be scratched out at the last minute because someone whispered words of caution in certain ears? Why was there a mystery? The answer seems to be only that Boulton was unorthodox and said the wrong things; in many ways he was the right man, but when it came to the moment of choice he was seen to be quite wrong for a senior post in a cautious organization. 'You see, Boulton,' someone told him, 'we don't think you're a man of sound judgement.' It was damning and conclusive; it was as simple as that.

CHAPTER FOUR

BISHOPS

ASKED how a bishop could be distinguished from other clergy in church, a child in the diocese of Chester wrote in an examination that 'He would have a kind face and hairy hands. Red hair and a beard. He would have a chain round his neck. He has a robe and a sort of train. His collar would be back to front. He has a sort of crown. His hat is called a mighter.' Everyone recognizes that bishops have presence. 'Bishop', like 'girl' and 'ghost', is an effective headline-word; it has satisfying overtones, and Methodists have been known to complain that while a district chairman can say something startling and have it ignored, a bishop has only to say that sin is prevalent or nuclear bombs need careful thought, and he can be sure of three inches in the paper. History was full of bishops: they are part of the fabric of the nation, and as such demand, and receive, serious notice.

Bishops are addressed as 'My Lord' and are described as 'the Right Reverend', not merely 'Reverend'. On becoming a diocesan bishop a clergyman has traditionally been made a doctor of divinity by the Archbishop of Canterbury if he is not one already, and it has always been safe to prefix his name with 'Dr'. There's no reason why a bishop should not be addressed as 'Mr' but somehow he never is – though this may change, since the present Archbishop has said that in future 'Lambeth degrees' will not be awarded automatically.

In many ways, bishops conform to the times, just as humbler subjects do. But within the Church they remain figures of traditional grandeur, ruling by influence rather than by authority. Always, beyond their legal, official powers, is the authority of their titles and traditions.

The Prayer Book's service for the consecration of bishops has a tightly-knit group of questions and responses to cover all aspects of behaviour. Having agreed to the doctrines of the Church, a bishop must promise 'with all faithful diligence, to banish and drive away all erroneous and strange doctrine contrary to God's Word'. He must 'deny all ungodliness and worldly lusts, and live soberly, righteously, and godly'. He must 'maintain and set forward . . . quietness, love, and peace among all men', as well as punishing those who are 'unquiet, disobedient, and criminous'. Finally he must be 'faithful in Ordaining, sending, or laying hands upon others', and must 'shew yourself gentle, and be merciful for Christ's sake to poor and needy people, and to all strangers destitute of help'.

A bishop is supposed to be wise, authoritative, sympathetic, and accessible. He is supposed to know what's happening in all the parishes of his diocese, and usually manages to be well-informed about outstanding efficiency and incompetence among his clergy. He knows a lot about their private worries; he must be able to notice an incipient breakdown, or decide whether a clergyman who asks for money is as desperate as he sounds.

Doing much of his work from his residence, which may be anything from a modest suburban house to a stately home with a gravelled drive, the bishop is a central figure around which the diocese can group itself. His overseeing crystallizes in occasional 'visitations' of the diocese, in which every parish must answer a detailed questionnaire, and the bishop visits many of the parishes in person; this is followed by a 'visitation charge', a kind of spiritual communiqué to his clergy. But the routine is more important. Much of a bishop's time is spent in finding clergymen for vacant livings; many parishes have a bishop as patron, and he may also be consulted when he's not the patron. In addition, he has absolute authority over the assistant clergymen, the so-called curates, licensing them to work in a parish. Dr Hunter, the former Bishop of Sheffield, once wrote, rather irritably: 'I suppose more hours are spent on trying to fill livings nowadays than on any other item of administration. This is not made less frustrating by the time some people take to make up their minds and to answer letters.'

For the last hundred years, bishops have been growing busier, as the Church, like all organizations, has learned to appoint committees, produce memoranda, have endless phone conversations, and engage in democratic and public-relations activities. A bishop must sit on many committees, study statistics about finance and reports on the state of buildings, attend fêtes, and listen to fools, saints, sinners, and large numbers of average men. Even his special spiritual functions become part of a routine. Only a bishop can ordain priests and deacons, and confirm Church members. Confirmations can become especially monotonous, making some bishops feel, and complain in print, that they are 'confirmation machines', hurrying between churches to lay hands on 'those that are baptized and come to years of discretion' (Suffragan bishops, aware that by their consecration they are no less bishops than their superiors in the eyes of God, are sometimes irritated at being given most of the confirming to do).

Beyond the diocese, another set of duties take a bishop's time – perhaps twelve days a year for Church Assembly meetings in London, and another twelve at Convocation and the regular bishops' meetings. Dr Hunter adds more detail to the imposing list: 'There will be two or three consecrations of bishops in which he ought to take part. If his interests are not narrowly ecclesiastical, he may be involved in this or that at national level, and he may like to feel there is some obligation to put in an occasional appearance in the House of Lords.' The routine of being a bishop is such a usual complaint among churchmen that it takes a sophisticated bishop like Glyn Simon, the Bishop of Llandaff (a diocese of the Church in Wales) to remark that people use 'administrator' almost as a term of reproach – but that 'However rightly a bishop may delegate work he will not be any the more a spiritual man if he shirks administrative detail'.

The Bishop of Llandaff was writing in *Bishops* (Faith Press, 1961), a book he edited in which most of the contributors were themselves bishops. Simon wrote of the popular suspicion aroused by 'the Bench of Bishops' as opposed to 'our bishop'. He suggested they should be more in touch with the world; they should speak plainer English and live in smaller houses (Simon himself, to his own amusement, has no option but to live in a large establishment in the Cardiff suburb-village of Llandaff. It has an unoccupied look, and a notice on the heavy door says 'Please do not ring bell unless answer is required'. There used to be four servants; now a woman comes to clean five mornings a week). But Simon, despite the cool appraisal, is no less aware of his unique role as a bishop. He may mutter at traffic as he drives himself through Cardiff in the rush-hour, be a well-liked clubman, and say gleefully that 'I am regarded as irresponsible and a hopeless revolutionary'; but in his mind he carries a picture of the episcopacy as something laid down by God, not a useful way of managing things. One of the essays in the book is by Robert Morgan, Bishop of Truro till he retired in 1960. Morgan writes that the three orders of ministers in the Church – bishops, priests, and deacons – are a 'reflection of the Order of the Blessed Trinity'. That is, 'the mysteries gathered round the Being of God are to be reflected in the Holy Order of the Church'. Expressed in secular terms it sounds vaguely utilitarian: that we have deacons, priests, and bishops because there is a divine Trinity of Father, Son, and Holy Ghost. But Morgan is not expressing it in secular terms:

In this Trinity of Eternal love the Father glorifies the Son and sustains him in his perfect obedience and the Son glorifies the Father by the perfection of his obedience, both alike in the power of the Holy Spirit of love. . . . It is this mystery of authority and obedience and mutual indwelling in Being of the Blessed Trinity which must be reflected in Holy Order. It is this mystery which is to be reflected in the relation of the bishop with his priests and deacons. . . . We may say that Holy Order is the tireless energy of love under stable control through the mutuality of authority and obedience.

All this is endorsed by Glyn Simon, who, brushing aside any idea that Christian Churches can be reunited if they lack proper bishops, says flatly that it is God's will that bishops should govern the Church. 'Bishop Morgan's essay,' he asserts, 'throws light on the ground on which such a belief is based; it is based on nothing less than the Nature of God Himself.' Bishops might not all be prepared to go as far as this; but they take themselves and their function more seriously than many people, deluded by cheery extracts from diocesan newsletters or brief, smiling appearances on television, might suppose. A well-worn fact in this field is that nothing changes a clergyman more than becoming a bishop. Dean Inge, the sardonic Dean of St Paul's earlier this century, had an aphorism: 'When an Evangelical is made a bishop, the transformation is even more rapid than that of a Labour member who is made a peer.' Low men become Higher, High men become Lower, radicals start to conform. Even William Temple, who became Archbishop of Canterbury in 1942, and whose death two years later is still mourned by churchmen who think he might have 'changed everything', is said to have been subdued. There is the sense of dignity; there is the responsibility for souls, of being answerable to no one on earth (except for offences against Canon Law, in which case his fellow-bishops judge him) but the Crown; there is the massive and theatrical atmosphere of the cathedral; there is all that history; there is the unending expectancy of one's hearers. There are the insignia – the throne in the cathedral, the dome-shaped mitre for the head, the pectoral cross of precious metal for the breast, the golden episcopal ring with the great amethyst, the heavy staff shaped like a crook. Even a piece of correspondence can have a certain dramatic quality when the little upright cross is written alongside the bishop's signature. It is not surprising that men find it awe-inspiring, or that, in the case of ambitious clergy – who probably occur no more or less frequently than ambitious men anywhere – the signs of appetite for these things can often be read. There may be that unsettling mixture of warm charm and glazed stare – except when a bishop, a peer, or an M.P. arrives, causing the eyes to concentrate and the charm to be replaced by vigour and deference, with a trace of outspokenness. There may be a compulsive need to talk about bishops, and conversations with bishops, and intimacies shared with bishops. Some years ago a clergyman talked to me in his study – whisky, slippers, fire, books – for a quarter of an hour about his recent dealings with bishops and archbishops: quoting verbatim the letter from a high place ending 'Yours ever', telling an anecdote about an archbishop's sense of humour that turned into an anecdote about how a dean and a bishop were kept waiting while the archbishop and the clergyman hobnobbed together. Later, after talking about the amount of time bishops had to spend on the thankless task of filling vacant livings, the clergyman drank his whisky solemnly and said: 'To be a bishop? I think it's the most ghastly fate that could befall any man.' He didn't sound very convincing even then, and six months later it was announced that he had accepted a bishopric.

Everything conspires to cut the bishops off. They must be one of the most annotated bodies of men in the world, providing copy for any writer who cares to spend an hour with *Who's Who, Crockford's Clerical Directory*, and *Whitaker's*. Their high average age and the large number who went to public schools are the most commonly quoted statistics; D. L. Munby, in *God and the Rich Society* (Oxford, 1961), said the average age (of forty-one) in 1958 was sixty-one, that eighteen went to one of twelve leading public schools, that of the rest all but three went to minor public schools and grammar schools. The Rev. Maurice Wood, the Principal of Oak Hill Theological College, produced a kinder view for an Evangelical conference. Complaining that parts of the Press caricatured the Church, with 'ancient angry bishops . . . only emerging in gaiters and funny hats to complain about divorce', he said that 'The truth is that only seven out of the forty-three archbishops and diocesan bishops live in palaces, while six of the rest of our diocesans live in houses with street numbers on the door. Their average age is sixty-one; seven have been decorated for gallantry; one has been a prisoner of war in the notorious Changi camp.' Other writers point out that there are never more than two or three diocesans who have served in country livings; or that none of them are scientists; or that most of them went to Oxford or Cambridge. This close and continuing interest helps to set them apart. So does the traditional episcopal language that people keep deploring, in vain. The Bishop of Chester was quoted as having told a diocesan conference that 'The sight of the police being required to lug sit-down demonstrators into police vans is one which is neither profitable nor edifying. . . . Let Christians weigh well the issues and come to a sober judgement; and let them seek to propagate their convictions through the free and legitimate channels open to them.' At the start of 1962, the *Church of England Newspaper* quoted some New Year messages from unidentified diocesan leaflets. 'As we look forward to a new year,' said one, 'it is natural that we should wonder what it will bring forth.' 'As each year begins,' said another, 'the number changes, reminding us that we are moving forward into the new and unknown.' A third declared: 'As a new year opens let me express the hope that it may be for you all a happy and prosperous one. At the same time we must face facts and not assume the habits of the ostrich, which is said to bury its head in the sand.'

It's true that bishops are less remote than they were. A number of newer bishops would never dream of beginning an article or address with 'My dear people' and sprinkling it with similes about ships in stormy seas. They are no longer wealthy in the old sense, though they are still 'comfortably off'. A hundred years ago many of them had great estates and princely incomes. Even in 1939, Canterbury got £15,000 a year. But he had to pay for nearly everything himself. Now the Church Commissioners own bishops' houses, palaces, and gardens. They pay bishops a salary, and provide them with a black Rover apiece and a chauffeur, gardener, and secretary (but no domestic help). Canterbury is paid £7,500 a year, York £6,500, London £5,500, Durham £4,500, Winchester £3,500, and the rest £3,000. The differential is partly because of the historical status of the top five sees, partly because the Archbishop of Canterbury, say, is involved in heavy entertaining, and this may not be entirely covered by the expenses allowed him. A bishop has to pay for his own heating, except where the Inland Revenue can be persuaded to allow the Commissioners to heat a chapel in the palace, or a little-used state-room where the fabric might otherwise deteriorate. A new bishop must provide himself with robes, which could cost

£300 or £400, and such items as his episcopal ring, perhaps £50 or £100. There is no tax allowance for such things, except when they have to be replaced; but friends and parishioners often present a new bishop with much of what he will need (when Cosmo Lang went from York to be Archbishop of Canterbury in 1928, J. Pierpont Morgan, the American banker, who was a friend of his, gave him 600 tons of earth to supplement the soot-soured soil in the gardens of Lambeth Palace).

Modest though his earnings are by past standards, a bishop's salary is large enough to irritate many clergymen. Bishops' pensions are particularly irksome. The Church's latest pension scheme, put into effect in 1961, sets seventy as the retiring age. Clergy with forty years' service receive £400; archdeacons, £600; deans and provosts, £700; diocesan bishops, £1,250, except for the Bishops of London, Durham, and Winchester, with £1,750, and finally the Archbishops of Canterbury and York, with £2,000 apiece. An even sharper statistic for the clergy to swallow is that widows are entitled to one third of their husbands' pensions, which means that a bishop's widow draws more than a retired parson. When the scheme was debated by the Church Assembly, the bishops decided, or were prevailed upon, not to speak. A number of people sounded unhappy about it, but the measure was approved and received the Royal Assent. The former Bishop of Winchester, Dr Haigh – a bachelor – wrote to *The Times*, and refused to accept his increase. Some months later, at the start of 1962, Mervyn Stockwood, the Left-wing Bishop of Southwark, broke his self-imposed silence on the matter to say that 'I know now that I should have refused to toe the line, because I believe our [the bishops'] silence gave the impression that we approved the racket'. He added that 'It is not surprising that the world questions the integrity of the Church when it realizes the extent to which materialism has caught us in its grip'. Some thought it curious that bishops could be made to toe the line on any matter, let alone one of conscience.

Stockwood's presence at Southwark is the best illustration in the present-day Church of how a bishop can influence his diocese and give it a sharp image. There are some clergy in this part-industrial, part-suburban, and part-rural diocese who are distressed to find that in the few years since Stockwood became bishop in 1959, the name 'Southwark' has come to mean innovation and controversy. But a bishop's powers are great, and with a handful of key appointments he can make a diocese alter course. Stockwood came from Great St Mary's, the university church at Cambridge, where he had been a brilliant performer. He is urbane and clever, an honest radical, a good showman, and a shrewd judge of talent. What he seems to look for is social conscience allied to intellectual capacity. Parish clergymen who care about, say, housing and nuclear disarmament (both matters that concern Stockwood very much) can complain, and sometimes do complain, that it's one thing to make statements from on high and quite another to work at these things among the sour and distressing grass-roots. The Rev. Bill Sargent (see Chapter 7), who has a hard East London parish, is one of those who thinks that a social conscience is something you use to give people a roof over their heads, and intellectual capacity is a useful weapon for dealing with London County Council officials. But Stockwood's talent, which he uses to the full, seems to be one for producing the conditions that will enable ideas to breed.

Sermons, books, and television interviews issue regularly from the circle of Southwark liberals. Canon Stanley Evans makes Left-wing assertions about nuclear disarmament. Canon D. A. Rhymes preaches against a narrow morality, suggesting, among other things, that what is unnatural to the heterosexual is natural to the homosexual. A new Vice-Provost, a cathedral official, protests against the Thirty-nine Articles at the very ceremony held to appoint him. Unorthodox schemes are encouraged – for instance, a night school for businessmen who want to be ordained – but it is the steady flow of ideas about Christianity in a secular society, rather than the practical instances of application, that make Southwark important. The Bishop of Woolwich, Dr John Robinson, is one of the subsidiary bishops in the diocese, and much of the thunder against Stockwood has been on Robinson's account. But Stockwood has strongly defended the author of *Honest to God* (he says he has read it three times), declaring that 'hysterical criticisms of what has been termed "South Bank Religion" leave me unmoved'.

Many churchpeople, even those with liberal inclinations, are afraid that this is going too far – not least because of the difficulty of conveying complex ideas. The Church is proud of the amount of 'rethinking' that is going on, but at times there is an uneasy feeling that religion, which used to be full of simple certainties, is becoming intellectualized, and needs to be carefully presented to ordinary people. This need seems to be recognized in some of the appointments of bishops in recent years – for although the appointments system creaks and gives offence, it can show a computer-like wisdom in knowing what's wanted. The Bishop of Guildford, Dr Reindorp, who was appointed just before the Provost row broke out, was described by one magazine as 'ecclesiastically the Prince of PROS'. Forty-eight years old when he went to Guildford after being Provost of Southwark, George Reindorp is impressive chiefly for his enthusiasm in making contact with people: the Christian message is taken for granted, and his effort goes into conveying the information, not re-examining it. He shines at schools, clubs, meetings, and recording sessions; his manner is light and chatty, and his appearance, with thin silver hair and bony features, is episcopal yet curiously boyish; his spry manner is a sort of ironical comment on the purple cassock and the episcopal ring on the right hand, just as his way of speaking seems to be a comment on the way he knows bishops are supposed to speak. If he should happen to let slip a phrase like 'In my judgement', he apologizes and says: 'That's always used by bishops when they mean "What I think".' He is an ardent communications-man, leaning forward to murmur: 'I would be so grateful if you would make a note for your book. People ask why it is that bishops never speak out on big issues. But when they do, nobody likes it!' As yet, he thinks, the Church isn't awake to the possibilities of radio and television – 'We're stirring in our sleep.'

I happened to mention the liturgical movement (see Chapter 11). Reindorp said it was all a matter of communication. Its importance didn't depend on 'whether I should stand facing westward or wear red trousers on the Feast of St Leger . . . I'm thinking of a particular clergyman now – *splendid* man – he thinks, "This is it, you can pack another flock in around the courts of Heaven." But a year later he says, "My policy's failed." I said, "I knew it would. You don't convert the kingdom by just moving the altar down from the west end and standing behind it."

'There are people who've got carried away by it. Some bishops were carried away by it – because it's exciting, you see. But the vast majority aren't carried away.' They see the movement, says Reindorp, as part of a general awareness. 'I believe, in other words, that the interest in the whole liturgical business, in making the Prayer Book and the services of the Church relevant – that's the word – is an offshoot of people being aware of the need to put the Gospel over.'

But although Reindorp is perhaps the most obvious publicist among the episcopate, the latest generation of bishops is information itself by the standards of a few years ago. There was the remarkable affair of the Faith and Coggan interview on B.B.C. television in January 1962, when one Sunday evening the pop-singer Adam Faith and the Archbishop of York, Donald Coggan, discussed God, sex, and the teenager. The programme was the result of some remarks by the Archbishop, who had been quoted as saying a few days before that 'Adam Faith tells youngsters that the meaning of life is sex – the propagation of the species. Adam Faith tells us nothing about the life hereafter or why we are here at all'. Faith objected to this, and the Archbishop agreed to a filmed interview. The result was to present disagreement in the guise of tasteful concord. Dr Coggan is an Evangelical, probably the nearest to the Conservative Evangelical position among the bishops; his sister, Norah Coggan, works with the Church Pastoral Aid Society, which is on the immoderate wing of the Evangelical group. He was Bishop of Bradford before 1961, when, on Michael Ramsey's translation to Canterbury, he replaced him as Archbishop of York, who comes second in the Church's hierarchy. Coggan has a high reputation as a preacher and Biblical scholar; but for the Faith interview, he kept the big guns out of sight. While sex was 'one of the greatest and most wonderful things in life', said the Archbishop, it was important that 'all of us, youngsters and older blokes, should begin to think out a faith which is strong enough for this life, and for the life to come. . . . Religion is so jolly relevant to this life'. Pressed by the interviewer, Ludovic Kennedy, Coggan said: 'I'm one of those who feel that sex is a thoroughly good thing, an instinct implanted by God. I'm not one of those who belong to the generation who thought it was a sort of smutty thing that you only talk about hush-hush.'

Faith, 'speaking as a teenager, just as a teenager', asserted earnestly that 'love is the most important thing, and this is what most of my songs are about – teenage love, and it's a very delicate and beautiful thing'. 'And a harmless thing,' said the Archbishop. 'And a harmless thing,' agreed Faith, who shortly went on to ask whether the Church was the only way to meet God, and complain that 'I don't feel that the Church really gets to teenagers. There's no communication.' The Archbishop disagreed gently: 'In a way religion is a tremendously personal thing . . . I couldn't agree more. On the other hand it's also a family thing . . . it's a corporate thing – a get-together.' Later they talked about archaic Church language, class distinctions, and the H-bomb:

– What is the Church's view on atomic warfare and the fact that we keep a stock of warheads? . . .

– The only answer to that is we're divided. Let's be frank, it's no good glossing things over, we're divided. . . .

Altogether it was too polite and euphemistic for an encounter that implied such obvious multiple disagreements. 'Teenagers and the Church' was the headline in *The Times*. 'God and the Pops' was the *Sunday Pictorial*'s version, which suggested sourly that 'National publicity of this kind, with an Archbishop playing straight man, is not going to harm the young Adam', and listed a number of pop singers who 'seem relentlessly determined to get in the groove with God'. In the *Guardian* Michael Frayn presented an interview between Rock Richmond and the Bishop of Twicester.

Twicester: As you probably know from my Press releases, I'm a great fan of yours. My wife and I have often rolled back the carpet after the day's episcopal business and enjoyed a jolly good rock together to one of your recordings. And I can tell you, Rock, that for rocking in, gaiters are every bit as good as drainpipe trousers. (*Appreciative laughter*.)

Newspapers carried photographs of Faith and Coggan sitting

side by side, deep in conversation. People felt vaguely that here was a teenager giving a creditable performance. In the *New Musical Express*, a columnist mentioned how well Faith was doing with his latest release, 'Lonesome'. 'What with his new all-family appeal on disc,' he said, 'plus his informal chat with the Archbishop, Adam Faith is really maturing by leaps and bounds.' From the Church's point of view the gains were less obvious. An Archbishop had been shown as friendly and reasonable; in a way he had made more contact than a bishop like Robinson could ever hope to do; but the message conveyed had no teeth. It has become a bishop's duty to be a publicist, even when the conditions make it probable that his impact will be blunted. The simple, positive, believe-or-watch-out! message is dated and unfashionable; the more intricate intellectual approach to Christianity doesn't translate into goggle-box terms; Coggan had no option but to take his chance in the studio – except the option of refusing to appear, which, since refusals are sometimes as well publicized as appearances, could have done obvious damage.

Many bishops are 'personalities' who would have distinguished themselves whatever their job; but however outstanding they are, diocesan bishops are satellites to the chief bishop, Canterbury. 'The Arch' is the one man who can set the tone of the Church, and there have been complaints this century that Archbishops have been doing it all too successfully. Randall Davidson (1903–28) and Geoffrey Fisher (1945–61) are the most complained-of in this respect. Fisher (now Lord Fisher) was at one time the headmaster of Repton. He was a success at any gathering, whether it was a garden-party or a committee, but he had no time for fools, or, on important matters, for those who disagreed with him. He remembered names, he gobbled up paper-work, he reorganized the Church's administration at a time when it was badly in need of it; and

93

left with a reputation for being both efficient and imperious. (A bishop reported in a letter from Lambeth Palace, written while he was attending a meeting there, that 'the Headmaster has just caught the Bishop of — smoking and given him a whacking'.) No one man can speak for the Church, but most people, especially in other countries, regard the Archbishop's word as official, whether he is speaking in the House of Lords or talking to reporters at London Airport. Fisher came through as a crisp no-nonsense man of simple faith, who understood top people rather better than bottom people, respected Establishment, and liked nothing better than the smooth hum of a well-made committee at work. As soon as he retired and Ramsey was appointed in his place, churchmen began to say that, while Fisher had been exactly right for 1945, Ramsey was exactly right for 1961: where Fisher's strength had been admin., Ramsey's was going to be holiness. It was taken for granted that this single appointment could alter the climate of the Church. Less than six months after his enthronement, a bishop explained to me how Ramsey was making himself felt: 'I can see it in things like the diocesan conferences – they're becoming increasingly democratic. Bishops are more likely to call the clergy together. There's more time for discussion than ever before.' He was unable to say how, exactly, the new spirit filtered down: but it did. It was said that at his first bishops' meeting, Ramsey had suggested they all waste as little time as possible, so that the bishops could hurry back to their dioceses, where the real work lay.

Ramsey has the air of solid, reliable holiness that belongs to the popular idea of monks. Most photographs show him laughing, and the big, happy mouth, together with the wings of soft white hair and the bushy eyebrows, make an agreeable picture. For years he has been widely mimicked in the Church – the high, mumbling voice, the habit of repeating things, the disconcerting boom when he laughs, the furiously wiggled eyebrows, the facial contortions. When he talks he thumps with his heel or his hand for emphasis, and he is fond of phrases like 'sort of' and 'smashing'. He is a bulky man but his movements are quick; aged fifty-six when he went to Canterbury, he looks, in repose, a good eight or ten years older, though he is said to have looked like this for at least ten years previously. I met him soon after he had accepted Canterbury, while he was still at Bishopthorpe, the modest palace in a village a few miles from York where the Archbishops of York live amid traces of splendour. Over lunch, at a long table in a dark room with a log fire at one end, he sat slumped over the food, alert under a surface of words; his wife joked about a tear in his cassock that would have to be mended before the photographer arrived; his female secretary, another woman, and his chaplain responded to his remarks without initiating much themselves. It was a still house. In his study, with gulls from the Ouse flashing past the windows, Ramsey burbled happily but anticipated any question that was worth his effort before it was properly asked; later he sat patiently, moved his chair about, and held lamps for the photographer, while three reels of film were shot.

He is a congenial man, but he says uncompromising things about religion: 'Watered-down versions of Christianity are likely to be more popular, but the deepest human needs are likely to be met by beliefs which are more worrying but which have a sharper edge . . . a sharper edge!' He has been at pains to deny that religion is a 'sort of cult of happiness. Religion is loving and serving God. And loving and serving your neighbours and forgetting yourself in the process. And of course, a person who is really self-forgetful has a chance of being immensely happy, but happiness is a by-product'. As well as expecting to meet atheists in Hell (Chapter 1), Ramsey has given due warning about the place: 'I regard it as my business to give the warning to myself. Whether it will mean perpetual pain or something like the dissolution of my consciousness, I don't know. The analogy I would use is that if a man really wants to stew in his own juice, he can and will.' (He said this on television, where he has been a success through taking a strong line. It would be hard to imagine him saying, like Coggan, that 'Religion is so jolly relevant to this life'.) He once warned a group of ordinands about the dangers of being dominated by friendships in the parish: 'Beware of thinking too much about being liked, approved, and admired by the people . . . you are sent to be the teacher of the truth, and it is easy to be popular for superficial reasons.' Do not, he advised them, 'by sophisticated attempts to be contemporary at all costs, blunt the force which lies in the universal imagery of the Bible: bread, water, light, darkness, wind, fire, rain, hunger, thirst, eat, drink, walk. . . .' Ramsey has been lukewarm about the parish Communion, preferring the 'quiet, early celebration' which 'keeps alive, and gives real place to, the *meditative* element in religion'. What is likely to have a more positive effect on the Church of England, he has been lukewarm about Establishment. From the many interviews that followed his translation to Canterbury there emerged the fact that, while he wasn't prepared to campaign for disestablishment, he hoped to see it come, preferably through the Church having disestablishment thrust upon it by an irritated State. A new Prayer Book, with new forms of worship, is what Ramsey wants. The Church last tried to revise the Prayer Book in the 1920s, when, after years of argument and preparation, a draft was prepared that was supposed to be more suited to the Church as it had developed since the 'Anglo-Catholic' movement that began in the nineteenth century. The Church approved it, though far from unanimously, and it was sent to

Parliament in 1928. The House of Lords passed it, but the Commons threw it out by a small majority, invoking the old cry of 'Popery', and exposing the Church's ultimate dependence on the State in humiliating fashion. At the heart of the controversy were the fears of Low churchmen that a High variety of Prayer Book would be imposed on them, with Anglo-Catholic practices not simply tolerated (often illegally, as they are now) but given authority. They still fear this, and rely on Parliament to preserve the *status quo*. In the early 1960s the Church was preparing a detailed plan to ask Parliament to allow experimental variations in the Prayer Book – nothing so drastic as 1928, but enough to cause a full-scale row when the time comes. Ramsey had no sooner been enthroned in Canterbury Cathedral, on the grey marble chair of St Augustine, than he was preaching an enthronement sermon in which he blandly asked for 'greater freedom in the ordering and in the urgent revising of forms of worship'. If the link between Church and State were broken, he said, the ones responsible would be those who denied the Church its freedom.

He could have chosen few more dramatic moments. The Lord Chancellor was there, the Home Secretary, the Chancellor of the Exchequer, and the Leader of the Opposition; the Prime Minister, who was supposed to be there, was 'prevented from attending', an absence that provoked a certain tension. Four thousand people were in the nave, with another thousand clergy in the choir. There were bishops, deans, canons, monks, nuns, peers, and knights. There were officials with strange titles – the Apparitor General, the Commissary General, the Actuary. There were taperers, cross bearers, precentors, and singing boys. There were representatives of the noncomformist Churches, the Old Catholic Churches, the Lutheran and Reformed Churches, the Armenian and Orthodox Churches.

There were Anglican bishops from, among other places, Borneo, Gibraltar, Sudan, New York, and Quincy, Illinois. There were mayors, chief constables, vergers, lawyers, and schoolboys. There were soldiers, university teachers, and the 'coronation barons and officers of the Cinque Ports in their robes of scarlet'. There were leading churchmen and their wives. There were some of the country's leading politicians. It was the mixture of Church and State that to Englishmen is the most natural thing in the world, with striped trousers, rich robes, expensive hats, fanfares on trumpets and peals of bells; and it was precisely at this mixture that the Archbishop's words about freedom were aimed. Soon after, in the Church Assembly, he was agreeing to a commission (the third in thirty years) to inquire into Crown appointments, and it was duly set up by early in 1962. The Church of England seemed to be making one of its periodic changes of direction. The pressure has been building up for years among Anglo-Catholics, but it has taken a like-minded Archbishop to make it effective; and since it was the State that appointed Ramsey, the State must either believe that he won't go too far, or must be willing to consider some degree of disestablishment. As a well-dressed woman said to a friend on the steps of Church House, a few days after the appointment was announced: 'We are expecting *great things* of the Arch.'

CHAPTER FIVE

PARSONS AND PARISHES

AMONG the 13,000 or so Anglican clergymen who work in English parishes, there is enough variety to prove almost anything. To generalize about them is to bring down wrath from bishops, just as to ignore them is to be accused of missing the point about the Church: that what matters isn't the machinery, the learning, the place-seeking, and the rest, but only the man in the parish, praying for his people, consoling them in trouble, and sharing their everyday life. It sounds easy, and is said to be extremely difficult. It is an old ecclesiastical half-joke that God calls the weakest men to be clergy because these are the ones who need most looking after. But parsons are as mixed a bag as any profession, and to complicate matters there is (say many clergymen) no secular means of measuring their ability and success. What is 'weakness' in a clerical context? Is it 'Overworked Vicar Vanishes to Take a Rest'? Does it mean men of little personality? What is 'personality' – does a clergyman need the force of will that makes a man successful in a boardroom? Or is this forcefulness the very weakness he must fight against?

On the whole, clergymen seem to make the best of what they have, exactly as they would do if they were bankers or dockers; only the objective is different. Because they have been pushed on to the margin of society, away from their central position in the parish, they sometimes tend to speak lightly of important things – they don't do themselves justice, they make self-critical remarks that, when reported by journalists, have a bleak and hopeless ring that may not have been intended. No one has found a foolproof means of reconciling the simple life of the clergyman with his complex surroundings. Perhaps the clergyman's life isn't simple, and never was; but people like to regard it as such. They resent it, for instance, when he complains about money. Roman Catholic priests in England are paid a trifling sum as pocket-money, but have their expenses, down to whisky, laundry, car, and telephone in the better-off districts, paid by the parish; it is possible to combine a commendable image of poverty with a sensible degree of comfort. The Anglican (who probably has a family to look after as well) has whisky on the sideboard at the peril of being called 'middle-class', and if his car is more than a modest saloon, someone is sure to suspect him of being secretly rich.

Money worries many Anglican clergymen, sometimes to the point of obsession. Some cripple themselves with public-school fees, and some are crippled anyway, by low stipends, or heavy parochial expenses, or even by an ineradicable taste for better living, inherited from a middle-class childhood before the war. Now that the Church Commissioners have been able to raise stipends to a point where £20 gross a week, plus a house, is becoming common, Anglican clergy are not as indigent as they were a few years ago. But clerical poverty is a real factor in the Church. Rural clergymen, in particular, may have a thin time. They earn less in marriage-and-burial fees; they are more likely to have a rambling vicarage that needs a lot of heating, and to need a car for visiting, yet have an impecunious church council that can't afford to help with expenses. The privately run Poor Clergy Relief Corporation (not the only one of its kind) gives away £30,000 or £40,000 a year to clergy and their widows, to help with everything from school uniforms and domestic help during illness, to holidays and the cost of moving from one parish to another.

Another £11,000 of clothing is distributed, and altogether more than 1,000 cases are helped annually. A dealer in second-hand clothes and goods for the clergy reported excellent business. His current list covered sixteen sides of foolscap, typed in single-spacing, with several hundred items, some of them quite expensive, others rather seedy-sounding:

CASSOCK Priest's black russell cord D.B. cassock. 61" long, inside sleeve 17", 40" chest. Might do for Server as there are a number of moth holes. Looks sound enough. 25s.
and
BIRETTA Black stuff. 6⅞". Slightly mucky. 2s. 6d.

(The dealer added that if he put an unusual academic hood, of a colour and design that weren't identifiable, in his list, he might get as many as thirty applications, from, he believed, clergy who wanted to pretend to some obscure academic distinction).

Parsons who complain openly about money are a minority, but a vocal one. It is not always a personal complaint. 'A key parish should be filled by the best man available, whether he has private means or not,' an influential clergyman wrote to me. 'That is impossible under present circumstances. The thing of course is perfectly fantastic but it is not realized by churchmen as a whole. When the Archbishop of Canterbury writes to me as he sometimes does his threepenny stamp costs him nothing: on the other hand my reply costs me threepence. Naturally my Bishop at no cost to himself writes to me very frequently but my replies cost me each time threepence, and this correspondence with a single correspondent must cost me fifteen shillings a year. This is not a complaint but is an illustration of something which is fundamentally wrong.'

Others make a minor industry out of their despair. Bishops

groan when they see the letters. One young clergyman, with three children and a complicated domestic set-up that involved owning either two small cars or one small car and a scooter because his wife needed transport to get to her job, accompanied his letter with appendices setting out a detailed budget. These were headed 'APPENDICES, both FINANCIAL (Make to yourselves friends of the Mammon of unrighteousness, Luke xvi, 9) and THEOLOGICAL (Look unto the rock whence ye are hewn, and to the hole of the pit whence ye are digged, Isaiah li, 1)'. Appendix A concluded: 'That only leaves £423 a year for the expenses of my work, and for five of us to live on.' Appendix B listed out-of-pocket expenses:

£3 for help with services while I had flu.

£10 Stamps and Stationery (including Christmas cards to parishioners).

£9 Robes.

£37 Proportion of cost of servicing and repair of car.

£92 Petrol and oil for the 11,600 miles travelled on parochial duty in the year.

YOU WILL NOTICE THAT I HAVE *not* BEEN ABLE TO INCLUDE ANY MONEY FOR THEOLOGICAL BOOKS.

£2 5s. Hire purchase on scooter

Written in as an afterthought was: 'Thank God I have a wife who can and will work.' In another appendix he remarked that it was 'Sub-Christian Stoic nonsense that parsons, nurses, and others with a special vocation do not need to be paid'. Appendix E was headed 'Odious Comparisons', and declared: 'On one point I would like to ask for your advice, my Lord Bishop. Would I be right to give way to my anger?' Appendix I was headed 'That Christ did not intend us to be beggars'. It began: 'I wash all the nappies, sheets, and other things that can go into the Hoover washer, my wife washes all the woollens and fancy things. . . .'

There is a shrill note about clergymen who work too hard and feel their isolation and lack of privilege. 'In constantly increasing measure,' wrote a parson in a city in the North, 'the Church of England is represented to the world in general in the terms set by the official aristocracy who hold all the big jobs, and appoint to the lesser positions of influence. It is from this aristocracy that all speakers on radio and TV are selected. The rest, those who for some reason or other – mostly because they have dared to step outside the limits which that aristocracy have arbitrarily determined – have been pushed into the outer darkness, left to rot or overwork themselves without assistance, sneered at, ostracized. . . .' Anyone who has much to do with the clergy collects weird letters, full of capitals and underlinings, guilt- or hate- or fear-ridden: 'We are a miserable gang of humbugs and hair-splitters and twisters and money-grubbers. We are an uneducated lot of pretentious PHARISEES and SCRIBES. The Nonconformists are at heart SOLID and sincere and TRUTHFUL.' This letter was written on the back of cyclostyled copies of letters written to the clergyman by his bishop, suspending his permission to officiate in the diocese because of 'prejudices and obsessions' in his sermons. 'Judas Iscariot' had been written in red ink beside the facsimile of the bishop's signature.

Most clergymen escape extremes. The oddity of the parson's situation may be what strikes the outsider, but its absolute normality is what strikes the parson himself. It is society that is ignoring him and his all-important work. Behind him is not only his personal conviction but the weight of centuries of church-going and belief – thousands of buildings, tens of thousands of books, millions of sermons. There are the scores of millions of souls that the Church has saved in four centuries. His isolation is apparent, not actual; he is the one inside. In the parish, whether it is rich and old-fashioned, and so appreciates the vicar, or average and urban, and so coldly unspiritual, he retains his special place. People still cross the road when they see him out walking, perhaps to talk to him, perhaps to keep out of his way. No one, apart from policemen and known criminals, can dry up a conversation so quickly. No one has so high a reputation to maintain, even in the most ungodly district. No one's absence from work or estrangement from wife is so quickly seized on by gossips and journalists. No one's work in the community is so difficult to report, except in polite terms that no one bothers to read apart from church-people who know anyway.

The parson's formal duties are few. 'And all Priests and Deacons,' says the Prayer Book, 'are to say daily the Morning and Evening Prayer either privately or openly, not being let by sickness, or some other urgent cause. And the Curate* that ministereth in every Parish Church or Chapel, being at home, and not being otherwise reasonably hindered, shall say the same in the Parish Church or Chapel where he ministereth, and shall cause a Bell to be tolled thereunto a convenient time before he begin, that the people may come to hear God's Word, and to pray with him.' This twice-daily office becomes embedded in the parson's life, though 'reasonably hindered' is a convenient loophole; more than one clergyman says Evening Prayer upstairs in the vicarage, as a lullaby for his small children, knowing that if he says it in church there will be no congregation. The parson must administer Communion to those who are in a position to receive it; he must marry, baptize, bury, and visit the sick, a simple matter in most small or rural parishes, but an endless grind, sometimes operated on a rota system when it comes to funerals, in a large city parish with perhaps 20,000 parishioners. If there is no pressure of weddings and funerals, he will have time for methodical visit-

* Technically, the incumbent is the curate.

ing, for reading, for preparing sermons, for talking to people. Only his time and energy limit the number of things he can organize. He can start coffee-bars, open youth clubs, write to *The Times*, edit the parish magazine, run bingo, write pamphlets condemning bingo, instruct engaged couples, practise amateur psychotherapy, take part in local politics, pester the town hall to accommodate ill-housed families, run film-shows, make films, produce plays, speak on a soap-box, take pensioners to the seaside, campaign against smog, write hymns, draw posters, mend the organ, march in processions, sit on platforms with neo-fascists or unilateral disarmers, run Scouts, make contacts and plan strategy with neighbouring clergy. He may believe in bustling from meeting to meeting, firing advice at schoolgirls and councillors. Or he may believe, with a substantial minority, that the Church is too busy, that it talks too much about 'strategy' and 'involvement' and 'identification' and 'missionary situation'. He may believe in sitting still and concentrating on things that are said in one word but need hours of patient explanation before an inkling of them gets through to strangers – 'prayer', 'fellowship', 'spirit', 'love'. He may believe in nothing much in particular except God, who is so much a part of his life that to disbelieve in him would be like disbelieving in the shiny collar round his throat or the stones in his church.

But with 'God' and the clergyman's feelings on the matter, the outsider reaches the point where he can no longer follow. The most unprofitable question he can ask a clergyman is 'Why?' Some of the reasons that clergymen give for entering the ministry were mentioned at the end of Chapter 2 – phrases like 'inner urges' and 'to serve the Lord Jesus'. To try and look behind such answers, the questioner must either remain on ground he understands, or let discussion pass to territory where the words mean nothing. If he wants to make it a secular inquiry, the outsider can listen to psychiatrists. One, whose patients include clergy and their wives, said he had told Church House that 'we want more people whose basic characteristic is secularity, not religiosity, and then perhaps we'll get a more balanced clergy'. In his experience, 'many of the clergy are moralists, they are intellectuals, and their personal sense of Christ as a person they live with every day just ain't true'. Some had problems of homosexuality – 'this is very common at some of the theological colleges. There are the other old problems – dislike of women, of the flesh, of matter'. And there was pride. 'Many of the clergy regard their university honours and the theological degrees as part of their justification. But when a man breaks down, he may realize for the first time that all he has to bring is the sin and the mess. The moment of brokenness is a sacramental moment of great importance.' A clergyman himself, a young man with some knowledge of psychology, remarked of breakdowns: 'St Paul had one. The time may be coming when people will say of a clergyman, "He's not had his yet".' As an afterthought, he produced a couple of possible reasons why men might enter the Church: 'So that they can be alone whenever they want to. So they can fight without getting hurt.'

But to understand a clergyman's reasons, as most clergymen would have them understood, means entering a world of mysteries. Clergymen believe they are called to do work that will result in the triumph of Christ; but even to try and understand a statement like that can mean reading a library of devotional and theological books, only to find that the explanation is still enclosed in a skin of faith. A thousand clergymen will express it in a thousand different ways. All seem to draw strength from a conviction that while most men's work is dust in the wind, theirs is nearer the heart of the matter. But this suggests pride, and would be denied by many clergymen. It is impossible for an outsider to make the allowances that insiders demand.

*

Some parsons prefer not to talk to journalists, but most of them are quite willing; as a rule they are very hospitable, and provide food and beds in a way that sometimes make a reporter uneasy when he comes to write about them later.

The Rev. Peter Sterne (not his real name) has a parish in a city suburb. It sprawls over a hill and down towards a valley, looking away from the city towards further hills, where amid the blur of brick are still a few squares of green containing cows. Sterne's parish has thousands of council houses, crisscrossing over the hillside, the pattern varied now and then at intersections by three or four fluorescent-lit shops, a pillar box, and a telephone booth. Scarcely any of his 16,000 parishioners are professional people; not a single dentist practises there. The men work mainly on the railways and buses and in foundries and steelworks, and have inherited a reputation for toughness from the city's harsh industrial past. Many of them wouldn't know where the church is – an unhandsome brick building on the main road that runs across the hill. Fewer still could find the vicarage, an ordinary-sized, between-the-wars detached house, a hundred yards from the church, with a big rank garden and a broken drive. On the front lawn, parallel to the overblown privet, is the lady parish worker's caravan, with its piano, piles of devotional books, and bottled gas. 'I used to say – I'm changing a bit now,' said Sterne, 'that if a parson's going to be among his people, he ought to live in the same sort of house, if it's only for meetings. But I've heard people on the bus say, "Poor? That something parson's got a thousand-pound caravan in his garden".'

Sterne is a small, dark, middle-aged man, his face small and yellowish, his fingers slight and bony. Around the house, bathing one of his two young daughters or writing in his downstairs study, he wears unclerical clothes – a blazer with brass buttons, a check shirt, an orange tie. No clear line separates work from domestic routine. When Brenda, his wife, pretty but harassed, takes the older girl to school, Sterne is left in the kitchen drinking tea, shaking out cornflakes for the remaining child, trying to read his mail. Every level surface is covered with crockery, newspapers, groceries, dolls, and vests; the bus journeys take his wife a long time. But Sterne seems not to mind, any more than he minds when, having been up at six in the morning to take early Communion, he sits up late at night, talking, smoking, and rubbing his eyes, leaving himself five or six hours for sleep.

It counts as a good parish, with an active congregation of two or three hundred, and a sense of purposefulness that radiates from Sterne. What separates him from most of the 16,000 is indifference to his message, not antipathy to him. His accent is strong, his manner friendly, and he is impatient with the upper echelons of the Church: 'The House of Laity's no more representative of the laity than my Aunt Fanny's goldfish pond. The people in this diocese who are in the Church Assembly are either heads of firms or heads of departments.' The suspicion that the Church is associated with landowners and industrialists (which is true) and that this taints and stifles the Church (which is arguable) is especially strong in a parish like this. Sterne is on the side of the people, instinctively opposed to the Church Commissioners. 'People here are utterly convinced that we are maintained by the State. They say the Church tells them not to keep up with the Joneses – but here's the Church keeping up with the Clores and Cottons. Do you know that the Church Commissioners are the biggest shareholders in one of the steel companies here?'

It is about such things that Sterne is partisan: not about High or Low doctrines, or Canon Law revision, or the reform of ecclesiastical courts. His aim is simply to establish contact with parishioners, generally through women and teenagers, and encourage them to come to church and have faith in God. He himself believes in divine intervention, in the sudden coincidences and oddities of behaviour that are not really coincidences, but the inflexible unfolding of God's plan. He once rang an influential vicar for no reason, called to see him, confessed that the impulse was inexplicable, went with him to see a new church that appealed to him instantly but had been offered to someone else, and, when the other man later backed out, was offered the church himself. What plan was this part of? Sterne couldn't say. Like so many Anglicans, he makes as few claims as possible. 'Recently I was in a prayer meeting, and I was shocked and almost reduced to fits of laughter and had to leave – it was raining at the time, and someone asked that it should be stopped by the time we went out. I thought this was asking too much of the Almighty. But then I thought: Am I wrong?'

The years slip by, and Sterne works too hard. He has no car – the garage is rented to a neighbour. He has a curate ('what a curate needs is a thick skin and a sense of humour') and is trying to establish a 'group-parish' set-up, with four or five adjoining parishes working together, coordinating services, meetings, visiting, and campaigns. Things happen slowly. The enthusiastic literature of recent years on the liturgical movement and the 'house-church' movement has affected the parish without sweeping it. Five years ago fifty parishioners took Communion every week; now it's 140. Sterne said in a letter:

The way in which we are trying to reach the unchurched masses, is through 'house-meetings' or 'house-churches' and through the training of lay-people. We have house-meetings and conferences for young people, adults, and members of other churches. Once a month there is a Healing Service – and from time to time the Sacrament of Holy Baptism is administered at public worship. Perhaps one of the most frustrating aspects of our work here is the sheer unresponsiveness of the people – who at times are as hard as the steel they produce – and of course, the laity in the Church are on the whole fifty to a hundred years behind in theological understanding.

Four questions keep coming up in discussions with younger people: Is there a life after death? What is the Church's attitude to divorce? Why should I go to church – I'm as good as people who do. And race relations. Teenagers seem to like him, and crowd into a sitting-room to discuss the Christian view of sex or apartheid; a few sound unnaturally pious, but are diluted in the general conversation. They once discussed crime and punishment. 'When I found what these kids wanted,' said Sterne, 'I had the shock of my life. They wanted flogging reintroduced, and stretching on the rack, and boiling oil poured on them. It was then I realized we were in the post-Christian era.'

An afternoon house-meeting in a council house was attended by the vicar, his parish worker (a middle-aged woman), and eight wives and widows, who would normally have been discussing a passage from the Bible, but were having a general conversation because a journalist was there. It was a small, hot room, with much polished wood and bright cushions, and everything displayed on little tables; half the television's eye was visible in a corner. The youngest woman was about thirty, the oldest well into her sixties. Tea and cakes began arriving almost at once, and a woman in a lemon jumper, on a sofa against the wall, looked anxiously at a piece of jam sponge and whispered: 'Is it seedy, love?' Sterne was talking about life after death: 'People say to me that no one ever came back from the dead. But Jesus did.' A middle-aged widow with sad features, still pretty, said she had taken great comfort from the saying of Jesus that 'In my Father's house are many mansions'. There was desultory conversation:

'There are no marriages in heaven, Mr Sterne's told us that.'

'Well, you'll be an angel.'

'I'm too busy living my life on earth.'

'We had a very good sermon.'

'I heard about the darkness and how dramatic it was. It must have gone home, that sermon.'

The women began to discuss the life of a clergyman, and Sterne told them about the opposition he had met in his family when he announced he was going into the Church. 'They said, "We've had some bloody funny things in the family, but we've never had a bloody parson."'

'That's the first time I've heard a vicar swear!' said the woman in the lemon jumper.

'He was only quoting,' said someone.

'I sometimes wish I was a butcher,' said the vicar. 'Because everybody wants meat.'

Ah, said the women, but you're held in awe: the vicar is always held in awe.

'I'll tell you what awe your vicar's held in,' said Sterne. 'I'm afraid I'll have to swear again. There's a woman in this parish I'd go anywhere to avoid. I once rode twice round the estate because I was upstairs on the bus and she was downstairs. If she sees me in the street or anywhere, she shouts: "You bugger!" That's the awe your vicar's held in.'

There was general laughter, some of it shocked. Sterne admitted that people often showed respect, sometimes of a curious kind. If there was a Littlewoods coupon on the mantelpiece when he called, they might go to great lengths to stand in front of it. Soon after this the meeting broke up, because the children would be home from school; there would be another one next week.

Sterne's parish is bleak, though by no means the bleakest in England. Urban society and the local church occupy different worlds; it is by wandering through the countryside that the outsider is most likely to catch the lingering flavour of the Christian community. Christian writers sometimes complain that the village's attachment to its church is sentimental, and that villagers are just as pagan as townspeople. But the structure remains. More than a third of England's parishes have a population of less than 1,000. The rural diocese of Hereford has one clergyman to every 1,000 parishioners, London has one to every 5,000. Vicar and villager have a chance of knowing one another. The Bishop of Taunton, Frank West, wrote in *The Country Parish Today and Tomorrow*:

> In the country he can still be the Persona – the parson. He can still exercise the kind of ministry which the compilers of the Ordinal [the rules for the ordering of priests] had in mind, and it is only because so many country parsons have an incorrigibly urban mentality that they fail to realize what a privilege and opportunity this confers. The country congregation, though sometimes disconcertingly small, is often fairly representative of the village. During the week the parson has time to make himself acquainted with the labours of the agricultural part of the congregation, and at such times as harvest he can actually share in them. . . . The country parson can do, without making himself a public spectacle, what many town parsons would like to do – that is, share in the daily work, think the same thoughts and breathe the same air as many members of his Sunday congregation.

In a large, comfortable vicarage in a quiet village, the Rev. John Marvell (another pseudonym), who has a reputation in the Church, spoke of the meetings of rural clergy that he has initiated – 'little companies of the spirit'. Marvell's reputation is for goodness, holiness, saintliness; he is a stocky man with wavy soft brown hair, a big straight mouth, and dark eyes, and speaks in a deep, rich voice about the power of love: 'This amazing power that comes from love, really.' What he says and writes is not always meaningful even to clergymen; Peter Sterne thought a newspaper article by him had been 'a bit pi'; but there is no denying the warm, steady pressure of his conviction. Large numbers of priests in his diocese now meet, talk, and pray regularly. 'We've found what things are on our minds. Churchmanship is one – party matters. A feeling of failure is another. When I was on a housing estate I used to meet other clergy, and we'd ask each other how things were going. Then you say, "Very well" – but they're not. You talk to the other man and you agree you're both hammering your head against the wall.' As for prayer – 'The power of prayer! The lonely man being caught up! The cranky man feeling he can air his quirk! We must learn to love one another – not to be commanded from above but to grow into it from below. Not to do this is the central failing of the Church. If we could become the sort of Church where we love one another and know how to pray, we wouldn't need golden-tongued oratory. Then, I feel, if the Church can have learnt some of these lessons of prayer and love in itself, it can't help but spill over.'

Marvell's vicarage was in sharp contrast to Sterne's. The country one had a foreign girl to look after the children; people spoke with Southern English accents, and there was an air of good connexions and expensive education. Mellow garden, fields, trees, and near-by church all added to the atmosphere. The previous Sunday had been Harvest Festival, and the church was filled with a sharp, barnlike smell; at the front were laid fruit and vegetables, tinned food, bags of sugar, a lump of coal, a tube of toffees. 'In the village,' said Marvell, 'there is a lot more goodwill and friendliness because of the Church. There isn't much looking beyond our frontiers – but then, that's the countryman. My harvest sermon at evensong was about world hunger. Some of the villagers didn't think much of it.' Some of the villagers also didn't think much of a proposal by Marvell to move the organ so as to hear the choir better, and a few were refusing to contribute. He was taking this in his stride, as he was the controversy about that night's harvest supper in the village hall, which was being attended by the whole village, including Methodists, who objected to the presence of strong liquor; even cider was out, so Marvell was compromising with Cidatone, which was in flagons but contained no alcohol. When the time came, the supper went off very well, with plenty of friendly interchanges between villagers and the commuter-dwellers who lived in done-up cottages, and worked in the city ten miles away. The hall, a single-storey building decorated with grasses and coloured paper, had a clock with a brown face and a framed list of subscribing members, dated 1938. Cold meat, salad, and little trifles were eaten off trestle tables. A young man with sideboards said it was very nice lamb, and an old farmer corrected him sharply: 'It's wether! It eats better than lamb!' Later a lawnmower manufacturer with rimless glasses sang 'There is a lady, sweet and kind', accompanied on the piano by his sister, who went on to guy a romantic ballad – this performance caused the vicar, his wife, and one or two more to choke with laughter, but was received in silence by most of the audience. The dancing, to records, would have gone on long past midnight if the vicar had allowed it. To an outsider it was a cheerful few hours. To Marvell it was 'One of the moments when unity is being achieved: a profoundly Christian moment'. But it was not possible, Marvell suggested kindly, to report on the reality of the Church, any more than one could report on the reality of family life: you could live it, but your jokes and customs, so important on the inside, would be meaningless to someone outside the circle. There was about the Church, said Marvell, an unreportable intimacy.

Men of Marvell's calibre are rarer in the countryside than in the towns. Many rural parishes cosset men who are old, tired, broken, or merely want peace and quiet. The Rev. James Thynne (a pseudonym), a curate who lives with his wife in a cottage, became a clergyman because from the age of thirteen he wanted to be a university teacher, and failed: 'I'm a pseudo-intellectual. I'm interested in intellectual things but I'm rather third-class at it.' So he makes do with a corner of the parish, where the vicar and the vicar's wife (who calls him 'Thynne') leave him alone, and he has 800 souls to look after. Oxford is not too far away, with its books and its eminence; the dean of a college once told him he suffered from Morbo Oxoniensis. 'I have lived,' he says determinedly, 'fifty years too late – the country-house atmosphere, the silver, and all that. The vicar's wife is always on at me because I tend to be too polite, jumping up and down when ladies come into the room. But I must say I like old-fashioned courtesy.' He has told the bishop he is terrified of leaving (the bishop replied: 'What does a bishop say to that?'). If he must go, he would like it to be a parish in Bath or Cheltenham, or deep in a southern county. Ideally, though, he wants to stay where he is, with £400 a year, smoking a pipe for a treat at Christmas and Easter, mustering Sunday congregations of twenty or thirty (which is a far higher percentage than Sterne can ever hope for), functioning at low pressure, honest about his deficiencies, amiably conscientious: 'I would rather sit down and read a book on philosophy, but if I did the Boys' Brigade would go to pot.' He has the Ever-green club for old people, the Guides and Brownies, the Women's Institute, the parties of village boys to take to have tea on the river at Oxford or up to the Science Museum in London. There are the disappointments. 'I often think a young man will grow up into the life of the Church, but his friends say "He's a friend of the bloody parson". Still they have kindly thoughts towards one.' There is the outsider's interest that never seems to reach the flash-point of conversion; it has taken him twelve years as a clergyman to get three families 'interested' in the Church. Much of his time goes in correspondence with Christian eccentrics – a Brother Somebody on the south coast, a healing woman in the west, a movement in the United States. Living on the edge of the Church, he is more at ease with farmers and villagers than with other clergy. Sometimes he spends a morning working on a farm. He can't understand why the country parson is supposed to be lonely. It makes his day when, out walking, he meets a farmer on horseback. 'There are so many things happening – and there's the loveliness of the countryside.' He wants to be buried there; within the shell of his failure, he seems to be happy.

Lifetimes can drowse away in the countryside, or come to an unsensational end there. The Rev. Morton Gervaise (a pseudonym) has a parish in the West Country, in a village that might be part of a film-set for a bitter travelogue of rural decline. The vicarage is behind elms and poplars, at the end of a long stone drive. Most of its nine acres are rented to farmers. The lawns are cut but the flower beds are ruined, and the kitchen garden, inside crumbling brown walls, has only a few strips of herbs and fruit bushes. There is a fine wine cellar, without wine. The kitchen is big enough for a choir to eat in. One wing of the vicarage is empty, the ancient wallpaper is peeling, a few toys lie around sealed with dust, a bird's nest has fallen into a grate. Gervaise, who has a tall, pointed body and stiff grey hair, lives with his sister in a few large, centrally heated rooms, where there are comfortable arm-chairs, thick striped curtains, books and flowers, and many ornaments. Gervaise is a widower. He beckons and points to a mildly daring reproduction of a Hogarth painting in another room, away from the rest of the bric-à-brac. 'I keep it a little *sotto* on the sideboard.'

The vicar was once a naval chaplain. He was once on the staff of a university, he was once the vicar of a society church, where 'people hardly read very much, but they knew everything. They attached more value to their opportunities of hearing the latest conversation'. There, Gervaise had thrived: for, as he put it, 'one of the real advantages of being a clergyman of the Church of England is that you're absolutely all things to all people. It was quite the thing to dine with so-and-so in great style, then go down and have a cup of tea in the basement'. But that had been a long time ago. He had married late, travelled, had children and put them through public school – one was still there, costing him nearly £500 a year all told, paid for by the 'private means' that he and his sister retained as a bulwark against the 1960s. His kind of clergyman's insulation is becoming rarer now, the old self-sealing conviction, proof against experiments and enthusiasms, that the parson is a king-pin, that people are a pretty dull, venal lot, that life will go on as it always has.

I was advised when I came to the country, never use a word that a child of thirteen can't understand. I never reproach and I never scold: they'll probably see it, in time. It's no good thundering in the pulpit. All you can do is strengthen the attitude of the faithful. It's a bit platitudinous, but you can't be concrete in a small community. People bring their children to be baptized, even though they never come to church. Ultimately one feels the outcome of these things is in the hands of Heaven. One's only an underling, a deputy and all that.

The words have the clarity of honest hopelessness: it would be possible to fight the apathy of the parish, and thousands of clergymen do, but it would be easier to sit still, spend the morning doing household chores and writing letters, visit a few cottages in the afternoon, read and watch television after dark. Visiting is less onerous if you visit only the hard core of original villagers. 'You know, I don't go to the council houses. I feel they know all about it. If they want the church, they know where to come. Mind you, if anyone mentions religion, I'm on to it – in a nice sort of way.' The parson is accepted. 'There's perfect good will to the clergy. They ask if there's anything they can do – sharpen the tools, or come in if a bit of electricity goes wrong.' As for the life of the village, the parson is a fixture, like the war-memorial drinking fountain and the county policeman's notice-board showing wanted men, used very little but somehow integral. There is no demand for clubs and organizations; a flower show and a fête suffice, together with Sunday School, attended by about twenty scholars, and cricket matches in summer. Gervaise's speciality is his preaching: 'I preach well, I know I do.' A dozen or so people receive Communion at eight o'clock on a Sunday morning; Gervaise passes efficiently and devoutly along the row of parishioners, there are the small sounds of clothes and shoes, the wind blows under the great oak door with its face of studs. This is why the vicar is really here, though no more than a handful of villagers are present. Three hours later the church has about twenty-five in the congregation for matins, when Gervaise preaches his main sermon, and for evensong at 6.30 there may be as many as thirty or forty. On a Sunday the vicar comes into his own. During the week he sits back and observes from an eminence. 'If they come to you, you can give consolation, which I like very much to do. But some of them are so brazen, you know.' It was, said the vicar, nonsense to talk about the sleepy English countryside. A girl had been taken from a near-by village school, pregnant. He had known of a plumber's wife who was not a plumber's wife at all but a brazen mistress whose child by her real husband (who kept another woman) lived at the other end of a village. There was the accountant who had come to the countryside, who was said to be not a real accountant at all; the letter-heading was a tax dodge, and what he really did was to deal in second-hand furniture. His daughter drank like a fish. 'Well, I'll get nowhere there,' said the vicar. As an evangelist Gervaise isn't much good. But he sympathizes with people, especially the old. He is probably no more and no less than most of his parishioners expect.

More acceptable to the Church as a picture of its work in the countryside is the South Ormsby group of parishes, in Lincolnshire, which is too distinctive a place to be concealed with pseudonyms. Methods of joining parishes ('unions') or of having more than one served by a single incumbent ('pluralities') are of long standing; nowadays most schemes come under the Pastoral Reorganization Measure, which was approved by Parliament in 1949, and which is sometimes held to have saved the parochial system from collapse for want of clergy. In the last ten years the need to join up parishes has been made a virtue by some vigorous churchmen, who condemn the parochial system as inefficient and out of date, and experiments with various degrees of amalgamation are going on. At its most elaborate it calls for the cooperation of patrons of livings, parochial church councils, and parishioners; together with a clergyman who can rush around, be tactful and imaginative, and organize his group of parishes and team of curates with the slender administrative resources of a vicarage. It doesn't always work. Suitably forceful clergymen are rare, and many people hate to see parishes fade away. The Bishop of Southwell, Dr Barry, wrote in 1958 that group parishes should not be regarded as 'an ideal to be pursued by beagle-nosed administrators nor as a final or permanent solution, but rather as a regrettable necessity which has been imposed upon us by circumstances'.

This passage was quoted regretfully in a book called *The South Ormsby Experiment* by the Rev. A. C. Smith, who began his scheme, the best-known of the Church's group-parish experiments, in a run-down stretch of Lincolnshire countryside in 1952. Smith (later made an archdeacon) found Barry's strictures 'a little disturbing'. He sees the group-parish not as a makeshift imposed on the Church but as a means of giving the countryside what it lacks in the way of leaders and initiative. While men like Barry suggest that 'The parochial system is what we understand', Smith and those like him claim that his particular kind of grouping has the best of both worlds: the group provides an overall strategy, companionship for a team of clergymen, and opportunities for training young curates, but the parishes within the group keep their identity. 'I am quite sure it must have been divine guidance,' wrote Smith, 'which caused me to set my face against any form of obvious central direction and to do all I could to see that each parish retained its own freedom within the framework of the larger family.'

Smith has gone from South Ormsby, made into an archdeacon and perhaps marked out for still higher office – the Church is full of schemes left behind by talented incumbents whose talents are needed higher up the ladder. It took a long time to find a strong enough successor, and when I went there in 1961, some months after Smith had left, the group was still without a rector. It was coasting along quite happily, with three curates for the fifteen small parishes that cover seventy-five square miles of thinly populated countryside. Something over 1,000 people live in the parishes, which have the names of an A. E. Coppard story – Ruckland, Oxcombe, Farforth, Bag Enderby, Driby, Brinkhill, Harrington, Salmonby, Maidenwell, Tetford, Worlaby, Somersby, Ketsby, Calceby, and South Ormsby, where the central rectory has the traditional site: on a slope facing south, backed with trees, looking out on gentle, chalky hills. Twelve churches serve the group, and blue-painted boards outside each listed the monthly rota of services, from South Ormsby, which had one or two each Sunday, down to the remoter ones like Farforth and Ruckland, which had to make do with one service a month. A green single-decker bus, presented secondhand by a transport company, toured the parishes at least once a Sunday with a curate at the wheel to collect parishioners for a central service, usually evensong, at one of the larger churches.

Alan Glendining, the curate who was living temporarily at the South Ormsby rectory (he wasn't in charge of the group) also drove a van, paid for partly out of his own pocket – he said all the curates had some kind of modest private means. He said he wasn't overworked: there was a routine. The atmosphere at the rectory was cheerful, not what people refer to, sadly, as 'churchy', and the Glendinings were aware of their lack of churchiness. He and his wife once ran a farming magazine, before he was ordained, and he talked about ordination as a solution to his life that dawned on him gradually. He was a pale, handsome man, still young, with thick black hair that was starting to grey. Mrs Glendining and the children had family jokes about 'bish-hops' and 'archbeacons', but despite the freedom from ecclesiastical atmosphere, there was the inevitable feeling that inside the rectory was a very different world from the seventy-five square miles of lanes, farms, and cottages outside. One curate's wife said a lot of people called her 'Madam'. It embarrassed her that 'the women round about will laugh at a joke I make, however crapulous'. The status of the clergy and their wives remained high. Mrs Glendining said:

If I go to a house where I'm not particularly well known, a chair is brought out and dusted, and I must sit down first – the woman will stand and wait till I have. Actually, a lot of the women don't do it now because they've got used to me drifting in in rather unconventional clothes. I generally wear trousers – but that, in a curious way, doesn't matter in the slightest, you see. Because I am ostensibly the 'rector's' wife, I can get away with murder. They wouldn't be seen dead in here [the rectory] in their trousers. When they come here to sew they've all changed into the most immaculate clothes. You could take them to Buckingham Palace – they look absolutely delightful, charming. But it doesn't make a bit of difference that I wear my trousers.

Alan Glendining said:

I should hate to have caps raised to me all the time. The point is here that there's no middle class anyway, except the clergy. We're not trying to foster the illusion that we're gentlemen. But you don't want to shock parishioners – well, you do, but you don't want to shock them socially by stepping grossly out of what they consider should be the parson's part. The best thing to do is to behave and talk as is natural to you. And if your pastoral work is carried out with love, and it's a prayerful one, you do get close to your people. Wear gumboots and keep pigs if that's the way you want to live, but not just in order to get under their skins.

Whisky is what the parson is expected to drink: definitely not beer. His children are not expected to attend the village school, and the first clergyman's child who did, when the experiment started, was given a rough time by the rest of the class, who weren't prepared for such an alien. This part of Lincolnshire is a few years behind the times. Many of the women do their own baking and bleaching; shops have a faded look, communications are poor, some of the most enterprising inhabitants have gone off to Scunthorpe or Nottingham. It has a kind of decaying calm and remoteness. Effort, even the effort of one clergyman to every 300 parishioners, is easily dissipated. No one on the staff boasted about results. One of the curates said it took him three months to work his way round the five parishes, with about 100 houses, that were his quota. It was hard to get people to talk about themselves, except when it came to illness: 'They start talking about the terrible time they've had, and they become spiritually off their guard.' It was usually through talk about their children and their families that they became approachable. And if any contact was made, it was generally with women. 'With the men,' said the curate, echoing the thought that worries many clergymen, 'I find that one is more superficial. Christianity is largely a woman's religion here, as it is in other places. Whether the men are lazy or because there's an aura of soppiness about religion, I don't know. I don't know how to get hold of the men, and it's a terrifying thought to be a woman's clergyman.'

There were plays, fêtes, and outings to organize. There were people to be taken hospital visiting, and each curate was averaging about 300 miles a week in his car or van. There were house-Communion services, well attended. There were children's meetings. One of the curates stopped his car on a high road overlooking a valley: a shining wind-wheel, a few cottages, a couple of farms, an isolated church. ('One feels,' he said, calmly, 'the best thing would be to knock some of them down.') Children went to one of the farms on Friday evenings – perhaps twenty or more, to have a hymn practice and a general sing-song. 'They don't come because they're terribly good,' said the curate. 'There's nowhere else to go.'

To measure the success of the experiment is impossible. More people go to Communion, though the number fluctuates year by year; the previous Easter, it was about one in six of the parish. But some parishioners, especially the old, say they get fewer, not more, visits from the parson. Most people

seem to agree that the group has achieved a certain unity. But
the parish bus can drive for twenty minutes on a mild summer's evening, and collect no more than three old ladies for
the service at South Ormsby. Much of the pattern (in summer,
1961) was still the quiet pattern of the sleepy parish. In one of
the little churches, screened from the road by trees and an
overgrown churchyard that was due for mowing, matins at
eleven was attended by the local squire (an important man,
travelling to London most weeks) and his wife, together with
a young man and a boy in his party, one woman on her own,
and myself. Before the service, squire, boy, and curate were in
the vestry, which was simply a partition at the end of the nave,
ringing the bell and talking audibly. There was no organist.
The church had a dry, stony smell, and two candles were
burning on the altar. The squire read the lessons loudly and
expertly, and the curate preached a plain, earnest sermon on
the dangers of formalism. His text was a passage pointing to
the legalism of the Pharisees, and from this he went on to say
that the danger now was of making religion an affair of formal
worship. Christianity, he said, was a thing for every day.
There were one or two literary references, including a reference to a volume of Victor Gollancz's autobiography which
(the curate said later) he would remove from the sermon, as
being obscure, when he preached it that evening to a larger
congregation in another of the churches. After the service,
squire and curate had a chat outside the porch. They talked
about the appointment of bishops. The curate thought the
present system was wrong; the squire, who did most of the
talking, thought it was all right. He didn't agree it produced
stooges. He named a go-ahead bishop. 'I don't know anything
about him, but I believe he's a very good man. He's always in
the papers, he's always thinking out some new crack. I suppose
he's considered the sort of bright and new and unstooge-like

chap.' He thought about this. 'Anyway, I'm not sure this bishop is really right, you know. I'm not sure that the chap who goes on in a rather simple Kiplingesque – not showing his feelings too much, not putting everything in the shop window all the time – isn't right.'

There is also the more private aspect of the group: the meetings and general friendship of the clergy, who at this time were strongly influenced by a movement called Servants of Christ the King. It involved silence and controlled discussion. They would meet on a Monday morning, and one of them would expound a passage of scripture. Then they would sit in silence before starting to discuss it – 'learning to be a small group together, waiting on the Holy Spirit'.

The three South Ormsby clergymen had been discussing healing, and the concept of 'the healed Church', and the idea that ill-health was contrary to God's will. In the sitting-room of the rectory, the windows facing south, his colleagues sat back to hear Glendining's exegesis of two passages, Acts ii, 42–7, and Luke iv. Glendining was using a commentary. After a few minutes he said: 'I don't think much of this geezer, do you?' The others agreed they didn't. 'Every time he takes one step forward he takes two steps back. It cost me twenty-five shillings, too.' Later, after the formal exegesis and prayers and the long silence (it was probably about fifteen minutes), everyone lit cigarettes and the room filled with smoke. It had a high ceiling and yellow wallpaper; the grate was tiled, and beside it were china bell-handles to summon servants who no longer existed; there was a fourteen-inch television, an address-stamper on a desk, and an upright piano. The passage from Acts had begun: 'And they continued steadfastly in the apostles' doctrine and fellowship, and in breaking of bread, and in prayers. And fear came upon every soul: and many wonders and signs were done by the apostles.' The Luke chapter contained 'Christ's temptation and fasting: he, over-coming the devil, beginneth to preach: the people at Nazareth admire him; he cureth one possessed of a devil, etc.'

The senior curate, who was older, and who had been described to me by one of his colleagues as 'a holy man', said: 'Where the Church is being the Church, the same marvels and signs will be found today. This healing comes about in a proper Church, and in the absence of this, the healing can't be done in a proper way.' But he said that one had to interpret the community life, described in Acts, in modern terms. 'Church people may get beyond thinking the Church is a building. Some get beyond thinking it's the parson. But few get beyond thinking it's a small group of people.' They had had a meeting in Lent, prayed for the sick and had 'a feeling of being concerned with other people. We must somehow make the Church have a common life. What that means today, I don't know. But it means sharing meals and praying together. I feel if we can create that sort of community, then the sort of healing that our Lord did will become available to the Church in the way it was in our Lord's time.'

They seemed as uncertain of the means as they were certain of the end; they had met for breakfast together, they had prayed, they were talking, and now there was nothing else to do but wait. Glendining said he wondered if a modern term mightn't be 'the compassionate community. If we can, or if God can in us, start the compassionate community, then one of the reactions will be the same as with those who saw Jesus – they noticed his authority, and his holiness was noticeable to the unclean. Now we don't have much of either: authority or holiness. The fact that there is a recognizable Church with authority and holiness is going to help. The rather encouraging thing is that none of these healings need be inexplicable miracles in modern terms. They're miracles of faith, but they're not interference with the physical process, which is what sticks in so many throats.' He referred to Luke iv: 'He cureth one possessed of a devil, etc.' 'Simon's mother-in-law's fever might have been a family reaction to Simon stopping fishing and going off.' He liked to think their prayers in the past winter had been effective: there had been people on the edge. 'It may not be due to prayers. It may be due to our prayers and the loving care of the family. But it's very encouraging.'

They talked about psychiatrists, and the second curate said he thought doctors shared in the ministry: 'We all share in it according to the gifts we have been given, because in essence it is Christ's ministry.' In a sombre voice the senior curate said: 'We're inclined to write off evil spirits, but should we?' It was like a stone in a pond; the ripples went through the room. He said there had been an evil influence in one part of a village. 'When I went into any house in that particular part, I felt there was an evil influence of some sort. There was something there which seemed to affect everybody. It was what you might term a bad spirit. There was one individual there who I would say was the Devil's advocate in the village, and I would say it probably stemmed from his influence. As there was a particularly bad spirit in that part of the village, and as this person lived there, I put two and two together and maybe made five. But we tend to throw out demons entirely, and maybe we've overdone it a bit.'

The feeling of patience persisted: of waiting for the mysteries that ran parallel to everyday life to reveal themselves, and change everything. 'You sometimes get a tune going round in your head,' said Glendining. 'You can't get it out. You sometimes get an evil thought going round in your mind, you can't get it out. Well, these patterns can be explained as electrical patterns, impulses, in a certain part of the brain.

These can be isolated, and doctors do isolate them when they do a pre-frontal leucotomy, but this doesn't give you the primary cause, which could well be interpreted as devil possession.' The second curate said: 'Yes, it could be. But I don't think that in the present climate of opinion we can talk very sensibly, and be looked on as sensible people, in terms of devil possession. We don't have the holiness to do so.' They talked for another half-hour, about the need for the clergyman's authority, to avoid becoming a 'holy huddle', and to give people the strength of belonging to a committed body. It was nearly time for lunch when they broke up, discussing services, churchyards, choirs, and sick parishioners.

The countryside offers long stretches of time, and the chance to concentrate on a few people at once. The towns are where problems become acute – the numb parishes where enthusiastic clergymen are caught up in activities that often seem to isolate the Church by the very degree of their success, since outsiders view it coldly (if they view it at all) as an excess of private, specialist enthusiasm. Mr S., the rector of a vast suburban parish, could do no more than he was doing. His face was stamped out of hard flesh; he had a heroic war record, a sweeping presence, a blazing enthusiasm for God. His three predecessors had broken down under the strain of the parish. 'One was a militant pacifist, a thrilling man. Another put a clean hot knife through the rather buttery amalgam of things attached to St Mark's. It was either Yes or No to Christianity. He got caught up in controversy over whether clubs should be open to all or only to Church people – it's very parochial, very perennial. We open the sluice gates a little. Another lost his seat in the saddle for the last two years, and waffled around.' Mr S. had two churches and four curates. The rectory, a 1930s house with small, steel-framed windows, was next to a red brick church, with a clangy bell, a thin brass weathercock,

and green copper sheeting on the spire, blackened at the peak.
The Scouts' hut alongside was inscribed:

No defacing these walls please
NUTS!
What we want is guides
No gypsies
No circulars
No hikers
No hawkers
No scouts
But guides
and
No!! rude
remarks please

It was Ascension Day, and the rector held a children's service
at 10 a.m. He stood in the aisle giving instructions: 'All
stand!' and 'Sing louder!' Then he hurried to one of the
daughter churches for a schoolgirls' service: 'In our Lord's day
the earth was a flat plate and Heaven was like an inverted
pudding bowl on top.' His energy was prodigious. 'Ideally,'
he said later, 'we've got to care for the multitude, we've got
to find *time*.' He talked about Christmas – 'A terrific carol
rally and a tableau' – and Easter – 'Three twenty-three-foot
crosses and three processions of witness'. There was the pressure of weddings: 'Two hundred and fifty a year, sixteen a
day at the peak. I see every couple for an hour and a half in
church. That's an excuse for getting them here. They won't
admit they want to know anything, but they won't risk
making fools of themselves, so they come to a rehearsal.' It
was, he said, a parish that could last him till his dying day, and
twenty other priests as well. There were so many people who
thought that 'Christianity is to do with the small print, with
things they don't understand'. His curates were hand-picked:

'This is a tough parish, spiritually tough. So I've got to have someone who doesn't need to be spoon fed.'

It didn't look especially tough, yet the indifference of those miles of council houses would be the reason for his predecessors' breakdowns. It was not a lack of respect ('Everyone on the staff,' said a curate, 'gets called "the rector", except if there's someone in the Forces, and then it's "padre"'). But the usual answer when you called, said the rector, was either 'No' or 'Mum's not in'. It was shattering, he said, when someone committed suicide, and the clergyman knew nothing about it until it had happened. There were plenty of parishioners who worked for the church, and made it an active place. But almost without exception, they were people who lived in 'one of the better parts', not on the council estates. A curate, living on an estate, said how difficult it was to have friends there: 'Not that one's snobbish, but because of the terrible dangers of jealousy if one does make friends. If we have someone to baby-sit, we must have them all. The doctor is the only one we can have as a real friend, because he's in rather the same position.' It seemed only natural that the rector's children should be away at boarding school.

The rector thought himself that they were succeeding in making the church a central institution. What had his activity achieved? Well, he said, for instance, they had had missions, carefully prepared with letters to newspapers, and visits to pubs, and coffee parties. They had achieved better organization, and they had inculcated more respect for the Prayer Book – 'Catholic in the best sense of the word, without being frilly or fussy or spiky.'

The trouble is that to the outsider, the achievement is less exciting. What catches the outsider's sentimental interest is the middle-aged curate whose speciality is hospital visiting. His bachelor's bedsitter has a packet of cornflakes on a shelf, alongside a plaster statue, highly coloured. He rises at six in the morning. He gets round the parish on a scooter. He lives on a small income. Curate: 'I've bought myself a little notebook in Woolworths.' Rector: 'Let me pay you for it.' Curate: 'No, no!' His cuffs are bound with leather. He is happy, he likes people, people like him. He is *there*: which is perhaps what matters.

CHAPTER SIX

BUREAUCRATS AND LAWYERS

To find a geographical spot in the Church where power resides and decisions are taken is impossible. Lambeth Palace and Bishopthorpe have a good deal of authority, so does every bishop's house and palace, and so, in a way, does every vicarage. The nearest to a centre of authority in the secular sense, with bureaucrats and politicians working and meeting regularly, is Church House at Westminster, close to Westminster Abbey and the Houses of Parliament, where for forty years a bureaucracy has been developing on Civil Service lines.

In the block of streets to the west of the river and south of the Abbey, which contains Church House and many other ecclesiastical offices, clergymen are often to be seen with books and brief-cases. One of the most famous of missionary societies, S.P.G., the Society for the Propagation of the Gospel in Foreign Parts, is in Tufton Street. So is the Mothers' Union. The Friends of Cathedral Music are near by, and the Poor Clergy Relief Corporation. There are a couple of hostels – Church Army and Salvation Army – and the parish church of St Matthew. There are religious bookshops, and shops where clergymen of all denominations can equip themselves. Even more than an archbishop's enthronement, a shopful of clergymen's clothes and necessities seems to be concerned with a special kind of religion. An altar cross in hand-carved Perspex stands next to a pair of candlesticks (£20), a 'missal cushion in Louis XIV Brocatelle' (£11 5s. 0d.), a 'walnut wafer box with grid' (£3 complete), and a 'hand-carved Christmas Crib set' (£65 complete). Hymn boards, brass vessels, plaster animals, and wooden saints are on sale, and 'Lincoln' rayon damask is obtainable at £1 5s. 6d. a yard, 'in gold and Roman purple only'. It is not big business – most Anglican clergy wouldn't touch missal cushions or purple vestments even if they could afford them – but such shops have a powerful atmosphere that extends to the window and the street outside.

At Church House there is concentration of a different kind. The Church is organized in layers, and everything tends to overlap; but basically it has its Parliament of long standing called Convocation, which deals with matters of doctrine, and its modern Church Assembly, in full the 'National Assembly of the Church of England', set up in 1919, which deals with everything else. A variety of boards and councils carries on the work of the Assembly; and their small full-time staffs, part lay and part clerical, make up the Church House secretariat. The new secular techniques of management and business efficiency have had their counterpart (though rather a pale one) in the Church, and in theory a great deal of planning is now centralized. The Convocations – there are two, Canterbury and York, meeting separately two or three times a year, and occasionally as one body – have no similar administrative unit. Convocations are the senior bodies, with more ultimate responsibilities, but in the daily life of the Church, the Church Assembly and its bureaucracy do the work. As far as the Assembly itself is concerned, this is composed of the same people as the Convocations, with the addition of several hundred laymen and women.* The forty-three diocesan bishops who form the Assembly's House of Bishops also form

* A plan to virtually do away with the Convocations by merging them with the Church Assembly in a 'General Synod of the Church of England' was proposed in May 1962. This would give laymen a say in matters of doctrine and ritual, at present discussed only by clergy in the Convocations.

the Upper Houses of the Convocations, and the 340-odd clergy in the House of Clergy are also the Lower Houses of the Convocations. Democracy is not the Assembly's strongest point. The bishops are there because they are diocesan bishops; more than a third of the clergymen are there *ex officio*, as deans or archdeacons. The 200 or so who are elected have been chosen, by the vote of their fellow-clergy in the dioceses, whenever there is a General Election – another aspect of Establishment; the Submission of the Clergy Act of 1533 laid it down that Convocations can assemble only by authority of the Crown, and for the sake of convenience this authority is made to coincide with political elections. An election to Convocation produces a good crop of candidates, who canvass with manifestoes that are generally more garrulous and un-buttoned than those of politicians. Occasionally they are printed, more often run off on duplicators.

One said at the 1959 election:

Dear Brother . . . I groan at our poor showing in Press, on Radio and Television, and in the Film and Literary world, where it is becoming accepted as beyond discussion that the only intelligent apologists for the Christian faith are Roman Catholics, while Anglicans are paraded merely to display points of view. I want to see boldness and moral courage in imaginative schemes for diocesan and parochial organization. I do not believe in the parson's freehold . . . I should not mind a bit if we found ourselves disestablished . . . I am sick of the Reformation settlement, and I think that the Lord is calling us beyond it.

The most democratic part of the Assembly is in theory the House of Laity, all of whose members – 340-odd, roughly as many as in the House of Clergy – are elected every five years by the lay members of the Church, 'member' having been defined by the Convocations in 1919, when they created the Church Assembly and much administrative machinery in parishes and dioceses. Leaning towards the principle that parishioners are people who live in the parish and that therefore everyone is or ought to be a member of the Church, the 'Electoral Roll' was invented, and declared open to those who had been baptized, whether or not they had been confirmed and so become Church members by most people's definition. Anyone aged seventeen and above who has been baptized, who isn't a member of a religious body that is not in communion with the Church, and who either lives in the parish or has attended the parish church regularly for the previous six months, can have his name put on the roll. These electors then vote for the parochial church council in the parish, and the lay members of the diocesan conference in the diocese. It is these lay members, forming the diocesan 'Chamber of Laity', perhaps 400 or 500 strong, who in turn elect the House of Laity of the Church Assembly. Inevitably, middle-aged and elderly middle-class men and women predominate. Such people form a considerable proportion of the small number who bother to get their names on the roll in the first place. The diocesan Chamber of Laity can elect whom it likes, but as a rule elects from within itself. The well-known retired schoolteacher, bank manager, or colonel is more likely to be there, is more likely to be elected to the House of Laity, and is more likely to be able to afford the time and money to travel to London three times a year and stay there for a week at a time.

The age, composition, and general remoteness of the House of Clergy, and to a lesser extent of the whole Asssembly, is an old grumble in the Church. The Assembly was intended to be a Parliament – Bishops, Clergy, and Laity can sit separately, though more often they sit together – but the fact that all its measures have to be submitted to the real Parliament, and that the independent Church Commissioners control the Church's capital, weakens its status. What happens there means little to the majority of churchpeople; a vicar in a Lancashire town, or even in a London suburb, is likely to be indifferent to most of the Assembly's debates; I happened to be travelling in the North at the time of an Assembly, and some of the clergy I spoke to didn't even know it was in session. Its debates are reported, dutifully and without much prominence, by newspapers. A verbatim record is made but not published; the official report is an edited version, cut to half the original, and sold at the uneconomic price of 2s. 6d. a copy – it costs about a guinea to produce. Even to interested churchpeople, the debates often seem irrelevant. The world it deals with is too often private and ecclesiastical, with days devoted to such matters as Church discipline or redundant churches. It assumes the Church to be composed of the educated and well-informed. Agendas are loaded with the reports of the councils and committees that the Assembly has under its wing. Specialist phrases crop up – 'ecumenical cooperation', 'the place of the laity'. The anonymously written *Commentary on the Church Assembly*, a short digest of each session which is sold as a pamphlet, has such sub-headings as 'Reluctant Church-wardens', 'Dedication to Pastoral Duty', 'The Occupation of Ministers', 'Of Full Communion', 'Hospital Chaplaincies', 'The Archdeaconries (Augmentation) Measure, 1953', and 'New English Bible'. Debate is often to the point ('The sick atheist,' said a speaker on Hospital Chaplaincies, 'hardly exists'). But churchmen have been known to feel that time is slipping away, that the world is prospering or perishing while the bald heads bob up and down and the Archbishop sits in his high-backed chair, doodling (so they say) in Greek. 'The Church,' said a Birmingham clergyman in one debate, 'is suffering from the disease of democracy – too much administration by too many people.' He was seconded by a colleague from Chichester: 'We are all desperately busy, but what are we busy about? How much is devoted to bringing God home to the people?' A Hampshire vicar wrote to me that Church Assembly, diocesan conferences, and the rest were 'a farce and a waste of time', because they were 'based on the false conception that democracy is Christian and therefore the Church should be democratic. The truth is that the Church is authoritarian and always has been. Our Lord ruled his followers with absolute authority; they did not form committees! . . . It would be far better if the Bishops ruled their dioceses on the Apostolic pattern and had a cabinet of advisers such as their Suffragans, Archdeacons, Rural Deans, etc., and a sort of civil service of duly qualified laymen to deal with finance and other administrative duties.'

Perhaps people expect too much of the Assembly. It prepares straightforward measures dealing with such matters as pensions and the reorganization of dioceses, and passes them up to Parliament, where they are usually approved. It debates the reports of its councils and committees, and when the subject is important, like sex or education or Establishment, it can help to crystallize the Church's views. It is when the Assembly is expected to do more than this, to be a microcosm of the Church in action, that disappointment sets in.

Meanwhile the Church House men are more influential than they were, perhaps more influential than the Church Assembly, their master, realizes. As a civil service it's small – fewer than twenty clergymen, with a similar number of laymen. Between them they cover everything the Church does apart from saving souls – training clergy, relations with monks and nuns, relations with the Roman Catholics and nonconformists, Press and broadcasting, pensions, Church law, care of churches, Anglicans overseas, industrial chaplains, unmarried mothers, hospital chaplains, deaf and dumb, ethics and social problems generally, fund-raising, statistics, and adult education. Money to study or help with these things, at present well over £500,000 a year, is contributed to the Church Assembly by the dioceses under what is known as the 'quota'. Sometimes the departments are 'boards' – the Central Board of Finance, the Board for Social Responsibility. Sometimes they are 'councils' – the Central Council for the Care of Churches, the Youth Council. Most of them occupy Church House itself, with a few in outbuildings near by, working in offices that tend to have drab yellow walls and harsh shades round the lights.

Some of the smaller units are virtually one-man shows. One hears the view that 'in the early days there was a band wagon, and people jumped on it. There were a lot of bodies when the Church Assembly came into existence, they wanted recognition, and affiliation to the Church Assembly was the easiest way of getting it'. Attempts to reorganize have been partly successful, but there has been, and is, stiff opposition from some of those who are due for reorganization. The larger councils are where significant planning and thinking can be found – in CACTM, the Central Advisory Council for the Ministry, which decides how men shall be selected and trained; or in the Board for Social Responsibility, which looks after matters affecting 'family, social, and industrial life', and issues papers and pamphlets on everything from divorce and suicide to artificial insemination and homosexuality, as well as being responsible for moral welfare workers and industrial chaplains. All boards and councils have their written constitution. Members are drawn partly from the Church Assembly, headed as a rule by bishops and archdeacons; they may hold several meetings a year, but unless they have time as well as ability, most of the work and many of the decisions fall to the secretaries and their assistants at Church House. An official said: 'The theory is that the council runs the staff, and the chairman of the council is like a Minister in politics. But it doesn't always work. In politics Ministers are professionals, but here bishops have other things to do. So you tend to get chairmen who just preside over meetings.' The secretary of one body, a clergyman – not one of those quoted elsewhere in this book – thought that 'not many members of the Assembly know what's going on'. He said it would be overstating things to suggest there was a 'powerful secretariat' at Church House; but it was where much of the Church's initiative now lay, and it would be better if the Assembly queried more of the bureaucrats' decisions – 'But then,' he added thinly, 'many of them at the Assembly are really concerned with having a holiday in London, meeting their friends, and engaging in ecclesiastical intrigues.' He thought the issue of who would control the bureaucrats was important: 'Some of us ask ourselves whether it's our function to make policy. Apart from anything else, we're not as able, many of us, as civil servants in the administrative class. Most of us don't make a career of it – we just serve for a few years.' He also suggested that unlike the Civil Service, which had to cope with the 'enormous corporate intransigence' of the Treasury, the ecclesiastical bureaucrats found it a shade too easy to have their schemes financed.

. Their importance is recognized in their salaries. This is a sore point with many clergymen, especially clergymen in drab parishes who earn £800 a year. Salaries at Church House are around £1,400, and linked with scales in the Civil Service, so that if civil servants with a similar salary receive a five per cent increase, then so does the Church Assembly staff. The £1,400 is explained as:

The average income of beneficed clergy, roughly £790 [the figures refer to the end of 1961], on top of which the Church Commissioners are providing another £50, and in some cases a further £50. This makes £890. The latest Government statistics say the cost of living in London is 38 shillings a week more than in the provinces. You've now virtually reached £1,000. Add to this the fact that the parson in a parish has a free house, he lives over the shop and therefore has no travelling expenses, he goes home to lunch and so on – this is getting into the realms of guesswork, but it's reckoned to cost a married man who has to come to London £400 or £500 a year to pay rent and rates, travel to work, and buy his lunch. Part of this has already been included in the 38 shillings, so the lower figure of £400 is used, and it's reckoned that if a man is brought from a parish he must be paid £1,400 a year or he's worse off.

What many parsons find more irritating than a salary differential for bureaucrats is the fact that the bureaucrats are there at all. Annoyance erupts over an incident like that of the Statistical Unit and the 'breach of confidence'. The Unit is a small but expensive department at Church House, costing about £15,000 a year. Before it began work, under a professional statistician, in 1954, no accurate figures about the Church of England had been collected between two covers. Churchmen were always regretting this. The Bishop of Southwell called it 'incredible' in 1958. 'Statistical records would matter for the intelligent running of a business or industry. Why not for the business of the Church?' asked the Bishop of Sheffield. The Unit prepared a 4s. 6d. booklet, *Facts and Figures about the Church of England,* in 1959, and followed this with a revised and expanded version, costing a guinea, in 1962. It is a massive collection of tables, charts, and graphs, from such obvious classifications as 'Ages of parochial incumbents in sizes of livings; analysis for each province, 1959' to the more esoteric 'Diagram XXIII. Sunday-school children per 1,000 population aged three to fourteen inclusive, 1891–1958; private motor-cars currently licensed per 1,000 adults, 1922–59', from which it appeared that 'the decline in Sunday-school attendances is inversely related to the increase in the number of motor-cars'. The Unit draws its information from newspapers, bishops' registers, and other bureaucratic departments, but chiefly from the clergy themselves, who in recent years have complained, with some success, about the forms they have to complete for the Unit's parent body, the Central Board of Finance. But at the end of 1961 a stronger charge was laid against the Unit, when it was said to have divulged information about individual parishes that had been supplied on forms marked 'confidential'. The *Church Times* in particular breathed fire, and two months later the Central Board was apologizing and saying it wouldn't happen again.

The row (though this was not explained to the Assembly) arose from the bureaucrats' concern at the amount of money that parishes give to the Anglican Church overseas. The Overseas Council of the Church Assembly suggests ten per cent of income, but when the parishes' figures were being analysed in 1961, ready for the 1962 *Facts and Figures*, they showed that even including money given to 'home missions' – that is, missionary work within Britain – parishes were handing over only five per cent. The solution, as an official put it, was to 'tell the Overseas Council which parishes weren't pulling their weight, so they could chase them up'. This admirable piece of efficiency resulted in a list of the 27.8 per cent of churches in England which gave nothing to missions in 1958. It was duly marked 'confidential' and sent upstairs from the Statistical Unit to the Overseas Council, who passed it on, still marked 'confidential', to the secretaries of missionary councils in the dioceses. Some of these diocesan secretaries then complained that in many parishes, where there are 'daughter churches' as well as the parish church, all missionary giving is channelled through the main church; this gave an unfair impression of meanness in the final figures. The result of the row was that the figures were amended to show the number of *parishes* that gave nothing; it was too late to change the table in *Facts and Figures*, and the new information had to be gummed into page 80; even calculated by parishes, it showed that 18.8 per cent gave nothing to missions. But a second and louder row overtook the first, when a parish clergyman discovered that the names of the non-giving parishes had been circulated by the Overseas Council. The Central Board of Finance tried to point out that details of parochial expenditure were public property anyway, to be fixed annually on the church door; but it was true that these particular lists had been based on those particular forms marked *confidential*. The *Church Times* said that 'A continuance of the present practice can only lead to damage both to the moral reputation of the Church and to the efficiency of the Statistical Unit', and eventually, out came the apology. Meanwhile *Facts and Figures*, with the amendment inserted, had been published, and described as 'gloriously glossy' by the *Church Times*, which went on to question the need for 'so elaborate an undertaking, in which the Church of God apes the way of the world in the latest fashion of business efficiency'. Presently the 'confidential' row was being written about in the *Church Times* as though it had confirmed the darkest suspicions of sober men. Urbanus, a columnist who fancies his turn of phrase, wrote sarcastically of 'the wealth of ingenuity coffered in the brains of Mr Neuss's nameless gnomes' (Mr R. F. Neuss* is head of the Statistical Unit). 'The raw material for this public show-off,' added Urbanus, 'was, as parochial incumbents know all too well, the confidential information which they were pressed to compile for the Central Board of Finance.'

* As a result of *Facts and Figures*, Neuss was elected a Fellow of the Royal Statistical Society.

The Statistical Unit was privately indignant; some of the bureaucrats sympathized. 'But they're getting their own back,' said one, just after the 'confidential' affair. 'An incumbent wanting to move has written to ask for details of a parish, but they said, "Sorry, old boy, it's confidential".' Secular newspapers were generally impressed by *Facts and Figures*. But it got off to a slow start, and in the first month after publication, only 1,000 of the 5,000 copies printed were sold.

The critics of Church House bureaucracy use phrases like 'our real work among the people' and 'what we need is spirituality', which suggest that the bureaucrats are wasting valuable time. What strikes the outsider more sharply is the amount of time the Church wastes on Canon Law revision, which has created a bureaucracy of its own since it began in 1939. The Church has inherited an internal system of laws, some of them going back more than a thousand years, many of them so at variance with the facts of present-day Anglicanism that the net result is less, not more, Church discipline. No one knows how much Canon Law there is, though the phrase is usually taken to refer to the 'Canons of 1604', when 141 canons drawn up by the Convocations were given the Royal Assent; most of the 141 simply put on record what was already in operation. Canon Law grew up with Christendom, rambling and overlapping, mixed up with forgeries and the mistakes of copyists, some of it as old as the fourth century A.D. It was founded on the civil law, and, says Halsbury's *Laws of England*, also upon 'holy scripture, Christian tradition, and various canons or rules made at different periods of the Church's history, both in the East and West'. Some of it has become the law of the country, and the most important elements for the Church were codified in 1604; the remainder still exists, a mass of legislation never entirely identified and separated, and, because of the time and trouble involved, likely to remain so. Confusion about what is meant by Canon Law is nothing new. The authorities cite such cases as that of Shipden *v.* Redman in 1622, when Redman, an ecclesiastical law-officer, said that all women going to be churched should wear a white veil, and Mrs Shipden, safely delivered of a child, refused, and was excommunicated. Eventually, the King's Bench had to rule on whether this was ancient custom or a new law (they decided it was ancient custom).

The uncollected Canon Law is not touched by the present revision, which is concerned only with the 1604 canons. To revise and simplify them has occupied hundreds of men for thousands of hours. It is an unreal subject for an outsider, but many determined and intelligent men sit on committees, write books, and suggest that behind the fought-over details are important theological issues. In 1604, for instance, the Church was far 'Lower' than it is now. Attempts to take this into account come up against the wrath of the Evangelicals – who seem to be losing the battle, though not without obtaining sizeable concessions. Clergymen who wore vestments in the nineteenth century, in the early years of the Anglo-Catholic movement, were often prosecuted. Vestments are now common among clergy without strong party feelings, but to the extreme Evangelical they are still 'garments adopted in medieval times by a superstitious and corrupt Roman Catholic Church'. The revised Canon B8 spells out the legality of vestments, adding hopefully that 'The Church of England does not attach any particular doctrinal significance to the diversities of vesture permitted by this Canon'. The Evangelicals refuse to be mollified, and insist that vestments are a sign of 'High' doctrines.

The unrevised canons were often quaint. 'No Ecclesiastical Person shall wear any Coif or wrought Night-cap, but only plain Night-caps of black silk, satin, or velvet,' said the old

Canon 74. Canon 75 declared: 'No Ecclesiastical Person shall at any time, other than for their honest necessities, resort to any taverns or ale-houses, neither shall they board or lodge in any such places. Furthermore, they shall not give themselves to any base or servile labour . . .' The new version calls only for 'apparel . . . suitable to his office.' Canon 75 becomes: 'A Minister shall not give himself to such occupations, habits, or recreations as do not befit his sacred calling, or may be detrimental to the performance of the duties of his office, or tend to be a just cause of offence to others.' The change from old to new is not always so smooth. Sometimes, where the wording was harsh and precise, it has become woolly. Canon 5 said: . . .'Whosoever shall hereafter affirm, That any of the Nine and thirty Articles . . . are in any part superstitious and erroneous, or such as he may not with a good conscience subscribe unto; let him be excommunicated *ipso facto*, and not restored, but only by the Archbishop, after his repentance, and public revocation of such his wicked errors.'

The new Canon A2 is much blander. It merely says: 'The Thirty-nine Articles are agreeable to the Word of God and may be assented unto with a good conscience by all members of the Church of England.'

The language of the revised canons is a compromise which bears the marks of much drafting: 'except he shall be' and 'unto' and 'thereof' have crept in alongside the plainer English. Since 1946, when an archbishops' commission which had been sitting since 1939 produced its suggestions, the draft canons have been circulating between steering committees, the Convocations, and the House of Laity. By the early 1960s the work was coming to an end, and the opponents of revision were mounting their campaign to have the objectionable canons blocked by Parliament, when they are presented for the Royal Assent. Only the expert can spot the explosive ones:

the canon defining the 'lawful authority' that will allow clergy to depart from the Prayer Book, the canons that are alleged to give more power to the bishops, the canon about vestments, the canon about altars – whether they should be 'altars' (High) or 'Communion tables' (Low). Behind the detail is the reality of the Church's need to have more discipline, of a kind that can reasonably be enforced. With their eye on the next stage, which will be to attempt the revision of the Prayer Book in the face of furious Evangelical opposition, the reformers are doing all they can to strengthen the Church as a separate entity, free to manage its own affairs.

Short of full-scale disestablishment, the Church will continue to be served by courts that carry the authority of State as well as Church: one of the privileges of Establishment. The ramifications of Canon Law are equalled by the ramifications of the courts that are meant to interpret it; they are usually occupied with technicalities, when they are occupied with anything, but they are statutory courts and the law is behind them. Even non-churchmen can be involved. A few years ago it was proposed to enlarge an old parish church in what had once been the Hertfordshire countryside, but is now an expanding urban area. Some artists who lived in a house near the church read a notice displayed outside to say what was proposed, and imagined they were being invited to object, which they did – not on religious grounds, but because they thought it was vandalism to build on a nice green churchyard. Having objected, they found themselves appearing, not as witnesses at an inquiry but as 'opponents' at a consistory court, where they lost the case they had never intended to bring, and had to pay more than £100 costs.

But such bizarre episodes are rare. There is something very unmomentous about Church courts. The titles of many of them have a mouldering sound – the archbishop's court for the

trial of heresy, the archbishop's court for the trial of bishops
(there are two of each). Facts about them are hard to come
by – when they last sat, what the procedure is. Consistory
courts are the most practical; one to each diocese, presided
over by a Chancellor, an Anglican barrister appointed by the
bishop, who sits alone or with assessors to decide matters of
practice and behaviour. He grants faculties – licences required
to alter the ornaments, furniture, or fabric of a church. If the
church council wants to get rid of the coke boiler and install
oil-fired central heating, it first needs a faculty; in a straightforward case, with no one objecting, the papers go before the
Chancellor, and no public sitting is necessary. As one Chancellor put it: 'It's usually a matter of common sense. But it
avoids entrusting it to yokels and the incumbent on the spot.'
Even when a court is held, it's likely to be badly reported, or
not reported at all (this is why ecclesiastical lawyers find it
impossible to say when excommunication, which used to be
the severest punishment, was last imposed in England. Similarly with public penance. In theory it is probably still en-
forceable. But no one really knows). Occasionally a squabble
over a statue of the Virgin or the words on a tombstone will
find its way into the newspapers, still more occasionally there
will be full Press coverage of a case involving the discipline of
the clergy, which is the other kind of case that comes before a
Chancellor.

The system is being revised, so that when the new Canon
Law is ready there will be new courts to interpret it. In some
ways the new order will be more cumbersome than the old,
particularly where doctrine and ritual are concerned. One of
the new courts has the compelling title of the Court of Ecclesiastical Causes Reserved, and will call on theologians and
liturgiologists to help with expert advice. Some churchmen
find this a dismal prospect. But the High and Low wings have

been busy behind the scenes, as they have with Canon Law revision. A Chancellor said: 'The High Church are terrified lest they'll all be prosecuted for wearing birettas, and the Low Church are terrified lest they'll never be able to prosecute anyone at all.' The results of compromise are the panels of theologians and liturgiologists, added as checks and balances between one party and the other.

Further reforms have been suggested to save the Church from the damaging effect of trying its erring clergymen in open court. The Press finds the combination of sin and sex irresistible – as in the case of the Rev. Bryn Thomas, vicar of the Church of the Ascension at Balham Hill, in London, who appeared before Southwark Consistory Court in 1961. Thomas, who denied the charges, was found guilty of adultery with a Sunday-school teacher, of assaulting his curate's wife, and of trying to kiss two teenage girls in his study. The case was widely reported, Thomas was soon telling all in the *People* ('I became a prey to the type of women who flutter around priests like butterflies on the heather. Often I wandered through the very valley of temptation'), and five weeks after the eight-day hearing ended, he was deposed from holy orders – 'unfrocked'. This is the ultimate sentence against a clergyman. Sentences against the clergy begin with *monition* (a warning to do or not to do something),* and move through *inhibition* (partial disqualification) and *suspension* (for a limited period) to *deprivation* – that is, deprivation of a living, which was the initial sentence passed on Thomas.

Deposition is decided on by the bishop. Halsbury says that the bishop may depose a man 'by sentence and without any further formality'. In the case of Thomas, the Bishop of Southwark, Dr Stockwood, did it with ceremony at Southwark Cathedral. This was a far cry from the agenda-produc-

---

* An additional, lesser punishment, *rebuke*, has now been proposed.

ing bureaucracy at Church House, but it had an authority that suggested what the authority of the Church must have felt like in the past. It took place at 10 o'clock on a morning in May. The cathedral is a gloomy place, built on ground below the level of the main road and the high-level railway tracks. Trains and lorries pass incessantly. About a hundred people turned up, including a group of clergymen, a preponderance of women in the middle of the nave, and a block of journalists at the back. A man from the Church Information Office brought scts of cyclo-styled sheets headed 'SOUTHWARK CATHE-DRAL, MAY 4, 1961. A FORM OF SERVICE for DEPOSITION from HOLY ORDERS', ready to hand to the Press in the church-yard afterwards. Organ music boomed out, there was a scuffle by the door when a photographer tried to bring his camera into the cathedral and was hustled out by a man in a navy suit, and, to the chanting of the Litany, a small procession appeared from behind the high altar. The Bishop of Southwark was the principal figure, together with his Suffragans – the Bishops of Kingston and Woolwich – and the Chancellor of the diocese, wearing his full-bottomed wig. Some lesser clergymen accompanied them. No 'form of service' for deposition exists in the Prayer Book, and at the last deposition at Southwark, only the sentence was read. There is no need even for it to be held in a cathedral, though this is normal practice. The rule seems to be, as one Chancellor put it: 'The more notorious the matter, the greater the need for publicity.' This had been a notorious case, and it was made into an elaborate occasion. The Bishop of Kingston read from I Samuel ii, 27–35, where the fall of the house of Eli is prophesied: 'Behold, the days come, that I will cut off thine arm, and the arm of thy father's house, that there shall not be an old man in thine house . . .' Then came Psalm 51: 'Have mercy upon me, O God, after thy great goodness: according to the multitude of thy mercies do away mine offences.' The second lesson was read by the Bishop of Wool-wich: Matthew vii, 15–27. Trains rumbled, the women coughed, the thwarted photographers shuffled outside and Dr Robinson could be heard intermittently: 'Beware of false prophets, which come to you in sheep's clothing, but inwardly they are ravening wolves . . . every good tree bringeth forth good fruit; but a corrupt tree bringeth forth evil fruit. . . . And the rain descended, and the floods came, and the winds blew, and beat upon that house; and it fell: and great was the fall of it.' Then Psalm 130: 'O Israel, trust in the Lord, for with the Lord there is mercy: and with him is plenteous redemption.' Then the congregation knelt to pray, except most of the reporters, who remained seated, looking bored or glassy-eyed. Then Stockwood sat in his chair and read the preamble and sentence. The former vicar was to be deposed from 'the office which he hath misused and that publicly, that others may be warned neither to receive his ministrations nor to follow his example'. The sentence itself was like a voice from the past: '. . . THEREFORE WE MERVYN by Divine permission Bishop of Southwark first calling upon the Most High God of Heaven and Earth Father Son and Holy Ghost and setting him alone before our eyes do pronounce decree and declare that the said William Bryn Thomas having been duly ordained in the Church of England to the offices of Priest and Deacon be entirely removed deposed and degraded from the said offices . . .' The bishop signed the sentence at a small table provided at the entrance to the choir. 'Then,' said the special Form of Service, 'the Bishop shall move the people to pray.' 'The people', many of them there as sightseers, knelt again to hear the bishop say: 'And now, forasmuch as Almighty God desires not the death of a sinner, but rather that he may turn from his wickedness and live, let us pray to Him that He will, of His great love, grant to our erring brother true repentance and amendment of life, and to us and His whole Church, pardon and peace.' The Bishop of Woolwich prayed again, and the procession filed away behind the altar to add their signatures to the sentence. The Press hurried off to get their hand-outs, and a photographer, packing up his camera, grumbled to a colleague because neither the vicar nor any of the main figures in the case had been present. It had been a strangely theatrical occasion, overlaid with the wrapped-up mustiness that outsiders associate with the Church, however firmly they are told by the strategists at Church House that this is the age of 'new ideas' and 'exciting Christianity'. Here, it was the past that mattered. Even the precise force of the sentence was not clear. For there is a sense in which holy orders are indelible. Deposition stops a man from being a clergyman in the legal sense of the word. Yet although he is 'entirely removed, deposed, and degraded', this is held not to undo whatever it is that is done when, at his ordination, the bishop lays hands on him and says: 'Receive the Holy Ghost for the Office and Work of a Priest in the Church of God, now committed unto thee by the Imposition of our hands. Whose sins thou dost forgive, they are forgiven; and whose sins thou dost retain, they are retained . . .' He is still a priest, and theologically seems to be entitled, in emergency, to act as one: to administer absolution to a dying man, even to marry a couple if dire need could be proved. If an unfrocked clergyman were to be restored to favour, he would not be re-ordained. But the exact position, as with so much about the Church, isn't clear, and never can be.

CHAPTER SEVEN

SOCIAL CONSCIENCE

WHAT the Church thinks about present-day industrial society is poorly documented and often confused. Strikes, slums, contraceptives, road safety, and the Bomb are matters on which every possible viewpoint can be heard from the clergy, with only a limited amount of guidance being given at or near the top, and then often hedged about with qualifications that 'This is a private opinion' or 'This has only the authority of the committee'. Politically, the effective tendency is liberal. Where there is political movement, among action groups and intellectual clergy, it favours men, not managements. The bishops are against hanging. Apartheid is attacked, or at least quietly condemned, by the majority. But these are the convictions of most unadventurous liberals. When it comes to being outspoken or offensive, the Church has no more than a hard-core of convinced protestors who are willing to go further and faster than the popular tide (if the Anglican clergy had to vote for or against Britain's possession of the H-bomb, a large majority would probably be in favour of our keeping it). Various pressures work against reforming zeal. A hard-bitten blimpery lives on among a minority of middle-class clergy, who will sign any manifesto that refers to 'the threat of international Communism', as well as calling for the birch or condemning moral laxity at the least excuse. The growth of the Welfare State has taken the wind out of reformers' sails, in the Church as elsewhere. And there are subtler pressures. Capital punishment may be advocated theologically by a fierce young working-class Fundamentalist curate as well as politically by an elderly Tory canon. Priests on soapboxes and in factories may be condemned by their colleagues not because they are of the Left but because they are alleged to be wasting their time with things that shouldn't concern the Church. Young clergymen who are political are inclined to be Left, but many young clergymen make a point of not being political at all. Nick Earle, in *What's Wrong with the Church?*, writes about the 'popular fallacy' of supposing that the Church has the right 'actually to tell people how [their] daily life "ought" to be run'. Earle mentions the movement to boycott South African goods that was sponsored in 1960 by a group called Christian Action. After saying that he knows too little about politics to assess the movement, he raises 'grave doubts about the label which it used. The urging of a policy – however compassionate – in the name of Christ is to label the policy, not the motives, as Christian. . . . The epithet "Christian" can strictly be applied to two nouns only. The first is worship – a man is a Christian if he participates in it; and the second is faith'. Valerie Pitt, a caustic young churchwoman who writes in *Prism*, expresses the mood when she declares that 'The Englishman thinks of religion as "doing good", the committed Christian as a special kind of business called "church work", the modern-minded Anglican as "getting things done". The itch for action which sent our ancestors to found temperance societies in Borrioboola Gha sends us to wave banners in Trafalgar Square, to shove leaflets through letter boxes, and get under the feet of shop stewards.' For Miss Pitt, 'the Divine Work is not a scurry of endless doing . . . Christian action is not "meeting a challenge" or a species of athletics, it is "to stand and wait"'. Another variation on the point emerged from a radio discussion, where Valerie Pitt asked Canon L. J. Collins, the London clergyman who is chairman of the Campaign for Nuclear Disarmament (and also of Christian Action), what he meant by 'evolving a Christian way of life'. Collins said that 'the Assemblies of the Church of England spend hours and hours and hours and hours discussing new canons as to whether the wine should be called fermented wine or wine fermented or whatever it might be called, saying absolutely nothing, not even discussing, seriously, the question of nuclear weapons'. To which Miss Pitt replied: 'There are other things in Christianity, Canon Collins, besides nuclear weapons.'

One reason why Christian Ethics was dropped from the General Ordination Examination (Chapter 2) was that so few books exist to bring the subject up to date. 'In the middle of the twentieth century,' begins D. L. Munby's *God and the Rich Society*, 'one may be pardoned for thinking that many Christians are retreating into their fastnesses, and abandoning the unequal struggle with the world.' Munby pleads for a professional study of Christian and social ethics, and says the major issues that the Church should be studying are 'the use and abuse of our rich expanding economy, on the one hand, and, on the other hand, the problems of the poverty of the mass of mankind'. But the fact is that such calls for action, whether from laymen like Munby or (very different) clergymen like Collins, lack the resonance that they would have had between the wars, when William Temple was one of the dominant churchmen, and the 'Life and Work' movement was in the ascendant. Temple, an archbishop's son, became an angry young clergyman in the early part of the century, intolerant of secular poverty and ecclesiastical narrow mindedness. F. A. Iremonger's biography quotes from a letter he wrote in 1907: 'It is the system which is foul and rotten. Producer, capitalist, consumer – all are entangled in the meshes of its net. . . . We form Army Corps, we build "Dreadnoughts", we discuss endlessly what metaphysics are to be taught to children in our schools. But if we listen, there is still the desolate cry of the Son of Man: "I am hungry and ye give me no meat".' Temple, more than any other churchman in this century, became a power in the land – a power that always seemed on the point of connecting with society in order to change it, yet never quite performed this difficult feat. He was in the Labour Party for seven years. He opposed capital punishment before it was fashionable to do so. He annoyed Neville Chamberlain by writing to *The Times* when he was Archbishop of York, urging that the restoration of salaries cut as part of the national economy drive should have priority. He annoyed the City by his criticism of banking. But he was never a crank with a shrill voice. His wartime Penguin book, *Christianity and the Social Order,* was a best-seller, and is still in the bookshops (in the Preface, the first person Temple thanks is the woman who typed the manuscript). He became Archbishop of Canterbury in 1942. According to Iremonger he could 'fill the Albert Hall at a few days' notice, and was, beyond all question, the greatest moral force in Britain'. He was less revolutionary in later years, but by all accounts retained a rare stature and purposefulness. But he died in 1944, and the movement towards social awareness in the Church has lost its steam. Twenty years after the Malvern Conference of 1941, its intentions, as set out by Temple, have a museum look: 'To consider from the Anglican point of view what are the fundamental facts which are directly relevant to the ordering of the new society that is quite evidently emerging, and how Christian thought can be shaped to play a leading part in the reconstruction after the war is over.' Christian thought has remained on the sidelines, and the affluent society seems to puzzle the Church's moral theologians as much as it puzzles everyone. What one gets are statements, sometimes cheerful, sometimes gloomy. At Lent, 1962, the

Bishop of Manchester was telling his diocese that 'The Church has no concern in making the affluent more affluent. Its true concern is, or should be, for old-age pensioners, the homeless, the destitute, the prisoners, and those subject to the fierce poverty which exists in places beyond our shores'. Greer pointed to the 'heartening fact' that the previous year, British churches had contributed £658,000 to the Inter-Church Aid and Refugee Service. A few weeks later, at his enthronement, the new Bishop of Chelmsford was saying that 'there is so far little sign that our Church, in a day when young nations in Africa and elsewhere are coming to birth and looking for a soul, is buying up the great but fleeting opportunities of helping them to find a Christian pattern of life. Our missionary praying, service, and giving in the Church of England are still at a deplorably low level.' The bishop suggested that 'in politics, economics, and social life, in morals and religion, all is in the melting pot. The whole scene of human affairs is dominated by a question never before considered by men of affairs – what if the melting pot melts?'

Only the Church overseas – which is outside the scope of this book – can be socially effective in the old way. With more than 300 dioceses and 'missionary districts', and nearly 500 bishops, the Anglican Church is spread throughout the world; and despite the lack of support that the Bishop of Chelmsford deplores, and the difficulties of working in countries of Asia and Africa where white men and Western ideas have become suspect, the Church can go on doing simple, important things: converting pagans, teaching children, running hospitals. Its social role is more clearly defined than it is in England. Here, unable to play a 'leading part' in the new society, the Church has combined a dwindling amount of its traditional social work – running hostels, looking after unmarried mothers – with newer schemes and ideas that vary from printed cards in parishioners' windows saying, rather plaintively, 'I am a member of the Church. Can I help?' to large-scale industrial missions in London, Sheffield, Coventry, and other centres.

Here, in an industrial mission, where clergymen spend much of their time in engineering works and railway canteens, can be seen a detail of the Church in action, seeking to make contact with men whose families have been alienated from the Church since their ancestors left the countryside a century or two ago and settled into the bleak irreligiousness of the young manufacturing towns. (*Church and People in an Industrial City*, by the Rev. E. R. Wickham, is the classic on the subject. Wickham started the Sheffield Industrial Mission in 1944, and built it into the most elaborate in the Church before he became Bishop of Middleton.) An Industrial Committee of the Church Assembly now exists to coordinate industrial missions; but they are all autonomous, usually responsible to the bishop of the diocese, and staffed altogether by about twenty-five full-time and forty part-time clergymen, as well as a few Free Church ministers. All have their own ideas about training clergy and laymen, about magazines, about 'cells' and 'projects' and week-end conferences and study-groups with managements. Sometimes bad feeling is found among the non-industrial clergy because, they allege, the mission says nothing about going to church, and is too imprecise about its aims. From the missions' viewpoint this is a nonsensical objection, if only because it seems obvious to an industrial chaplain who stands in an echoing steel mill, watching his flock – whom he would hardly be likely to refer to as a flock – at some back-breaking or thought-deadening labour, that 'church' is a meaningless word for most of them.

Arthur Sainsbury (a pseudonym) had been doing it for years, and claimed no sensational results. There was a time when they were outsiders: 'Now we're too damned OK – no well-appointed diocese is without its industrial chaplain.' They had gone carefully with the unions, and now they went carefully with the managements. Managements, he said, always suspected they were a bit Red. He himself had once been an active member of the Labour Party; he had let it slide, though he had never officially resigned. Sainsbury was young-middle-aged, with a clerical collar and conventional grey suit. His house of blackened stone was on high ground with a confused view of smoke, slums, and acres of iron sheds. He was cool, intelligent, and suitably unshockable. It was a tough city. A trade union official once told him, referring to industrial disputes: 'I think Jesus Christ was lucky, he was only crucified once.' Relating it, Sainsbury said with satisfaction: 'That meant he'd understood what it was to be a human being.'

His approach to the works was bland, cheerful, and unpretentious:

I suppose in the end one is trying to make a man more of a man, full stop – to open up greater possibilities of living. It carries a lot of theological overtones. To look at the world from a certain point of view, to think this world a good place to live in – to widen their horizons, to reconcile them with each other a bit, to live more harmoniously.

Strikes? One gives a philosophical position, but one says: 'Use the usual channels – go on, be a layman, do your stuff.' I'm never consulted on this kind of issue. One hears the rights and wrongs, but people counsel themselves. You don't meet them as workers, you meet them as friends.

A lot of people think it's your task to stop them swearing. Go into any department and the men'll point at someone and say, 'Go on, he's the bloke you want to convert.' We're not trying to make people into churchgoers, though as a matter of fact many people think we are. We want to show what it means to be a Christian in industry. Take a man who thieves at work – it's going on all the time. He goes out of the works with precious metal. That doesn't matter, among his friends, but a man who takes a pay packet from a workmate is damned. We want to examine these codes of justice and fair-play.

In action, in a drop-forge at lunchtime, standing with polished black shoes close together on the pitted stone floor, Sainsbury attracted four men and three women at first; later, as the thirty minute break drew to an end, a few others drifted over to sit on a bench or the rim of a truck, and hear what was going on. It was an oblique conversation, shattered by the slam of hammers, the showers of sparks and sheets of flame, the steady roar of machinery. The shop was as high-roofed as a railway station, with sunlight cutting through the dust far above. Ostensibly the purpose of the gathering was to hear the report of an elderly man who had been to a week-end conference. But a heavily built younger man with an expansive manner, a union official of some importance, took over the conversation, seizing on a casual remark to demand: 'What do we mean by sincerity? Are we as workers sincere in our desire for true brotherhood, if one was to ask oneself that question?'

'That's the point,' said a woman in overalls, whose dusty nylon stockings protruded through the ends of her sandals. 'You should ask yourself.'

'When you say sincerity at work,' asked Sainsbury, 'what do you mean?'

'I mean sincerity of purpose in helping one another. It should be brought forward more.'

'If it's not there, it's not there,' said Sainsbury.

'That's what I want to know.'

A small man with a fierce expression, wearing a cap, whose name was Harry, broke in to say that if a friend had been ill, and on your way to the boozer you met him in the street, you'd say, 'How are you, Bill?' He'd say, 'I'm champion.'

'Have a drink?' 'No, thanks.' So you'd carry on to the boozer, and the man would go off along the street. 'But if you'd been sincere,' said Harry belligerently, 'what should you have done?' No one spoke. The official shook his head. 'I'm asking you a question,' said Harry. A man with sad eyes, munching a thick corned-beef sandwich, joined the group. 'Well,' said Harry, just as Sainsbury was opening his mouth, 'you should have given him the one and nine!'

Everyone made derisive noises. 'I'm of the opinion that the principle of sincerity is lacking,' insisted the union official, 'and I want to know what people are doing to expand that principle. It's my opinion of life that people are better at expanding untruths and half-truths than they are at expanding the truth.' Why was it, he asked, that one saw the same people all the time? 'I'd like to see these meetings attended by twenty or thirty people,' he said.

The conversation seemed to have a mysterious inner thread. The sad-eyed man shook crumbs from his polythene bag and said: 'I look at it this way. If a man can't do good, it's not for him to do evil. If you work with a man who's a wrong 'un, you'll end up a wrong 'un yourself.'

'My point is –' said Sainsbury.

'Excuse me. If you get someone convincing others, it'll be contagious.'

'Is that possible, Arthur?' asked the official.

'I'm more interested in a general reorganization of society.'

'It's no good having an organization and telling it you're going to be sincere,' said the sad-eyed man.

'Right!' said the official. 'That's right!'

'You can make it reasonably possible for people to have a good carry-on, a good framework,' said Sainsbury, smiling and opening his eyes wide. 'A small minority can have an effect. The House of Commons –'

'Hey!' said the official. 'We're drifting, Arthur. We're here on the shop floor, not in the House of Commons.'

'You shouldn't think the House of Commons is so far away.'

'Isn't it? It's further than two hundred miles . . . .'

Only a few minutes of the lunch-break were left when the older man gave his report. The noise of hammers and the crash of castings being tipped into trucks were becoming fierce. 'We were all agreed at the conference that the industrial mission is all to the good,' said the delegate. There had been useful discussions and interesting excursions: 'We went on a visit to Coventry, and it were really awe-inspiring to see the cathedral.' A minute later the meeting broke up, and Sainsbury went on to one of the offices, where nine young clerks and draughtsmen were sitting around, waiting to discuss the changing status of the white-collar worker in industry.

Here and at other works, men from the management were officially well-disposed towards the mission. Privately some were indifferent, as long as the clergy didn't make a nuisance of themselves; there was a lingering suspicion of 'socialism'; a few were genuinely interested. One executive who had come up from the shop-floor, a Presbyterian, was on the side of the mission, but saw the difficulties. He described how a chaplain had talked to the men about 'justice' when a dispute was in progress. The men said: 'Right, now we know what to do.' A union man had turned on the chaplain and said: 'I've been trying to hold these boys back for thirty years, and you undo all the good I've done.' We all laughed; it wasn't clear if the joke was on the Church or the union. On the whole, it was easier to find precise approval among the intelligent trade unionists than among the intelligent managers. 'A few years ago I had a poor view of the Resurrection,' said a foreman. 'I'm not ashamed to say that when I came to the Resurrection

I questioned the fact that Jesus Christ rose from the dead in a cave. The mission has given me a less jaundiced view of the Church.' An elderly union official, talking of meetings arranged by the mission, said: 'It stands to reason that a man who's been to an organization like that won't go home and give his wife a thick ear as he might if he'd been to the Anchor.'

Much of Sainsbury's time is spent with people who are at least nominally well-disposed; but to be properly effective he must pierce the lump of those who don't care – the men, by far the majority, who don't want to discuss the 'principle of sincerity' or attend week-end conferences, but have to be sought out and confronted in corners of the works. At 9 a.m. in a wooden hut, outside a foundry that was being rebuilt, a clergyman in a white safety helmet made a strange confrontation for half a dozen men having tea and sandwiches from the rough table. It was a damp, mild morning; earth-moving machines and gangs of men passed the open window; they all knew Sainsbury, and adapted their conversation, which was about women, to the occasion. A tall middle-aged man, described by the others as 'a proper atheist', began to denounce the leniency of Britain's immigration policy ('There's thirty-nine nationalities f—s a white woman in this country') and the Royal Family ('The Queen Mother ought to go to a council bungalow. Why should we keep her?'). The others shouted him down, and a man who was hanging his coat on a nail said as a joke: 'Love thy neighbour!' This infuriated the atheist, who began denouncing the interference of the Church, till an even bigger man, with an even louder voice, shouted: 'Now listen! Tha's got a short memory, thee. During the war they did a fine job – I'm talking about the Church Army.' The atheist immediately agreed. 'I'd give my last dollar to the Salvation Army. I'd sooner give to them than to him coming to the back door every Christmas for the upkeep of the Church. You've got a grant, I said. You get money every year for the Church.'

'There's nowt wrong with parsons,' said the big man. 'It's the congregations, mate.'

'You've only got to look at the *News of the World*,' said the atheist. 'They're perverted, half of them. There was a man the other day was bound over for three years for interfering. You and me would be over the wall for three years.'

A man passing the window stuck his head in, grinned at Sainsbury, and said: 'They daren't say them nasty words.'

'Mind you,' the big man was saying, 'we don't want parsons marching and saying Ban the Bomb. They ought to be in their pulpits.'

'They ought to ban vestries,' said the atheists. 'That's where the damage is done.'

A man going out of the door said: 'If my lad, who's in the choir, says anything about the vestry, I say: Home, straight.'

Sainsbury said only a few words. He sat calmly at the table, hands folded in front of him, looking at each speaker with interest. Later, talking in a café, he said: 'We've always respected industry. We've not tried to use it as a fishing ground. We've tried to judge it in the light of what we can contribute to industry. It's a pretty indefinable contribution.' Pressed for a definition, he said: 'I suppose what we're doing is a crude, informal kind of adult education. The Church has lost its way in industrial society. It hasn't got a consistent social ethic, so it bleats about morality. We don't bleat about morality.'

Where Sainsbury, and other chaplains, are less specific is when it comes to finding examples of decisions made on Christian principles. Talking about this in another town, with a chaplain and a minor executive in the executive's office, the executive said proudly that highly paid men who were being made redundant in an engineering shop were being paid lump sums in compensation, and given labouring jobs around the works. He admitted this was partly expediency but insisted it was partly Christian. A few minutes later the executive mentioned that he might be going abroad presently: some new machines were being installed, and the operators had to go to the continent for a month's training. The company had planned to send them to Germany, but had discovered at the last minute that the Germans used more men per machine than the English company intended to use. So the executive was hoping to visit Holland where it was understood that they used fewer men per machine and the operators would probably be sent there for training – nice and safe, where they wouldn't get ideas. The chaplain looked uneasy at this, but said nothing. Later, outside the executive's office, he said it bothered him because it did look a bit like sharp practice: but it would have done no good to start arguing.

A variation on the industrial-chaplain idea, which, it's claimed, gets round the chaplain's dependence on the good will of managements, is provided by a handful of worker-priests, who combine manual labour with the priesthood. But the idea has failed to catch on. Some bishops are afraid that worker-priests are illegal under the canon that forbids 'base or servile labour'; laymen are often hostile because they find their ideas of the priesthood being upset. Tony Williamson, who was the youngest at the time I saw him, working at an Oxford factory and living in a small house through the walls of which you could hear what was on television next door, was ordained in 1961. He has been elected to the city council. At work, he said, he drove a fork-lift, and on Sundays might be in church to take the parish Communion from 9 to 10, then at a union meeting by 10.30. What difference did the fact of being a priest make to him? 'The only real difference is celebrating the Sacraments. I felt it was right to be a priest before I felt it was right to be a workman' (though he worked in factories before he was ordained). If, he said, you were to ask a parish priest what was the difference between him and his parish worker, he would practically hit the roof: but what *was* the difference? 'I believe in prayer,' he said, 'and I think it's a good thing some people have got more time to pray than I have. But some clergy are living in a religious vacuum. They don't meet people, they don't live up to the realities of life.' 'They're church-centred,' said his wife, 'and most of the world isn't.' Williamson thought it was 'sheer nonsense to think that people like to talk about religion. They may talk about it with the parson because they think it keeps him happy. They don't say to the parson, "If you think you're going to get me into chapel in the next twenty years, you'll be lucky." But that's what they're thinking. Clergymen see people at their least real'.

Politically, Williamson is a Socialist: 'Someone should explain,' he said, 'how one can be a Conservative and a Christian.' Other people in the Church would like to have it explained how one can be a Communist and a Christian, a situation in which a few clergymen find themselves. The Rev. Alan Ecclestone, who has a parish in Sheffield, stood, unsuccessfully, as a Communist candidate for a seat on the city council in 1962. He saw no contradiction: 'I do not preach politics,' he said, 'but the social content of one's sermons is inescapable.' The *Church Times* reported him as telling a Press conference that the Communist Party took Socialism seriously, and proposed to end the exploitation of man by man. 'To give what help I can to the furtherance of such aims seems to me to be a matter of plain duty.' But there is no agreement, in the context of modern society, what 'plain duty' means to a Christian. 'It seems to my simplicity,' wrote a correspondent to the *Church Times*, 'that a widespread strike is thoroughly unChristian, in that it is aggressive. . . . If Christianity has nothing to say on this matter, then it had better pack up. If the Church approves, then it seems to me it believes that the end justifies any means. If it condemns but is afraid to speak, it is betraying its trust.' Much of the later correspondence attacked this view; but there was no unanimity. 'In an imperfect world, men are obliged to defend their interests,' said one letter. But 'The Church ought not to remain silent while this disease [strikes] spreads unchecked', said another.

What is the Christian's duty in the matter of war? When the Berlin crisis of autumn 1961 was at a dangerous stage, the Archbishop of Canterbury asked the clergy to lead their people in prayers for peace; he accepted the fact of nuclear weapons ('while they deter aggression, [they] provide the constant danger of war erupting') as he accepted the 'evil of Communism' and the 'peace of God'. Yet locked away inside his message was the suggestion that we should 'fight the evil of Communism . . . by practising urgently that love and respect for persons which Communism denies'. Most clergymen seem to feel that pacifism is splendid but impractical; disagreement is as great as it is outside the Church. At Southwark Cathedral one Sunday, during an ecclesiastical brains-trust held there after evensong, one of the congregation asked what subjects the panel would like to see on the agenda of the World Council of Churches, whose meeting in New Delhi was to take place shortly. The Chancellor of the cathedral, Canon Stanley Evans, who has strong social convictions (he was formerly a vicar in Dalston, in East London – mentioned later) spoke first. Nuclear tests were in prospect again. We were 'poised on the brink over Berlin', and 'for all our easy assurance that things will never go wrong, the risks are staggering. . . . We must bring Christians all over the world to stand together in the name of elementary common sense. If the World Council doesn't discuss this, it is so abdicating its responsibility as to make its work in the mission field impossible'. The next reply came from the Rev. Nick Stacey, a younger man, the Rector of Woolwich: a former Olympic runner, a frequent performer on television and writer of articles, always in the news because he has started a newspaper or opened a coffee bar or given up smoking ('It is a sin for a Christian priest to smoke,' he said, after the Royal College of Physicians' report on smoking and lung cancer). Stacey said briefly that if the Council talked about nuclear disarmament it would end in deadlock: so his chosen subject would be our responsibility to underdeveloped countries. 'I may be a very simple soul,' retorted Evans, 'but I've got more confidence in the World Council of Churches than Nick Stacey.' He referred to 'blasé moderns'. He said he was 'old-fashioned enough to believe that if one can get a chance of talking together, one gives the Holy Ghost a chance of operating'. The modern British attitude that 'it might be right to do it, but it won't do any good' was 'of the Devil – it demonstrates a lack of faith that is subversive to Christianity'. The temperature dropped a little as Stacey said: 'May the blasé modern or whatever I am be permitted to say a word?' Evans gave a small smile. 'What frightens me,' said Stacey, 'is another pious resolution about peace. . . . Politics is the art of the possible, isn't it? I'm sorry I'm blasé and modern and young, but there it is.'

In 1958 the Lambeth Conference, the gathering in London of Anglican bishops which takes place about once every ten years, is said to have come close to an outspoken statement condemning nuclear warfare; the conference is private, the published conclusions worthy but sometimes verbose and

THE CHURCH OF ENGLAND

platitudinous, and in the end what Lambeth had to say about the Bomb was that the nuclear situation 'makes a new challenge and demand upon us, both as Christians and as citizens', and that nuclear weapons should be abolished by international agreement. It is said that the American bishops played a big part in dissuading the conference from doing anything rash. Dr Stopford, now Bishop of London, who is supposed to have made an impassioned anti-Bomb speech at the conference, was one of twelve prominent churchmen – nine Anglicans and three nonconformists – who issued a five-point statement in March 1962, following the annual Defence White Paper, dealing with the Bomb. For nearly three years the group had been discussing the moral aspects of British defence policy, in a curious association with the Institute of Strategic Studies and a number of military strategists. The statement, when it came, was mild enough. The signatories urged that 'Britain must never be a party to waging any all-out, indiscriminate war, whatever any other Power may do' – though many of them said privately that no Government could be expected to declare this in advance. They suggested the Government should try to limit the spread of nuclear weapons, and be prepared to give up our own 'in a manner and at a time which promises to lead to this end' – that is, not on moral grounds but as a matter of expediency. In the *Observer*, 'Pendennis' gave an example of how the original wording had had to be toned down to make it palatable to all twelve* signatories:

* Bishop of London, Dr Stopford; Bishop of Chichester, Dr Wilson; Bishop of Manchester, Dr Greer; Bishop of Willesden, Right Rev. G. E. Ingle; Canon Carpenter, of Westminster Abbey; Canon Collins, of St Paul's – the most prominent of the nuclear-disarming Anglican clergy; Sir Kenneth Grubb, a leading layman; Canon Milford, Master of the Temple; the Rev. David Edwards, a young theologian and religious-books publisher; two Methodists, the Rev. Alan Booth and Dr Harold Roberts, and a Congregationalist, the Rev. Daniel Jenkins.

Point Five of the statement, 'H.M.G. should give first priority to the prevention of the further contamination of the atmosphere by nuclear tests' – hardly a clarion call – was softened still further to 'H.M.G. must never be discouraged from trying to prevent the further contamination of the atmosphere by nuclear tests'. The Church makes a better job of outlining the position than of petitioning the Government. *Modern War: What can Christians do together?*, a pamphlet issued by the Church Assembly's Board for Social Responsibility in 1962, described the differences of Christian opinion with lucidity. But even here, some central questions are not stated. The pamphlet divides Christians into old-style pacifists and old-style non-pacifists. The non-pacifists are then sub-divided into those who are new-style pacifists because of the 'indiscriminate and incalculable' effects of nuclear weapons; the 'better dead than Red' brigade, which, it is suggested, is very small, or doesn't even exist, as far as Christians are concerned; and finally those who accept, temporarily, 'something of a balance of power at all levels, including nuclear weapons', but aim at nuclear disarmament, and who would be prepared to support a limited war, though not all-out nuclear conflict. Later in the pamphlet these attitudes are consolidated in the phrase: 'There is substantial agreement that no Christian can possibly engage in, or support, all-out nuclear war.' But the point that worries so many, that the possibility of all-out war is implicit in the possession of nuclear weapons, and that once such weapons are possessed a small war may become an uncontainable war, is overlooked; the 'substantial agreement' becomes simply an agreement that war is nasty, not any sort of agreement on how to stop the process of 'escalation'. However, nuclear weapons have made the Church pay more attention to disarmament than it used to pay to pacifism. Old-fashioned pamphlets like *Article 37 and War*, published by the

Anglican Pacifist Fellowship in 1946, are still in circulation. The thirty-seventh of the Thirty-nine Articles is the only one that mentions war, holding that 'It is lawful for Christian men, at the commandment of the Magistrate, to wear weapons, and serve in the wars'. The Fellowship's pamphlet suggests that the Article refers only to 'just' wars, that it isn't binding on the laity, that it doesn't mean the Christian has a duty to fight, and so on. The Fellowship has about 2,500 members, less than one-fifth of them clergymen; pacifism remains what it has always been in the Church of England, a fringe activity, and even the nuclear debate is easily confined. The issue of the *Church Times* that reported the 1962 H-bomb statement, as its lead story, also carried, tucked away inside, a letter from the Bishop of Woolwich about the ordination of women (he was for it). The following week there were seven letters replying to the Bishop, taking more than half a page, but only one about the Bomb, urging that the statement shouldn't be taken too seriously, since it was not by experts.

Moral and sexual standards are probably the matters on which the Church, both in its individual clergy and as an institution, feels best qualified to pronounce. When the Rev. Leslie Weatherhead (the Methodist) started a correspondence in *The Times* in September 1961, with a letter suggesting that we were a 'nation in danger' because of our falling sexual standards, it was certain that many of the succeeding letters would be from clergymen (twelve out of forty-one, eleven of them Anglicans; the clergy were equally divided for and against Weatherhead). The controversies about a 'new theology' that began in 1962 and 1963 were often obscured by even more violent controversies about a 'new morality'.

'Moral welfare' has traditionally been one of the most active social interests in the Church. The organized body used to be the Moral Welfare Council – set up in 1939 to continue work being done by other Anglican bodies, concerned with unmarried mothers, and, to a lesser extent, other family problems. Its title and aims came to look increasingly restricted, and in 1958, to the accompaniment of upheavals and disagreements behind the scenes, it was made part of a newly formed Board for Social Responsibility, along with the Social and Industrial Council. At the end of 1961, the Social and Industrial Council became the Industrial Committee, and the Moral Welfare Council became the Council for Social Work. Its magazine, *Moral Welfare*, was renamed *Crucible*, and hopes were expressed that eventually moral welfare committees all over the country would restyle themselves accordingly. These committees obtain some of their money from local authorities and the rest from church funds and collections; they are understaffed, their social workers are underpaid, their offices are generally small and dingy; but they are still a major enterprise, helping people without regard to their religion or lack of it, and will probably outlast many of the Church's later schemes for social action.

At the centre, in Church House, the Council for Social Work has a different atmosphere: more intellectual and discussive, and concerned with a greater range of problems than 'moral welfare'. Study groups, which may include physicians, psychiatrists, and philosophers as well as theologians, consider such matters as nuclear war, artificial insemination, and suicide, and broadsheets and pamphlets are issued regularly, either directly or via the Church Information Office. *Ought Suicide to be a Crime?* was published in 1959, and according to an official of the Council was decisive in influencing the Government's Suicide Bill. 'Butler [then Home Secretary] was cautious. He didn't know which way the Establishment would turn. Then he got a copy of the Church's suicide pamphlet.

He thought, "If that's what the Church thinks, we're safe". The White Paper and the resulting legislation follow the pamphlet's recommendations closely' – the pamphlet having suggested unequivocally that 'attempted suicide should cease to be a crime'. The Council is a pressure group for reforming the law on homosexuality. This work began when it was still the Moral Welfare Council. It helped bring about the Wolfenden Committee, and hopes to have some part in moulding legislation that will eventually legalize homosexual acts between consenting adults. The relevant pamphlet here is *What Is Unlawful?*, another document with a tentative title but a straightforward message: in this case, that legislation should recognize that homosexual acts are immoral and unlawful, as are fornication and adultery, but not automatically punishable. In effect, the pamphlet suggests that the conduct of men who make love to one another should be morally censured but they themselves should be prosecuted only in certain defined circumstances. By the end of 1961 the Council had its own draft Bill drawn up, ready for consideration by the Church Assembly, and, no doubt, by whoever happens to be at the Home Office.

Next door to the Council for Social Work, the Industrial Committee's secretariat 'undertakes the promotion and co-ordination of the thought and action of the Church in relation to industry, including agriculture and commerce'. In October 1961 the Rev. John Rogan, one of the industrial chaplains at Sheffield, was appointed the first secretary: a youngish man with gold-rimmed glasses and a pipe, who, like Sainsbury, doesn't work on easy assumptions. Rogan takes it for granted that 'The world works on mediocrity, well-organized'. He is suspicious of phrases like 'written for the intelligent layman', where it turns out that 'what they've got in mind is people up to "A" level. I was in the R.A.F., and what people read was

Reveille. Or perhaps they wanted fewer pictures and longer sentences, so they read *Blighty*.'

Rogan shies away from any idea of an authoritarian Church; the Sheffield situation hardly encourages clergymen to think anyone would bother to listen if they did lay down the law. People, he says, should

think it out for themselves, using the insights of Christianity as their criteria. People come and say, 'What ought I to do?' The answer is, Get out and live, take the world in your stride, face up to life and the fact that there isn't a sort of pocket-book guide, as there was in the R.A.F., to say that when invited to dinner with a sheik you don't talk about pigs, dogs, or women. What the clergyman should say is: For pete's sake don't regard me as a sort of glorified dictator who's going to tell you what to do. It's like a weak child growing up, and asking continually what tie to wear. In the end you have to bang the table and say, 'I don't mind *what* tie you wear. Make up your own mind – don't pick mine.'

But what if the child growing up should say, 'I want to rape that girl?' Rogan said:

In that case you say, 'Is *that* what you think about human nature?' We lack a strong sense of community, of social restraints, so we've only got a sort of desiccated individualism to argue from. This is where the Victorian argument is so useful: Would you like this to happen to your sister? But neither children nor parents can articulate any ultimate reason for a code of behaviour. So if rape is what he really wants, then he won't be deterred by the moral sanction of his parents. What restrains him is either the prevailing morality, or understanding the consequences of his choice. Only when men have got a free choice, and can bear the consequences of their choice, do they understand.

What this means in terms of people who may not bother to ask or listen isn't clear. The lack of pretension over industrial missions, and social commitment generally, is impressive, but it is only too possible to imagine sage recommendations still emerging from Church House, spasmodically effective, in 1980, and the chaplains built into the background of the works, as Salvation Army bands blowing on street corners are built into the background of towns. The Church has its social conscience right enough. But the majority of clergymen, who have to cope with parishes, are concerned with the everyday situation rather than the thinking behind it. Among parish clergy, who are all social workers of one kind or another, a minority make it a full-time business. Such clergymen are usually Socialists, thriving (if that's the word) in slummy quarters of cities, where people are oppressed by bureaucracy and unhelpfulness as much as by poverty. What they achieve is often something small – a bed in a hostel, a pound to pay the rent, an appointment with a psychiatrist. Listening to a young vicar in East London, the Rev. Bill Sargent, of Dalston, E8, he sometimes sounds like a man from the Board for Social Responsibility: 'If you read the *Church Times*, you'd think we lived in a country where Lent comes round and we all say twice as many prayers – not a place with pensioners starving themselves, and petty restrictions on widows' earnings.' But Sargent has no time for the Board: 'What does it *do*? I think the Board for Social Responsibility is socially irresponsible. As far as the Board is concerned, I could be a Methodist minister.' He calls himself a 'local auntie, a kind of Coronation Street figure'. The cases that come to him are often long and involved, the facts garbled by the victim, the action called for not clear. He wrote to the Archbishop of Canterbury, in one of his frequent letters to the hierarchy:

Your Grace, When I came here in July 1960, among my people was a West Indian couple – young, with one child. The girl is very intelligent and educated, the husband was under confirmation instruction at the time. In due course he was confirmed, another baby was born . . . everything in the garden was lovely. Then it started to disintegrate. R—, the wife came to me in great distress in the early summer. C—, the husband, had been out of work for some time. He was lying in his bed for days on end, crying, talking to himself, refusing food, refusing responsibility for his family (R— was already carrying the third child). I went to see him (outside my parish) and talked to him. He refused to see his doctor to whom I had written and spoken on the telephone. I found out that he had been under treatment at — Hospital for mental illness in 1958. . . .

The National Assistance threatened the man with prosecution, health officials dithered, he attacked his wife and drove her out of the house, and she and her children went first to the L.C.C.'s Newington Lodge, and then to stay at the vicarage. After more confusion the husband was admitted to a mental hospital. Sargent wrote to the Archbishop:

I have spoken to dozens of officials, all of whom are concerned with their little area of responsibility and nothing else. . . . There are all sorts of problems brought to light here. What are we going to do about it? Instead of so many bishops writing the drivel they do about 'now that our material welfare is secured we have to watch out for spiritual temptations of wealth, security, blah, blah', they might instigate some proper social research into the Casualties of the Welfare State that end up on my doorstep every day. I have *no views* on Lanka [a Church-union scheme in Ceylon, then in the news] because I haven't had time to read the *Church Times* for weeks but I do have views on what is happening here, now, in London. . . . What are we to do is not the question that God is putting to us – it is 'What are we doing today?' Today's first lesson at matins ought to make us sweat blood – Zephaniah 3*. I see no sweat like great drops of blood falling down upon London's ground, sweetening the soil of the city's indifference. And if we don't sweat no one will.

* 'Woe to her that is filthy and polluted, to the oppressing city! She obeyed not the voice; she received not correction; she trusted not in the Lord; she drew not near to her God. . . .'

At a 9.30 parish Communion – brick interior painted white, bell rung by man in windcheater, candles, plain pews, brilliant green vestments, and incense-smoke shaken out of a brass thurible by a boy with an earnest expression – Sargent preached about Martin Luther King, the American Negro leader, who was in London that week-end. Tickets, he told the congregation, were available for King's appearance at Westminster Hall; they could also see him on 'Face to Face' on B.B.C. television. 'In the city of Montgomery, in the U.S.A., in 1955,' said Sargent, 'there lived seventy thousand white people. Most of them enjoyed that hall mark of Christian civilization, the indoor flush lavatory. Much of their standard of living depended on there being another sixty thousand Negroes. . . .' It was the twenty-second Sunday after Trinity, and the Gospel, as laid down in the Prayer Book for that Sunday (and read from a small altar in the nave, while boys stood around with candles) was Matthew xviii, 21 : 'Peter said unto Jesus, Lord, how oft shall my brother sin against me, and I forgive him?' About fifty people were in the congregation, including half a dozen children. Afterwards half of them went down to the basement – stone floor, gas fire, long table – for the parish breakfast of sausage rolls, bread rolls, marmalade, and tea, with a saucer to put the money in.

When everyone had finished eating they began to talk about housing, and Sargent said he was trying to find if it was possible for Christians to pay a voluntary rate to the local authority, the money to be used to house the homeless. This was in October, and some time between then and Christmas, Sargent heard from the Ministry of Housing that in law, there was nothing to stop it. So he wrote to a couple of bishops, and suggested the Church might try the voluntary-levy idea in London. But it must have been impracticable, because as far as Sargent knew, nothing ever came of it.

CHAPTER EIGHT

MINISTRY OF PROPAGANDA

THE Churches' Television Training Centre, formerly at Tooting Broadway and now nearer the middle of London, in the Marylebone Road, owes its existence to Lord Rank, who is a Methodist. 'The clouds parted,' suggested a clergyman, 'and God said, "Rank, open a TV Centre".' The Centre is used by all the main denominations except Roman Catholics, who prefer to make their own arrangements, and has a small permanent staff which is usually supplemented by guest speakers and one or more representatives from whichever church is having a course. At a three-day course for Anglican clergymen held in September 1961 the guest speakers were the clergyman who runs religious broadcasting in the B.B.C.'s West Region, and the religious-programmes adviser to A.B.C. Television. The chairman was the Rev. David Skinner, the Executive Officer of the Church of England Radio and Television Council – another of the councils whose secretariat occupies rooms at Church House, though in this case Skinner and his council are responsible not to the Church Assembly but directly to the Archbishops of Canterbury and York.

On the second day of the course, when I was there, the twelve clergymen had already heard two lectures and had two practical sessions, one on 'Lift Up Your Hearts', the early-morning religious talk on the Home Service, the other on television interviews. During the lunch-break they drifted in and out of a room containing visual-aid material, tape-recorders, and booklets, listening to a tape playing back recordings of their efforts for 'Lift Up Your Hearts'. The older men listened to themselves with arms folded, well-composed, but a couple of young curates became agitated, frowning and raising their eyebrows. One of the curates made notes as he listened to his voice saying: 'The town where I work has a famous Rugby team. . . . This morning I'm speaking to you as a member of one of the greatest supporters' clubs in the world. You see, I'm speaking to you as a Christian.' The Rev. Philip, a school chaplain, spoke of how a storm had frightened his daughter, and of human helplessness in the face of danger: 'Do you remember that sudden storm on the Lake of Galilee?' The Rev. William, who carried a brief-case, began with 'Good morning – I hope it is a good morning', went on to regret that it wouldn't be so for many, but added that whatever happened, we would be travelling another section of the journey of life. He made several references to 'short cuts' and 'the road of life'. Canon Peter, whose face was bland and rosy, said, astonishingly: 'I'm going to assume that you've had a good night's sleep, a good breakfast, washed up, and that you're sitting down and going to listen.' Canon John described a visit to a café and how he forgot who his waitress was, going on to talk about society's lack of proper communication. His message was: 'Really listen.' The good performers (John, Philip) would have sounded all right at ten to eight in the morning, but the bad ones (William, Peter) might have been caricaturing religious talks.

By 2 p.m. they were all in the classroom, which had a twenty-one-inch monitor screen, a blackboard, and a desk, being prepared for the minor ordeal of doing a closed-circuit Epilogue – the late-evening television talk transmitted daily by I.T.V. and less frequently by the B.B.C. The Centre's general manager said they should remember that mistakes couldn't be corrected in next month's magazine, and warned them not to look down when they were talking, since religious programmes were notorious for their views of skulls. One by one they went off to the studio, reappearing on the screen a few minutes later with an anecdote or a moral tale. The Rev. Daniel talked about a holiday abroad. One evening he was finishing a meal – 'Mopping up the fragments, this is what the Epilogue is.' Unknown to him, a cable car was close to disaster on the other side of the mountain. Whether life was exciting or humdrum, 'God has been with you all day'. It was rambling but reasonably effective. Canon Edmund asked that we imagine him with a table lamp: 'When I switched it on, rather a profound and wonderful thing happened. I got the power of the power station.' A Christian's life, he said, was rather like that: 'It's the switch that counts, the *I will*.' The Rev. Robert talked about fear: 'Many people are afraid to visit the dentist – but there are far worse pains than that.' Two clergymen said 'Hear, hear!' ironically. 'Most of our present fears spring out of a lack of some kind of love,' said Robert. Only with God was there final security.

It was all very homely, but that was the requirement. When it was over, David Skinner, a slight-looking young man with a firm voice, who was once a journalist, talked about the performances. 'Lift Up Your Hearts', he said bleakly, was a difficult exercise. It began in Scotland during the war with a metrical psalm, a hymn, and a short message; he didn't really know if it was possible to do it successfully. And the Epilogue was one of the hardest things in television: no actor would like to try it. He looked at his notes. Canon John had talked about the parson's deadpan face, and the lack of communication. 'It took you two minutes twelve seconds to make the point that God is remote from people,' said Skinner. 'It was incredibly loosely written. It didn't observe the disciplines of television.' The canon smiled weakly. The Rev. Ronald had held up a piece of Cornish granite, and talked about grave-stones and the people buried there. They had one thing in common – they were with Christ in glory. Skinner suggested that the way it was put would make a lay audience think: The one thing they've got in common is that they're dead. 'It was packed with theological nonsense,' he added, then corrected himself quickly: 'Not theological nonsense, I mean theological words the viewers won't understand.'

Next was the Rev. Charles, who had begun with an old Greek proverb: Know thyself. He told the fable of the man whose bride-to-be vanished, the day before their wedding, with a masked man. He tracked him down, removed the mask, saw the man was himself, and dropped dead with fright. Skinner said cheerfully: 'I suggest you don't use phrases like "rebelling against God's will". Ecclesiastical clichés mean nothing to most listeners. And always be afraid of phrases like "The next time you say a prayer", because for most people that's going to be in about forty years' time.' The rosy-faced Canon Peter, who had misjudged what the audience was like at 8 a.m., had been more effective in the Epilogue, discussing the nature of the twelve Apostles. There had been no conces-sion to viewers, said Skinner, but the sincerity came over: 'This is embarrassing to say – a goodness.' The table-lamp comparison was commended. So was the school-chaplain's opening line: 'Good evening. I don't know if she wore a polka-dot bikini.' But the anecdote had been over-elaborated. 'Beware of the children's-service idea, the "And now, my dear children, that story has an application",' said Skinner. 'Because then they become restless.' The Rev. William, who had talked obscurely about teenagers and 'beating the disc' and the search for thrills, was told to watch out for non-sequiturs: 'I was very conscious of the creaking machinery of dragging in Christianity,' said Skinner. 'I'm coming more and more to believe that the Epilogue has got to stand on its own. You don't use interesting examples unless they come in naturally. People wonder, "When's he going to bring in Christianity?" and then they say, "Ah, here it comes."' The Rev. Derek had talked about suffering. 'It's better not to use phrases like "capitulated in penitence",' said Skinner. By now the time left for discussion had gone, and after talking briefly about plans for the next day, the course broke up. Some of them went to the café round the corner for tea, talking jovially about the roasting they had received. 'Mind you, I think he was a bit severe,' said one. 'I agree,' said another. They all agreed: it was a good course, but the judgements were a bit severe.*

The trouble, as Skinner said later, is that 'you can't use a studio as an enormous brightly lit pulpit'. That clergymen who have been trained to elaborate themes to a congregation should find it difficult to make monosyllabic statements to a camera is hardly surprising; the remarkable thing is that so many of them have learned to do it capably. These are part of a Manchester vicar's notes for an intelligent explanatory sermon in church on the subject of the Litany (the 'General Supplication', one of the central prayers in the Prayer Book):

Need not be old-fashioned to value the Litany [the sermon begins]. Key – *to know what we are doing.*

History: First part of our Prayer Book to be in English (Cranmer

---

* The *Church of England Newspaper*'s television critic, writing on 9 February 1962, said: 'In my more cynical moments I find it difficult to regard the *Epilogue* (I.T.V. nightly) as little more than a convenient and inexpensive means of jacking up the number of minutes that I.T.V. can claim it devotes to religion. Be that as it may, here is a note for the TV clerics who give it: avoid like the plague the expression "We do feel, don't we?" (other verbs can be substituted for "feel"). It merely tempts me (and how many more?) to reply "No, we don't!" and to reach for the switch.'

1543), but far earlier than that. Litanies in English from 14th century. St Augustine & Companions sang (in Latin of course) at mtg. with Ethelbert in 597. But older still.

Begins with instinctive prayer 'Lord have mercy upon us' (so called 'the Lesser Litany'). cf. Psalm 51: 'Have mercy upon me O God'.

Responsive Prayer: Leader and people alternately: principle goes back before Christian times – *the way of a people united*. (c.f. modern 'A Man Dies' [the television Crucifixion-drama programme].) Still many heathen forms.

Associated with procession: but not necessarily. Story of Constantinople – Arians processed because not allowed in churches (398) so St Chrysostom replied with orthodox 'litany' processions, c.f. prayers at Whitsun procession. Procession of witness directed *for* people as well as *at* them.

This sort of thing would never do for the Epilogue, though occasionally it can be heard in straightforward broadcasts of church services, where there is less need to popularize. Religious broadcasting covers the whole range of ecclesiastical communication, from simple pep-talks for busy secularists to esoteric discussions (on the Third Programme) and detailed television observation of, say, Communion services that are meaningful only to churchgoers. The Church has always had a better showing on radio and television than in newspapers, partly because services are an obvious (and cheap) form of broadcasting, partly because Reith, who dominated the B.B.C. in its earlier years, was a religious man, partly because people are reached more easily by fine preaching than by fine writing. But the idea of using broadcasting, and especially television, to attack popular indifference to religion is comparatively new – religious broadcasting used to assume that Englishmen were Christians, and that what they wanted was Christianity as their forefathers knew it.

The Church was built into a privileged position in British

broadcasting. The rule was, and still is at the B.B.C., that Anglicans are in charge, with greater or lesser privileges for the rest. When Reith wanted advice on religious programmes in 1923, it was the Archbishop of Canterbury he went to, and eventually the present system of regional Religious Advisory Committees, with a Central Committee in London, was set up; an Anglican, usually a bishop, always heads the committee, which now advises commercial companies as well as the B.B.C. Within the B.B.C., the head of the Religious Broadcasting Department is an Anglican and his assistant is a Free Churchman; there is also a Roman Catholic, described as 'assistant *to* the head' – 'they have their reasons for wishing to seem separate', said a B.B.C. man. The department is staffed almost entirely by clergymen, with the emphasis on Anglicans; in England, about half the services broadcast are Anglican, one third are Free Church, one tenth are Roman Catholic ('between nine and twelve per cent is the hallowed figure'), and what time remains goes to lesser nonconformists. Producers in other departments of the B.B.C. sometimes resent the way Religious Broadcasting has a say in anything affecting religion (when René Cutforth was sent by a magazine-programme producer to watch the Bryn Thomas unfrocking at Southwark Cathedral, he declined to let his talk describing the occasion be vetted by the Department; the talk wasn't broadcast). The Department is also responsible for vetting pop records, to see if they contain any blasphemies.

This system of production-by-experts blunted B.B.C. religion. It wasn't until 1947 that an 'element of controversy' was permitted in religious programmes. The Church, especially the higher ranks, was suspicious of television, and sometimes still is – cathedral deans have occasionally been awkward over television cameras. And this suspicion has been fought less vigorously than it would have been by secular producers. Even the embarrassments of clergymen dealing with their ecclesiastical superiors may have had an effect: though religious producers are reasonably hard-boiled. 'There's more general humility among Roman and Free-Church broadcasters than among Anglicans,' said an Anglican producer. 'We try not to tell a man what to say, but we sometimes tell him what not to say. I've had to tell people that I don't consider it my duty to tell them what the Holy Spirit wishes them to say, but the Holy Spirit may wish them to put it another way.'

Commercial-television companies have established a different system. Their religious programmes are run by secular staff, who may have no particular pretensions to be Christians, backed up by small panels of clergymen as advisers. The result has been some good television – no better than the B.B.C. at its best, but more consistently uninhibited, and certainly better than religious broadcasting years ago, when, as David Skinner wrote in an article in the *Church of England Newspaper*, 'arguments raged about whether it was blasphemous to broadcast a dramatization of the Passion'. Nowadays, wrote Skinner, 'if there is any argument about a religious programme, it is likely to be about whether it was "relevant" or "true" or whether it "made an impact".'

On radio there has been a similar loosening up. There is the regular 'People's Service' on the Light Programme on Sunday mornings, a specially devised form of service, without liturgy – just hymns, Bible readings, and a sermon or talk, sometimes given in two parts. Its audience is more than five million, only two million or so behind the biggest audiences for religious television. The quality of the central sermon (often, but not always, given by an Anglican) varies. One Sunday a vicar will talk, with disquieting topicality, about God's willingness to turn everyone into 'radio-controlled sputniks', and say that we need to 'come in on the wavelength' of 'the master mind who makes things tick'. Another Sunday it may be a calm appraisal of morality: 'The Church never makes any spectacular advance in public morality, because each new generation has to be taught it. What is this moral law? Perfect charity – this is St Paul's idea, not mine. . . .' 'Five to Ten', another sound-radio programme, built around a daily three-minute non-denominational talk which is often suffocatingly pious, is another piece of popular religion; journalist writers contribute most of the material, which arrives at the rate of about eighty scripts a month; the audience is between four and five million.

Religion has become involved in the entertainment business, and the Church, despite continued mutterings about vulgarization, has been compelled to take the entertaining seriously. Archbishops (like Cabinet Ministers) make themselves available at short notice, Anglican monks have been discovered to be highly televisual, card-indexed lists of likely performers are ready at the Radio and Television Council. Candidates for the courses at the Centre are proposed by clergymen who make it their business to understand communications. The market is studied. 'The companies don't welcome an old man on the screen unless he's an eccentric,' said Skinner. 'There's a great demand for men in the thirties range – they may lack experience, but they know enough to make an impact.' The Council was made responsible to the Archbishops rather than to the Church Assembly so that it would be more independent and free of red tape. Ideas for programmes as well as people to take part in them are supplied to producers; the Council canvasses policies, especially the policy of spending more money on religious television, which is often run cheaply by the commercial companies. (This is why there are so many discussions, which are about the most inexpensive kind of television.) Thus companies are being prodded to spend money on outside-broadcast units that can look at 'the Church in action'.

In television as with the industrial missions, the Church is committed, in a modest sort of way, to the slow process of trying to teach the indifferent. The trouble with popular religion, as some clergymen point out grimly, is that if it communicates easily it may be all right, but if it bores the audience it has nothing else to offer: it lacks the backbone of a formal church service. Generally accepted as 'a good thing', one hears, now and then, a voice of dissent. The most important discussions and features go out early on a Sunday evening. 'Consequently,' said an I.T.V. producer, 'the clergy never see the programmes. If they did, they might have second thoughts about their value.'

Routine publicity for the Church is handled by the Church Information Office, headed by Colonel Robert Hornby. Hornby was the Army's Director of Public Relations for the Far East Land Forces, based in Singapore, when he heard that the Church was replacing its ramshackle information structure. He now presides over a unit for answering reporters, issuing hand-outs, organizing Press conferences for travelling bishops, publishing books and pamphlets, and liaising with B.B.C. and I.T.V. through a radio and television department. (This is distinct from the Radio and Television Council.) The idea is to present the facts without special pleading, though the Office suffers from the handicap of all P.R. departments by having to depend on its superiors for permission to give the facts about anything controversial; this is said to have severely inhibited the Office at the time of the Guildford row. *The Church in the News*, a booklet written by Hornby for clergy and Church laymen, takes a kindly view of the Press, and contains realistic advice about such things as the shyness of many reporters with clergymen, and what to do when asked silly questions ('The temptation to be short with a correspondent under these circumstances must be avoided'). Among regular material issued by the Office is a monthly series of 'Notes for Parish Magazines', made up of carefully unslanted items, with the number of words thoughtfully added, and suitable for magazines of every sort of churchmanship; and the weekly *Church of England News*, containing perhaps a dozen items for the Press, which is useful enough, but often emphasizes the private-world side of the Church – 'NARWHAL TUSK FOR COVENTRY CROSIER. A narwhal tusk which will form the staff of a new crosier to be placed permanently on the Bishop's throne in the new Coventry Cathedral was presented to the Bishop of Coventry (the Right Rev. Cuthbert Bardsley) by the Danish Ambassador (Mr Nels Svenningsen) in the Cathedral on Saturday last.'

Although Church House is learning how to publicize the Church (an Inquiry Centre for the general public is the latest addition), most Anglican propaganda is still unofficial, largely, no doubt, because of the cost of producing it. In 1943, some years before television was a power in the land, Archbishop Temple set up a Church of England Films Commission. It was run on behalf of the Church by S.P.C.K., the Society for Promoting Christian Knowledge – the oldest missionary society in the Church, which concentrates on publishing and distributing books and magazines. S.P.C.K. provided offices and £10,000 capital, and film-making began, in the face of suspicion from the clergy, who tended to judge religious films by the standards of some bad ones that had been imported from the United States. The Commission never really got going. After a few years it was dissolved, and the S.P.C.K. was appointed the 'executive film agency' of the Church; it now does its best as a centre for Anglican films and film-strips, where material can be bought or hired, and occasionally makes a film itself. 'Lambeth, 1958', a colour film of the Lambeth Conference, was made as an 'act of faith', according to an official, but sold 200 copies abroad. Inevitably it gives a tame view of Anglicanism at work. It includes shots of New Towns and African missionaries, but the Church emerges almost as a tourist attraction: old books at Lambeth, Big Ben and the river, green grass and white hats at a Lambeth garden party, even greener grass and larger hats at a Buckingham Palace garden party, coloured cloaks crossing Dean's Yard, the chequered floor of Westminster Abbey. The narration envelops the Conference (pronounced 'cunference') in phrases like 'vital issues in the world today' and 'take common counsel together'. 'Guildford Cathedral', made after the consecration in 1961, offers the same kind of spectacle, with soaring pictures and routine language ('battle of modern life', 'oasis of peace') that make the Church seem more decorative than anything else. Other films in the S.P.C.K. library, few of them as well-photographed as the Lambeth and Guildford films, are a strange miscellany. 'Your Inheritance', made by the original Films Commission, has a young man and woman coming across a country church, and seeing what goes on there: 'They [churches] were built as the spearheads in the war against injustice and evil . . . if busy men pass them by, they do so at their own peril.' 'Building Afresh' gives an unexciting view of how a temporary church on a housing estate brings people together. 'House or Home' contrasts a Christian family, where mother and father are always available, with pagan neighbours, where cigarettes dangle from lips, father goes off with the boys, comics and television are more important than the baby, and the son goes thieving in desperation. But 'Faith in Your Fingers', a colour film made by the Publicity Committee of the Diocese of Canterbury, is an ingenious view of Christians at work, seen through the movement of hands.

With books, the Church is on safer ground. A large proportion of the remarkable number of religious books published in Britain are about Anglicanism or by Anglicans. Small publishers' advances and a slow, steady sale are characteristic. Every conceivable aspect of the Church of England seems to be covered, and an outsider who goes into a religious bookshop, such as S.P.C.K.'s or the one at Church House, is overwhelmed by the shelves of advice, comfort, warning, and exegesis. The Church itself publishes, through the Church Information Office, a large number of reports. There are hundreds of religious paperbacks. There are Bible commentaries, biographies of bishops and missionaries, devotional work, accounts of experiments with house-churches and group parishes, compendiums on confirmation and nuclear war, and innumerable books of theology. The number of *practical* books is enormous. One corner of the Church House bookshop offered: *How to Look After Your Church, YOUR Parish Church, Organs in Parish Churches, Conditions for the Installation of Electricity in Churches, Redecorating Churches, Reading the Bible Together, The Church and the Atom, Liturgy and Doctrine, Gambling in Modern Society, The Position of the Laity in the Church, Baptism and Confirmation Today, How to Choose Stained Glass, Should Women be Priests?, Faculties and the Diocesan Advisory Committee System, Cathedrals in Modern Life,* and *A Handbook on the Installation, Preservation, and Repair of Bells, Bell-frames and Fittings, and other kindred matters.*

In addition to Anglican books, a steady flow of Anglican pamphlets and broadsheets is issued by societies, conferences, communities, pressure-groups, and individuals – these are often partisan, demanding that the Church honour its Protestant tradition or its Catholic tradition, or refuse to baptize the babies of non-churchgoers, or do something about Establishment. A huge number of titles must be in circulation.

Despite this, Anglican newspapers and magazines have a comparatively small sale. The *Church Times*, owned by a family called Palmer and published from comfortable Victorian-looking offices behind the Law Courts, with the printing works on the top floor, sells 65,000 copies a week. This is less than one quarter of the circulation of its Roman Catholic contemporary, *Universe* – a man at the *Church Times*, using one of those mysterious phrases that Anglicans keep for Romans, said that 'They have their own methods of persuading people to do things'. Until a few years ago the paper was firmly Anglo-Catholic; now, edited by the Rev. Roger Roberts, it considers it speaks for the whole Church, though it remains firmly in the Catholic tradition. It regards itself as a forum for debate and a guardian of the Church's good name; if it considers that to publish the facts might harm the Church, it will withhold them. An advertisement in the *Twentieth Century* said it 'plays an indispensable part in the public life of the Church of England . . . is read by all influential people connected with Church affairs'. It has an air of prosperity, from its sober front page to the lucrative columns of small-ads at the back, which, together with the ample display advertising, give a certain view of the Church – vestments, organs, lecterns, vacancies for curates, pilgrimages, public schools, holiday accommodation, headed notepaper, Communion wine, books, insurance, altar candles, hassocks, charity appeals, and mobile barbecues. Its comment can be radical, but it makes more assumptions about the Christian nature of England, and perhaps about the nature of a Christian, than the other weekly journal, the Evangelical *Church of England Newspaper*, which is thinner and carries less advertising, is weaker on news coverage and articles by Church leaders and book-serialization and book reviews, but compensates for this by a feverish concern with the non-ecclesiastical side of religion. Where the *Church Times* tends to look inward and dwell on aspects of the Church – the role of the parson's wife, the Church in Africa, the failings of theological training, the Anglican religious communities – the *C.E.N.* peppers its pages with articles about class distinction and churchgoing, what to do at work when people swear and tell dirty stories, the ethics of receiving business perks, honesty in advertising. The *C.E.N.* reviews television and films, and is scolded by its staider Evangelical readers for daring to have any truck with the world's wickedness; the film reviews, one correspondent suggested, were 'a blot on the witness'. A Slough clergyman wrote demanding 'No Parleying with the world, but instead every week Some Sermon in full'. To the outsider, and indeed to many Anglican clergy, the vein of Low-Church puritanism is unnerving; it doesn't sound like England (which, of course, is what the puritans are complaining about). Mention of a youth-club dance was criticized because 'some incumbents, to say the least, are uneasy about the running of youth dances in the parish'. A South London clergyman wrote: 'A live issue among many of our young people is that of Sunday football. The worldly ones will grasp at anything to justify it. Imagine then the concern of our youth leader when he finds in his first copy of the *C.E.N.* the report of a vicar who supports and encourages his young people in playing Sunday soccer, without any guiding comment.'

With theological commentaries, the *C.E.N.* is more inward looking than its rival. The *Church Times* knows that the Catholic revival this century has done its work. The *C.E.N.*, representing the Low Anglicans who have felt increasingly on the defensive as public taste and clerical practice veer away from them, is long-winded by comparison. Every week it has its teeth in some theological dispute: the nature of the Sacraments, the infallibility of the Pope, the significance of bishops, the position in which a clergyman should stand when taking

Holy Communion. One week, during a correspondence about the 'westward position', a churchwoman wrote to say that it all bewildered her. All she could find in the Bible was 'a frugal meal beautifully and simply described, and the straightforward command "Do this in remembrance of me". I can find no description of a table. . . . Anyway, does it matter?' She added: 'In my experience, many people think of most clergy as not only living in a tight little theoretical world of their own, but absolutely divorced from contemporary thought; men married to and preoccupied with thoughts which may have influenced theologians in Reformation times, but which seem to the man in the street in 1962 to be best described by Alice as "curiouser and curiouser".' This brought a number of letters the following week, agreeing that life was full and time was short and there was too much concern with 'clerical minutiae'. It seemed sensible enough, but the week after that, Qoheleth, one of the *C.E.N.*'s theological columnists, slapped them all down. He found the letters, he said, 'pathetic to read. It's rather like Fred Snooks writing to the *British Medical Journal* and complaining that a number of surgeons ought to cease arguing about how to perform a tracheotomy and simply try to make sick people better. It is, to be brutally frank, a prize example of the uninstructed glorying in their ignorance.'

When launched on a theological subject, the *C.E.N.* is unstoppable. It printed endless articles about Intercommunion, when (Chapter 11) this subject came into the news towards the end of 1961; it even conducted a poll among the clergy and laity (a man at the *Church Times* thought this was 'childish'). It is edited from cramped offices in Fleet Street, with a young editor, the Rev. John King, who has a couple of girls to help him (the *Church Times* staff includes an editor-in-chief, the editor, an assistant editor, and a news editor). Its basic rate of payment for contributors is three guineas a 1,000 – 'More,' says King, 'for bishops and Cabinet Ministers' – and the editor goes out with a camera and takes some of the pictures himself. The principal owners – Sir Alfred Owen, a Midlands industrialist, and John Cordle, M.P. – rescued it a few years ago when its circulation had fallen badly; sales are now believed to have risen to around 20,000, but details are refused. When the Church Assembly sends the new Canons to Parliament for its approval, the *C.E.N.* is sure to be in the thick of the dispute, taking a strong Evangelical, preserve-the-Prayer-Book line.

Besides this pair of newspapers there are a number of Anglican magazines. The party organizations publish several. Of the others, *Church Illustrated*, a magazine with an old-fashioned air, sells about 140,000 a month; it is published by Church Illustrated, Ltd, a non-profit corporation which in 1960 launched a handsome, glossy magazine, *Anglican World*, issued six times a year, and aimed at overseas as well as English Anglicans (the cover of the Easter number, 1962, is marked '3s. 6d.', with '70 cents' after it in smaller type). It has some striking illustrations and readable articles, but is not a magazine of ideas. The only Anglican ideas-magazine that means much to an outsider is *Prism*, which was started a few years ago by two Oxford graduates, and later bought by the Rev. Timothy Beaumont, a wealthy Anglican clergyman who moved into publishing in 1960. *Prism* is well written, radical, and High, given to occasional spoof articles (there was one on the ordination of children, intended as a satire on the theological objections to the ordination of women), and irreverent cartoons (priest beckoning from confessional, saying, 'Hey, Anthony! Come and get a load of this guy's night life –!!'). Faith, rather than good works, is what it seems to consider important. Ramsey is *Prism*'s idea of an archbishop. It sells rather more than 3,000 copies a month. Beaumont, who also owns a newspaper called the *National Christian News*, a children's comic called *Wonderland*, which he founded, and owned *Time and Tide* for two years, is one of the best publicized clergymen in the Church. Still in his early thirties, he inherited money from his father. He went to Eton, Gordonstoun, and Christ Church, Oxford, was ordained shortly after and spent four years in Hong Kong before returning to buy the ailing *Time and Tide*, which was soon carrying religious articles, and including bishops among its book-reviewers. Beaumont, with his full face, cigar, and carnation, has been an attractive subject for the Press, especially when he does unpredictable things like selling *Time and Tide* (in June 1962. He said: 'I now want to produce a completely different kind of paper'). Probably the richest priest in England, he lives in Mayfair, in a house with a moderately grand staircase, and manages to combine wealth and vocation successfully.

Most of the remaining Anglican magazines are more specialized. *Frontier* (circulation 5,000) is solidly intellectual, and frequently heavy going. *Junction*, 'A journal of Anglican realism', is thin but interesting, with a strong social conscience; Canon Stanley Evans, of Southwark Cathedral, edits it, and Tom Driberg is on the editorial board. *Theology*, not always as intimidating as it sounds, is a monthly with a wide reputation; a Cambridge theologian, the Rev. Alec Vidler, edits it (Chapter 11), and the ubiquitous S.P.C.K. publishes it. *Sobornost*, the 'journal of the Fellowship of S. Alban and S. Sergius' (circulation 1,700), is concerned to promote relations with Eastern churches. *The Vision* is the 'journal of the Association for Promoting Retreats'; it sells 2,500, as does the *St Raphael Quarterly*, a 'review of the Church's Ministry to the Sick'.

In terms of circulation, the journals that count in the

Church are the much-derided parish magazines. Eighty-five per cent of English parishes sell or give away nearly three and a half million magazines a month. They are widely criticized for their amateurishness, though to an outsider what makes a good one is not professional typography and production so much as straightforward prose on major topics. The 'parish newspaper' is becoming popular, generally a tabloid with big type designed to 'shock' and 'arrest'. Huge headlines like 'HARVEST HOME' and 'VITAL STATISTICS' dominate pages of unexceptional text, which, because it's more often comment than fact, has an oddly inflated look. Where the page has something to bite on, the result can be successful: 'IT PAYS TO ADVERTISE – OR DOES IT? Rumpus breaks out over meeting to discuss whether the Churches should advertise on a national scale,' which headlined the front page in a Portsmouth parish newspaper called *Community*, was followed by comment; but it was informed and readable. *Shire and Spire*, the Coventry diocesan newspaper, is one of the few that is both laid out professionally and matches its appearance with balanced reports and pictures. Inevitably it has been in trouble. A Coventry vicar cancelled his parish's order because 'a known Communist and an atheist' had been writing for it, and because (like the *Church of England Newspaper*), it didn't give a 'clear moral lead on current issues'. What fails to emerge in most of these parish newspapers is an editorial personality. But the *Dalston Dispatch*, the news-sheet of Bill Sargent's East London parish (mentioned in Chapter 7), achieves an impact in a single page, like a handbill. This contains condensed parish news and information, headed by a biting, unsophisticated article which takes the Cold War, tax fiddles, and the housing shortage in its stride. It uses doctrinaire language as well as more colloquial stuff: 'The high priests of American finance', 'the high priests of Massive Retaliation'. One article ended:

There's a crooked line of extortion and inhumanity connecting the deaths of those two little girls in Graham Road with the deaths of little girls in Angola.

If we don't see it and do something about it, we – YOU and I, mate – won't stand a cat-in-hell's chance of entering those heavenly mansions of our Father's Home.

There is also a character called Old Dick of Dalston who contributes a monthly aphorism: 'Wot djer expect from a Beat Generation but a Dead Beat Govermint?'

A near-by parish has an even smaller publication – the *Beauvoir Bulletin*, which consists of a piece of foolscap folded to make two sheets, covered in single-spaced typing and run off on a duplicator with a few titles in red ink. It makes the church (St Peter's, De Beauvoir Town) and its activities sound important; again there is a social conscience about things like housing; the parish news is reported without piety: 'Every day now until the twenty-ninth we shall remember PETER DAVIE in our personal prayers. . . . KENNETH FRANCIS also deserves our daily prayer as he prepares for his work in Africa. . . . ISAIAH MERCHANT fell some fourteen feet off a lorry as they were loading on Tuesday and cracked his nut. He is still in the Barnet General Hospital.'

Parish magazines, on the whole, are worse than parish newspapers. More magazines now have bigger pages and braver articles, but the standard formula is still ten or twenty small shiny pages, with a picture of a church or a rural scene on the cover, a vicar's letter beginning 'My dear friends' and saying nothing in particular, items of parish news, and a lack of interest in the problems or pleasures of the world at large. Often the vicar's prejudices rather than his convictions are what emerge, which is one reason why parish magazines are combed by journalists in search of clerical hobby-horses that will make stories for their papers. Money is frequently men-

tioned – usually the lack of it. A number of incumbents refer
to the amount of work they do, and give details. 'During
1958,' wrote one, 'your Vicar took some 300 services; prepared and preached 166 sermons; officiated at fourteen bap-
tisms, seven weddings, and twenty-four funerals; attended
over 200 meetings. . . .' 'I began keeping a record,' wrote
another. 'Week ending December 17th. Hours worked by
Vicar: 63½. Dec. 24th: 68½.' Often it sounds like a school
magazine; one offered 'Jottings from St George's', 'Echoes
from Emmanuel', 'Memoes from St Martin's' and 'St
Lawrence's Log'. There are many exclamation marks, and
paragraphs about bazaars, rose shows, autumn fayres, fêtes,
funds, and gifts: the reports of a private world that would be
acceptably cosy if it were not intended to be more than that.
'Insets', prepared by publishing firms and in a few cases by
party organizations, are incorporated in most magazines, often
with a diocesan news-letter. The news-letters vary, depending
on who the bishop is; both they and the insets usually reflect
an innocuous Christianity. The insets are gradually moving
away from indifferent fiction and paragraphs headed 'Historic
Oak' and 'Parson Bee-Keeper' – widening their scope to take
in competent articles on social issues and Church business.
Timothy Beaumont began an inset called *Outlook* in 1963,
which is a slight improvement. An earlier protest against
churchy journalism is the *Window*, begun by a group of young
clergy in the Blackburn diocese in 1946; within a year its
circulation rose from a few thousand to 53,000 and is now
steady at around 175,000, spread throughout the country. The
Window reprints articles from *Vogue* as well as from parish
magazines; its page of readers' questions, with answers from
'The Padre', is pointed and argumentative; it wouldn't be
read with the stunned incomprehension that many parish
magazines induce in outsiders. Its small circulation is hard to

explain. The editor suggested in a letter to me that 'many of the clergy are much concerned to maintain their magazine circulations and are terrified of adverse reactions from the least educated in their congregations. That is true of people who are quite revolutionary in their parish methods in every other field.'

A minority of parish magazines (taking a charitable view, twelve out of sixty magazines and newspapers examined) is interested in some aspect of non-Church life: road safety, elections, strikes, affluence, poverty, war. The best of these are better at writing about religion as well as being better at writing about the world. *Sanctus*, the magazine of All Saints, New Eltham, in south-east London, as run by the former vicar, the Rev. D. A. Rhymes, had articles on 'Corpus Christi: the relevance of worship and life' and 'The "Big Bang" and the Resurrection' as well as on 'The General Election – a word about Christian voting' and 'The Christian and nuclear warfare'. Rhymes was soon snapped up by the Bishop of Southwark and put on his headquarters staff.

While the mass of parish magazines remain low-powered communicators, probably read by few of the people who have them in the house, Christian journalists find a market in the secular Press. What they write goes beyond the devotional articles printed inconspicuously in *The Times* and *Sunday Times*, and the sticky good-neighbourliness of parsons' articles in women's magazines. Television may have helped to sharpen popular interest in religion; so may the political emptiness and moral hollowness of the times – Christians are never sure about this, but those who can write have found an expanding market in papers as different as the London *Evening Standard*, the *Daily Mail*, the *Sunday Telegraph*, the *Sunday Pictorial*, and the *Spectator*. On the same day, the Bishop of Southwark was writing on housing ('A SCANDAL: AND NO USE PASSING

THE BUCK . . .') in the *Standard* and the Rev. Nick Stacey was writing about unmarried mothers ('The schoolgirl on my doorstep') in the *Evening News*. Lay journalists like Monica Furlong write, not always on religious or moral subjects, but always from a Christian standpoint. In the long run this kind of oblique Christian propaganda, in newspapers and on television, is presumably the only kind that will be effective. A few uncompromising clergymen think there is no such thing as Christian propaganda in the modern sense. An Anglican monk, Father Jonathan Graham, head of the Community of the Resurrection, wrote in *Prism* that the Church didn't need columnists or television or to consult 'the best available organization', as previous articles had suggested. 'The general effect of the use of these media appears to be the diffusion of a vague familiarity with religion, without pressing the demand for crucified lives. This is incalculably harmful, and hinders the communication of the Gospel by the only authentic means' – that is, when 'the human agent concerned is suffering in union with [Christ].' But the mood of the Church is more in line with that of the archdeacon who told the Church Assembly with satisfaction that in its first few months, Colonel Hornby's radio and television department had 'arranged no fewer than eighty-three transmissions by co-operation with the radio and television authorities' (though, in fact, many of these programmes would have gone out in any case). The archdeacon estimated their worth at about £83,000 in terms of commercial value'.

The idea of actually buying television time or newspaper space has often been raised. Years ago it was laughed off as being 'American' and distasteful. But in 1961 came the announcement of an unofficial committee, with the Bishop of Bedford as chairman, that discussed the advertising of religion. An interesting row broke out, with the chairman of the

Church Information Committee (which controls the Church Information Office) dissociating the committee from the project: not because he objected to advertising but because of doubts about 'the type of material and the method of sponsorship'. One of the largest advertising agencies, J. Walter Thompson, was involved in the scheme, and there was talk of Thompson's handling an advertising campaign as a public service, without fee; this worried some churchmen, who said the Church might be inhibited if it 'accepted free publicity from commercial interests'. The scheme had been given the title of 'Religion in Britain'. Pained comments came from the Christian advertising and public-relations men – Anglican and of other denominations – who were behind it. 'We believe,' said one of them, 'that the Church should be in among the eight-inch double columns of the sweet firms and the eleven-inch treble columns of the brewers, speaking out for spiritual values.' The then Bishop of Bedford said they were 'only doing what church bells have been trying to do for centuries – with modern techniques'. Later he resigned from the campaign, saying he thought it should be run by laymen. Independent television put on a discussion programme called 'The Adman Cometh'. It began by saying that the people of England stayed away from Church more consistently than any other European nation outside Scandinavia, and continued with caricatures of religious advertising: 'I thought my soul was white till I used Denomination X – a Heavenly Product' and 'Vicars are good for you'. The trouble was that no one knew what manner of advertising was seriously envisaged. About the same time, a body that had existed since 1955, the Advertising Christian Group, announced that it had prepared 'three advertisements for use by one or more sponsoring churches in any given area'. The aim, said the group, was not 'to reflect any denominational viewpoint or to teach the

Christian Faith. Their sole purpose is to encourage readers to begin or resume church attendance'. The blocks, which cost £1 each, showed, respectively, a man on a scooter and a girl in a crash helmet about to join him; a man in a car about to be joined by a woman; and a man, a woman, and a boy leaving a house. All seven wore rigid smiles. The title in each case read: 'We know where we're going . . . we're going to CHURCH!' Each included about a hundred words of text: 'THESE TWO have found that God has a real purpose for their lives – and that's something worth discovering! You don't have to live in a monastery or run a leper colony to know God's purpose for *your* life. . . .'

Some people suspected that Religion in Britain would mount a more sophisticated version of such appeals. But when the first advertisements appeared, in *The Times* at Easter, 1962, they were seen to have avoided the obvious pitfalls. The highly professional committee of Religion in Britain wrote the ads and bought the 11-inch × 3-column spaces itself, using £1,000 given anonymously. 'The man who came back from the dead', announced the first of a series of three. It quoted from Mark, Chapter 16, in the New English Bible version: the Resurrection and Christ's commission to the eleven disciples to preach the Gospel: 'Then he said to them: "Go forth to every part of the world, and proclaim the Good News to the whole creation. Those who believe it and receive baptism will find salvation; those who do not believe it will be condemned".' The context softened the threat of damnation. It could hardly have been more dignified and reasonable – the layout was that of a prestige advertisement for steel or chemicals. It had the terrible sameness that advertising imparts to everything. It was another of those hesitant steps that the Church has to take, whether it likes it or not.

CHAPTER NINE

GOD, MONEY, AND PADDINGTON

MONEY makes the Church uneasy. If its clergy are poor, its
experiments foundering for lack of funds, it is forced to apply
secular standards and talk of failure. But if it is receiving and
making money in large quantities, a considerable part of the
Church feels guilty. 'Years ago,' said a bishop, 'the cry went
round: the Church is totally incompetent and nearly bankrupt.
Now the Church has appointed competent men and put its
house in order, the cry goes up: the Church is money-grub-
bing.' It irritated the bishop to be always in the wrong, and it
irritates the Church to be embarrassed by success. Is it flatter-
ing or disastrous when the *Investors Chronicle* writes that the
Church Commissioners for England are 'among the shrewdest
of the investing institutions in the U.K.'? Should the Church
be gratified or appalled because it is, through the Commissioners, one of the largest landowners in England? A Cheltenham parson wrote to a Church newspaper to 'express a strong
protest to the Church Commissioners for releasing their
Annual Report to daily and provincial newspapers as an annual
event. The clergy are extremely grateful for the wonderful
progress made, but what is the object in letting the average
newspaper-man get hold of such figures?' The result, as the
clergyman realized, was headlines such as 'The Church has
£204,000,000-worth of shares' (a local paper), 'Share boom
doubles Church income in 13 years' (*Daily Mail*) and 'More
money for clergy. Decision by Church Commissioners' (*The
Times*).

The ethics of Church prosperity are complex, and are not

made easier by the complexities of Church finance. The Church's capital wealth, if wealth is the right word, consists of what it has been given or has acquired. The original income of the parish clergy came from local gifts, usually in the form of land, the glebe, or a guaranteed proportion of the produce (and later the income) of someone else's land, the tithe. Tithes have been abolished – the Church received £70,000,000 of Government stock in compensation in 1936 – and much of the glebe is either rented or has been sold. The capital from such transactions, and from all the other gifts to the Church over the centuries, made in gratitude for life or fear of death, together with the interest that has accrued and the profits made on transactions, runs into hundreds of millions of pounds. Parishes retain some of their original endowments, and still receive them, for any purpose from increasing the vicar's income to looking after a grave. Each diocese has its endowments. But most of the inherited capital is now managed centrally in London by the Church Commissioners, a body which has a special relation with both Church and State. In the past the Church itself had no central treasury: the money belonged to the separate parts of the Church, the individual parishes, dioceses, cathedrals, and bishoprics. This meant that some clergy were impoverished while others were rich, and Queen Anne's Bounty (in the eighteenth century) and the Ecclesiastical Commissioners (in the nineteenth, when coal and industry multiplied land values), were attempts to improve the Church's management of money; Queen Anne and Parliament respectively set up the bodies, but the money being handled remained Church money, without subsidy from the State. In 1948 Bounty and Commissioners were joined and renamed the Church Commissioners for England, a title which was soon being spoken with respect in the City and gratitude in the vicarage. The Commissioners' duty is 'to make better provision for the cure of souls'. Among other things, this means forming new parishes, joining old ones, and helping to build churches. But chiefly it means using the Church's capital to pay the clergy, three quarters of whose income now comes from the Commissioners – between £9 and £10 million a year for something over 10,000 incumbents. From April 1962, when there was a substantial increase, the average gross income of parish clergy in England was about £1,100 a year, with the Commissioners paying something more than £800 of this, and the rest coming from various sources: 'surplice fees' for marrying and burying (on average about £30 a year), the parishioners' Easter offering (on average £37), perhaps rent for the glebe, probably grants from the parochial church council. Incumbents must pay income tax on their gross income, and some of them pay more than they should, because they fail to claim all their expenses. But after allowing for maintenance and rates – which incumbents have to pay – the average net income is more than £900. The range of net incomes extends from about £700 to above £1,500; curates are often considerably worse off, but where incumbents are concerned, hardship seems to be receding.

Though the sums can be calculated from *Facts and Figures about the Church of England* and the Church Commissioners' annual report, the Church, naturally enough, isn't anxious to point them out. Speeches and pamphlets tend to give the net amount paid by the Church Commissioners – that is, after rates and repairs have been deducted – and to ignore the income from other sources. A Church Information Office pamphlet,* written by a bishop, talks of dividing up the Commissioners' payments to provide 'an average income of £12 a

* The figures in it relate to 1958–9, when clergy were certainly worse off than they are some years later. But the pamphlet has remained in circulation.

week for 11,400 vicars (many of whom have to spend at least £2 a week on the expenses of their job)'. The point about expenses is valid enough, but there is no mention of income from other sources, which would have added several pounds a week.

It's not that parsons are opulent: only that they are not quite as poor as they seem to be before one examines the figures. This uncomfortable material improvement has been helped by the stewardship campaigns (mentioned later), but the Church Commissioners are the principal benefactors. There are ninety-five of them, including all the English bishops, and twenty-five deans, clergy, and laymen appointed by the Church Assembly. Rather more than a third are laymen, including such various persons as the Home Secretary and the Lord Mayor of York, and representing Crown, Government, law, City of London, and the universities of Oxford and Cambridge. The Board of Governors is the executive body, with sixteen clergy out of twenty-seven members. But the prime movers are a group within a group: the three Church Estates Commissioners. These are Lord Silsoe, who headed the War Damage Commission, was in charge of the Crown estates, and is chairman of the Cement Makers' Federation; John Arbuthnot, Conservative M.P. for Dover, and Sir Hubert Ashton, Conservative M.P. for Chelmsford; and the Secretary, Sir Mortimer Warren. First and Second Commissioners are appointed by the Crown, the Third by the Archbishop of Canterbury. The Second is always an M.P., so that he can be questioned in the House of Commons: it is Parliament, not the Church Assembly, that legally controls the Commissioners (who even handle their own Press relations, to the annoyance of people at Church House).

The small Estates and Finance Committee, which includes the Estates Commissioners, meets once a fortnight, the three Estates Commissioners once a week. Warren, who is in day-by-day control, can get hold of Silsoe at short notice if there is a quick decision to be made. A staff of more than 500 works in the large offices at Millbank, just past the House of Lords, but only ten or so are senior men; investment decisions are taken as swiftly as they are at the Prudential or Barings, and sales and purchases on the Stock Exchange come to more than £60,000 of business a day, channelled through about ten stockbrokers. Only a small proportion of the money is now in gilt-edged (Government) stock; industrial equities are the Commissioners' favourite, and the average yield per £100 on a total shareholding worth more than £200,000,000 in 1960/1 was £6 9s. 4d. The Commissioners' capital consists of £121 million 'held for the endowment of particular benefices, chapters, curacies, and diocesan stipends funds', and another £101 million which has lost its identity; it includes the endowments of bishoprics, taken over in the past, in return for which the bishops' property is looked after for all time. Besides the £200 million-odd in shares, there is property with a 'book value' of £69 million, and a real value that (said the *Investors Chronicle*) 'one can scarcely imagine'. The skilful handling of all this has brought down a steady hail of reproach. Phrases like 'the smooth Stock Exchange operations of the Commissioners' and 'associating with Messrs Clore and Cotton' (from an article in the *Twentieth Century* and a letter in the *Church of England Newspaper*) are brandished. The Commissioners stay aloof from the discussion. Sir Mortimer Warren was not available, but the official delegated to see the Press said to me: 'Let's get this straight, we regard ourselves as a completely commerical enterprise.' Someone else said that all the senior staff were members of the Church of England (a notice-board carried details of the Christian Fellowship, which operates in the offices), but added smilingly that he wouldn't mind an applicant for a job saying he liked beer and dancing.

The Church Commission executives, working in offices with carpets and heavy furniture that might have been imported direct from a merchant banker's in the City, see their work as a straightforward operation serving ends that happen to be Christian. Brewery shares are not bought, and the more obvious armaments shares are avoided; but as the official said: 'We try to keep our hands clean, only it's pretty obvious nowadays that if you're investing in equities you can't keep clear of armaments.' However, the important criticism of Church finance is not that money might be invested in a firm making parts for hydrogen bombs; it goes much deeper and concerns the nature of the Church's involvement in society. An apologist (a layman) said:

The Christian is living in two worlds. He can't escape – he must come to terms with the fact that this is a fallen world. It's by the motive of self-interest that God's people are preserved. Only that motive is strong enough, and we as Christians can't contract out of it. While as citizens we may try to soften the effect of economic forces and hedge the motives of self-interest with restraint, basically we're all in competition, we're all working for ourselves or our families.

If English Electric get the contract, A.E.I. don't. This is clear contrary to the teaching of our Lord about loving our neighbours. We therefore live in a state of inescapable tension. The whole economic system of the world is basically sinful, and we must be in a constant state of penitence – we are concerned with the redemption of the world. But as custodians of funds given by Christian people for Christian objects, we must preserve those funds so they're adequate for the purposes they were given. One would obviously avoid investment in something flagrantly immoral, but most business is pretty well conducted – they're all pretty decent to their staff. So one is looking primarily for the best investment.

It's basically an unChristian system. But without it the people would die.

Among those unconvinced by this argument is the Rev.

Stephan Hopkinson, formerly general director of the influential Industrial Christian Fellowship. Hopkinson said:

Is the right use of the Church's money simply to get the biggest return for the Church? Or is it to meet certain human needs? Of course, once you accept that the important thing is to get the biggest return for the Church, because the Church is a 'good thing', you're really on the road that leads to the Inquisition, to the belief that anything you do in the name of the Church is all right . . .

If the Church withdrew from the stock market and couldn't sustain itself? Well, greater poverty might be the will of the Lord for us all. If we really mean it when we call the Church the body of Christ, we must be ready to be a good deal more realistic about this application.

I think theologically there is a sound case for accepting the stock market as a part of the *status quo*, but we have the freedom and the right of making moral choices. In other words, even if we invest money, we have the responsibility for investing it where there's need and not just where there's profit. There are industrial and even agricultural potentialities that deserve investigating, even if they don't yield the easy gains of a take-over bid. I wish the Church would urge on the Commissioners its responsibility to such a degree that instead of congratulating them for the income that their financial skill makes available, we should hear them saying one year, 'Sorry boys, we've put all our money into low-cost housing because that was where the need was greatest'. I can see absolutely no justification for saying: We've got to get the biggest return we can.

But it's difficult to think of the Commissioners doing anything but utilize the money to benefit the Church as an institution. As trustees, with a duty to preserve their trust fund, they have no option. They have gone in for property development on a large scale, using a holding company with more than twenty subsidiaries, and cooperating with established property men; the Commissioners can afford to choose carefully, since the money at their disposal makes them attractive partners for financiers. With property and land, the Commissioners are on more traditional ground than with share investment. Factories, shops, and offices are owned in quantity. There are extensive blocks of housing, mainly in London, and a thousand farms, covering more than 200,000 acres, in thirty-eight counties; Durham has more than anywhere else, the remains of the great episcopal estates that once belonged to the 'Prince Bishops' of Durham. Some people wonder why the Commissioners continue to own so many farms. There are commercial reasons for spreading property investments; but the size of the farming interest probably derives from the snob value that attaches to landowning, together with the traditional link between Church and land. All the farms are leased to tenants, and annual tenants' dinners are held, with the local bishop, agents, and a few of the staff from London, to give the farmers 'a hell of a good dinner – all they can eat and drink', said a churchman. 'We're absentee landlords, let's face it, so the staff go down in force and give them a jolly good dinner, with speeches. There's a jolly good landlord-tenant relationship.' A tenants' dinner for a hundred can cost £300.

As well as paternalistic landowner, the Church is discreet urban landlord, anxious to see its image is not tainted. The old libel of the Paddington brothels, which once was not a libel, lingers on, to the disgust of the Commissioners. Labour M.P.s still say harsh things about slums. The history of the block of ecclesiastical land north of the Bayswater Road – with Paddington Station on the west, Edgware Road on the east – is another example of how the Church gets entangled in progress. In the Middle Ages the manor and parish of Paddington were owned by the monastery of St Peter at Westminster. When the monasteries were dissolved the estate went to the Bishop of London. At the end of the eighteenth century it was still undeveloped. On the left of the Edgware Road, going north, where there are now flats, shops, and cinemas, were fields and farms: Tyburn Field, Barretts Farm, Home Farm, Paddington Village, Church Fields, Pond Fields. West from Marble Arch along the Bayswater Road were St Georges Burying Ground, First Pightle, Second Pightle, The Mead, Home Close. In 1795 the Bishop of London granted a lease to a number of laymen which gave them two thirds of the rents and profits, leaving the bishop with one third, the freehold, and certain administrative powers. The laymen, later styled 'trustees', produced a development plan for the estate in about 1825, and between 1830 and 1880 the whole area was built up with tall, narrow Victorian houses, fit for gentlemen to live in. There were long waiting lists. People started making money, and a strata of leaseholders and sub-leaseholders, below the trustees, came into being. At first the leases that were drawn up contained few safeguards, or 'restrictive covenants': you couldn't spin catgut or boil tallow or skin hogs, but that was about all. No one thought about prostitutes. The solicitor at the Church Commissioners who knew the history in detail ('and the lease commenced on, I believe, the twenty-fifth of May, 1795'), said: 'If a lease for a house in a high-class district like Westbourne Terrace had contained a proviso about not using the house for immoral purposes, the purchaser would have burst a blood vessel.' Later the leases were tightened up, but by then it was too late. By the early part of the twentieth century, ingenious operators had realized that these large blocks of declining property, with only limited control exercised by the landlords, were ideal for brothels. The Church – by now the Ecclesiastical Commissioners had taken over the Bishop of London's interest – continued to draw its one third of the profits, the trustees managed the estate, drew the other two thirds, and distributed it to the holders of the forty-eight shares into which, for convenience, the estate had been divided.

The shares had become sub-divided; there were sub-profits and sub-sub-leases. If an undesirable tenant was evicted in the morning, he would probably have bought the lease of another house by the afternoon. Before the Second World War there was at least one street that had more brothels than houses. Things got worse during the war; brothels were raided regularly, 'the wages of sin' became a poor joke, and after 1945 the Church began a campaign to clean up the estate. Many of the shares, by now worth £100,000 each, had come into the hands of one man. After long negotiation the Commissioners bought them, and sought out the remainder. It had been possible to be a perfectly respectable shareholder (as most of them were) and have little control over what went on at lower levels. But now the ninety-nine-year leases were starting to fall in, and the Commissioners, gaining control, were able to take action against 'undesirables'. The operation was profitable as well as moral. Rents that had been £7 or £8 a site were now £200 or £300. The old rows of houses were ripe for development, and the Commissioners proceeded to develop them, this time taking rather more trouble with the wording of the leases. To root out immorality, and stop it infiltrating new properties, a special department was set up, run by a former police chief inspector, discreetly known as the 'welfare officer'. He and his staff spent four years, in conjunction with the police, restoring the fair name of Paddington. 'I made a study of immorality,' said one of them. 'I found that immorality is a highly technical subject – technical in the law and technical in its control. It was very interesting. A man would leap to his feet, cram on his hat and rush out to the *locus operandi*, or should I say *locus belli*. We evolved every possible means of making things difficult for them. By 1950 it was more or less eradicated.' Tenants are still scrutinized; abnormally high rents, offered or asked for, are regarded with suspicion; a private detective still looks at stationers' noticeboards to see if girls are offering their services via a Paddington-estate phone number.

'But we don't call it Paddington,' said an official, 'because that's bad P.R. We call it the Hyde Park Estate – the triangle between Bayswater Road, Edgware Road, and Sussex Gardens. It'll be the Mayfair of the future.' Working with property companies, the Commissoners, who in 1953 bought the last remaining shares, got the trustees to retire, and became absolute freeholders, have been tearing down and rebuilding the Hyde Park Estate, which is the southern section; and Maida Vale, at the northern end of the old estate. The middle section, Lancaster Gate, was sold in 1955 and 1956 for about £2,000,000 as being less suitable for development. With the brothels gone and 'Hyde Park' established as desirable, the square mile that was once 'Bell Farm' and 'Paddington Wood' has a promising future as a source of clergymen's pay.

While the Church Commissioners have used the devices of capitalism to push up their income, to a point where it is now above £16 million a year, parishes have been getting the same result from a complicated set of pressures on the ordinary churchgoer. 'Stewardship', the archaic word in general use, helped to add between £4 and £5 million to the annual income of parochial church councils between 1956 and 1960. In 1956, £11,500,000 was contributed; in 1958 it was £12,800,000 and in 1960,* by which time local stewardship campaigns had been properly under way for two or three years, it was esti-

* According to a two per cent sample taken by Mr Neuss's hard-pressed Statistical Unit. While he was getting out his figures, in the spring of 1962, he was sniped at again, this time by *Parson and Parish*, the quarterly magazine of the Parochial Clergy Association, which calls itself the 'watchdog of the parson'. Yet with stewardship, as with most aspects of the Church, the Statistical Unit is the only source of much important information.

mated at £16 million. The result was remarkable, and if the Church had been counting congregations instead of money, the pleasure would have been great. As it is, the Church is even more divided about stewardship in action than it is about the Stock Exchange. The idea behind stewardship is that people are stewards of God's creation, not owning the world's goods but simply looking after them. 'We are stewards, not owners, of all we possess,' say the pamphlets: 'our time, our talents, and our money.' The word 'stewardship' had been slowly gaining ground for years, perhaps as part of a growing awareness that what kept the Church going were endowments from the past, not contributions in the present. A 'Report on Christian Stewardship' was published by the Church Assembly in 1932, but it wasn't till some years after the Second World War that an effective movement began: initiated largely by laymen, and developing in several parts of the country at about the same time. Among its aims was fund-raising. What would have happened if the Church had been left to itself is not clear; 'in this particular branch of Christian conduct,' said the *Christian Stewardship of Money* in 1959, 'the heart of the Englishman is peculiarly stony ground.' But in 1955, large-scale religious fund-raising, long established in North America but regarded in Britain as alien, vulgar, and unnecessary, arrived in the shape of an enterprising company called Wells Organizations. Wells put a bomb under the movement and set it moving in a particular direction. Without Wells and the other companies that soon followed, the stewardship movement might have stayed small; or, less probably, it might have developed as a powerful movement with equal emphasis on 'time' and 'talents'. If so, it would have spared the Church the mounds of literature that have been produced since 1955 to prove that stewardship isn't just about money. What did happen after 1955 was a powerful movement for raising money by means of intense parish activity, based on the Wells-imported ideas of selecting key laymen and running an 'every-member canvass', which has brought in millions but been attacked for its methods and motives. Private conversations contain sharp and sometimes libellous remarks. Public documents explain stewardship at great length. Some of the critics attack stewardship campaigns in general, as a 'secular answer to a spiritual problem'. But most of the criticism is aimed at professional fund-raisers, and much of it comes from churchmen responsible for schemes of their own. One of the stewardship advisers that were soon appointed in most dioceses, the Rev. Brian Rice, of Derby, writing in *Home Words*, a parish-magazine inset, in 1961, conceded the companies' impressive list of satisfied clients', and went on: 'Sometimes there are spiritual benefits and by-products, but fifty-seven per cent of the parishes report that the general effects on Church life have been slight or not observable. Recently the companies have been making efforts to underline the spiritual aspects of their profession, and thus seek to avoid criticism and suspicion, which seem, however, remarkably penetrating and persistent. This is a target-raising movement, the language and method of commerce at its best. So the talk is of markets, clients, regions, fees, targets and so on.' Others deplore the 'untimely arrival' of the fund-raisers. 'I wish they'd never come at all,' said a layman, 'or not for another five years, till we'd begun to understand what stewardship is.' A clergyman at Church House said: 'We've learned a lot from Wells and the others, but we wouldn't be heart-broken if they went out of business.' He added that they showed no sign of this. Another said: 'Wells came here off their own bat. *Invited?* Oh dear no, they weren't invited.' 'There's a very harmonious relation between ourselves and the companies,' said a diocesan adviser near London. 'It's based largely on the fact that we avoid one another.' Many clergy-men come to the defence of the companies. The Archdeacon of Maidstone, the Venerable Gordon Strutt, who is an hono-rary director of a professional but non-profit-making firm of fund-raisers, Planned Giving, Ltd, wrote in July 1961 that the general attack which seemed to be developing on the pro-fessionals was short-sighted and un-Christian. 'It is ungrate-ful; it is unrealistic and it is certainly unkind.'

The 2,000 or more parishes that have had the fund-raisers in are, not surprisingly, the best advocates. Elsewhere incum-bents are inclined to talk facetiously of 'hired assassins' or nervously of 'American high-pressure methods' ('There is far too much Americanization in our country,' wrote a Hamp-shire vicar, 'and I think we can best pay our church bills and give to charity if we teach people to be true lovers of God'). Another complication is that 'time' and 'talents' are more difficult to handle than money. 'Stewardship's done nothing to bring the outsider in,' said an archdeacon. 'It's had an effect on the understanding of Church people, it's thickened Church life, if you like. But it's dangerous to talk of it as a spiritual movement. It's said fairly at the Board of Finance that they want a stewardship of time and talents, but it's exactly the time and talents that are hard to organize at the time they're wanted. I know of a parish where they organized a lot of people to read to the blind. But only a few of the blind cared to be read to.' 'You get a lady offering to play the piano,' said a London vicar. 'You get a *lot* of ladies offering to play the piano.' Other parishes have mustered sick visitors, road wardens, and hospital-car drivers, or built church halls and decorated churches. Suggest to the vicar of one of these parishes that 'time and talents' is an awkward phrase for a marginal activity, and he points confidently to the local evi-dence. But the fact remains that in practice, stewardship is mainly about money, and that a great deal of Church energy is expended on saying that the Church is less 'materialistic' about it than the companies.

At Wells Organizations Institutional, Ltd, the criticism is shrugged off as meaningless: missing the point, which is the inescapability of money. The vulgarity of money makes no one wince at Wells. The office is a suite on the third floor of a building in Hay Hill, off Berkeley Square. Frank Wells, in his early thirties, with straight blond hair and a resemblance to Billy Graham, has Kipling's 'If' framed on the wall, and on his desk an invitation, dated 1960, to a function in honour of his grandfather, a notable American fund-raiser. 'The International Fund-Raising Institute and the Rotary Club of Steubenville, Ohio,' were presenting 'The Distinguished Service Award for Fifty Years' Outstanding Service in Professional Fund-Raising' to F. Herbert Wells. In these circles, fund-raising is a wholesome activity. It was his grandfather, said Frank Wells, who had the idea of raising money for good causes by beginning with two or three leaders in the community, who would each find two or three near-the-top contributors, and so on down the line. 'My grandfather,' he declared, 'probably conducted more campaigns for hospitals than any other man in the States.' As for his father, Lewis Wells, 'he darn near went into the ministry'. Wells-organized activities have produced more than £1,000 million since 1911. After the Second World War they went into business outside the U.S., and at one time had companies in Canada, Australia, New Zealand, and South Africa. They came to Britain in 1955. 'My Dad came over here and said, "It's silly, it won't work here".' The English situation bemused them, with its assumptions, even among churchfolk, that the Church was somehow a charge on the State, and its weekly-gift envelopes that were too small for paper money. But no one else had entered the field. Wells opened an office in London, and before long were selling off their companies everywhere else, even in the U.S., in order to concentrate on England. In a few places at first, parishes were introduced to 'planned giving'. The canvass director came down from Wells, the small committee of key men was chosen – the business men, the lawyers, the accountants, 'the highest possible leadership that is available' – the Loyalty Dinner was held for the parish, the target was set, the canvassers were trained, then went visiting to get 'pledges' of so much a week for three years: 'The family's weekly thoughtful gift to the church.' The horrors of scientific fund-raising at a fee of £250 a week, plus campaign expenses, were seen not to be horrors at all when the income of the parish from direct contributions went up two or three times. A few nonconformist and Roman Catholic churches went to Wells, but it was the Anglican parishes, in England and Ireland, that really caused the theologians to flinch and ask if the Church knew what it was doing.

Frank Wells, who says fund-raising in Britain has barely started, knows precisely what the Organization is doing: raising a lot of money on a three-year basis, at the end of which, 'people who gave from more selfish motivation have learned to give more generously'. The Organization is not beginning with a spiritual approach to stewardship and going on to money, but the other way round: 'No one should sell spiritual results – they're a by-product. Money is the common denominator because it can be understood by the fringe families. We know that the interest will follow the money.' The first section in a Wells leaflet, *Creative Fund-Raising*, is headed: 'Raising an impossibly large amount of money.' The argument is that 'Anyone can see the truth that interest tends to produce sacrifice, but the larger truth is less apparent: that sacrifice produces interest'. Frank Wells marked a passage, and said: 'This is my answer to the Central Board of Finance.' The passage said that 'The church is freed for stewardship instruction on the highest plane only when its financial needs are being met. . . . Creative fund-raising alone can lay a foundation for stewardship instruction in which the motives of the teacher and the desires of the student will be fully honoured and respected'.

Stewardship isn't a plan, says Wells, with over-powering enthusiasm, 'it's a way of life. What we can do is to be a plus factor for a fund-raising campaign'. He uses adjectives like 'educating!' and 'pentecostal!' He explains how, if the parochial church council is moribund and his men can't work with it, they have to 'turn it over' and get the vicar to coopt new blood. If the parish is in a mess, Wells may decline to go there. 'They try to get us into parishes where they're grasping at the last straw. Why don't we go to these? Well, the diocese will do it just as well. We do better in good churches because they know what it's all about.' His twenty canvass directors – £1,500 a year basic salary plus £3 a day allowances – work at full stretch, leaving behind confidential files of pledge cards, and gratified vicars, sometimes with the annual budget of a small industrial undertaking. The future is pleasing for Wells, but not quite so pleasing, he thinks, for the Church's stewardship authorities: 'They don't know the problems they're heading for.' What are these problems? 'Fall off. The essence of fund-raising is to obtain funds with the least number of gifts. The Church authorities are happier to see a thousand families giving £10 each than a hundred families giving £100. We realize that families who give little are glad to get rid of the visitor. People die and go away.' And there are the building-fund projects, the raising of capital sums rather than income – the field in which the Organization normally operated before it came to Britain, and where it will turn its attention over the next decade. 'It'll knock the head off these people,' said Wells sadly, referring to the Church authorities, 'when they're completely committed to things they can't fulfil.'

Planned Giving, Ltd, the non-profit-making company mentioned above, was formed when a member of the Wells staff, running a campaign in the North in 1958, is said to have felt it wrong that a profit should be made out of stewardship. A wealthy industrialist, Kenneth Boardman, agreed to finance a new company; it's a private concern, with all the shares owned by Boardman. Five clergymen, all unpaid, are on the board of twelve, including the vicar of the first parish Planned Giving visited. Among the full-time directors, drawing a salary, are a former member of the Baltic Exchange and a former member of the Colonial Service; all are Church of England communicants. One of the basic Planned Giving pamphlets, *Christian Stewardship in the Parish*, emphasizes 'time' and 'talents' before it gets to money, but this part of the message is similar to that of Wells: 'Since this is a material world, money is the commodity most sought after. If, therefore, the Church member can first be taught to commit himself in terms of money the biggest obstacle to the further commitment of his whole life will have been removed. Similarly, the Church as a body must itself learn to give.' A director outlined the technique. The organizer arrives on a Sunday evening, and spends a few days getting the background and seeing leading church members. Four or five of the 'obvious leaders' in the parish are chosen – not necessarily churchgoers, and not necessarily better paid, though 'the odds are that the one who is the leader is also the one who is better paid' (Frank Wells also made the point that the leader *might* be a butcher or a baker). Then follows a series of meetings, the enrolment of canvassers, the parish supper – three weeks after the organizer arrives – and the canvassing: 'One expects sixty per cent or more to sign a pledge card for three years. Forty per cent won't touch it with a barge pole.' The Planned Giving charges are £50 a week less than Wells's. No guarantee against financial loss is given, as it is with Wells, though 'we have put money back – paid for a parish worker for a year, or cut the fee by £1,000. We don't believe a guarantee is right, because if we give one, the parish has nothing to lose. We find that if we put the onus smartly on their shoulders, there is a tendency to make them work harder'. Speaking at the end of 1961, the Planned Giving director said their latest results were better than Wells's. Wells dispute this. Comparisons are obscured by the lack of any agreed method of measuring pre-campaign giving, with which the new figure can be compared.

Although about 2,000 parishes had probably had campaigns by mid-1962, the last detailed figures go up to February 1961, when the total was 1,332: 610 with commercial direction, ninety-one with diocesan 'direction', 133 with diocesan 'supervision', and 498 'do-it-yourself' campaigns. Until the Statistical Unit processes the figures, there is little proof of which kind of campaign raises most money. 'If the dioceses can produce no more than the companies,' said one adviser, 'then there's no reason for our existence. Simply to set up an organization to copy them at a cut price savours of immorality – they're doing a good job. The crucial test for us is when someone says: "I will give £8 a week if I can do it by banker's order." Will the parish reject this? I've seen this happen, and the person told: "You must bring the money to church." Mind, I would say that if the visitor will collect the money himself, and regard this as a piece of evangelistic enterprise, and keep saying, "I hope to see you in church next week", that would be all right.'

This adviser said they set no target, yet their results were as good as anyone's. They paid no attention to status, as such, when looking for leaders in the parish: 'The chairman and other officers are appointed for their Christian sincerity coupled with their potential qualities of leadership. We don't attend the meetings where the leaders are being chosen.' There was no inquiry into people's income, or speculation about what they could give. He described how at least some professionals went about it; he said it was from personal experience:

They would produce, for the first steering committee, a list of about twenty names. They would have a sheet of paper ruled up into columns – (a), (b), (c), (d), (e), and (f). They would talk about sacrificial giving and about needing the right kind of leadership. In (a) they would write down the name of the most eligible person, then list the names in descending order of suitability. Then stop for a cup of tea. Then suggest changing the letters on top to amounts of money, and say: 'How much would you give?' Some of these people will be there – it's sometimes very embarrassing. Very soon there's one chap who's come up on top, and he's chairman.

Later on, families are grouped in OGA groups – order of giving ability. Say there are five hundred families. Everyone is allocated a card, with name and address. The steering committee meets. The cards are divided into four groups, and each group is told to go through them till they find a family that represents the average standard of living in the parish. You sort the cards above or below the norm. Then you swing them round *a la* whist, so that everyone checks everyone else's. You've then got low, middle, and high in each group. Then the middle cards are gone through again, so that you've got low middle, middle middle, and high middle. Repeat the exercise for high and low, so that you end up with nine packs, from low low to high high. This takes the best part of an evening, believe me. Then they set a price on the cards, perhaps from two and six a week rising to somewhere near £4 a week in some parishes.

When the visitors have been trained, racks are spread round the walls at their last meeting, and into these are slipped the cards of the people they'll be visiting. These visitors know what's on their own cards – what they've been assessed for. You might see you've been allocated to the fifteen-shillings. You can't visit outside your own group: if you're a twelve and sixpenny man and I'm a fifteen-shilling man, you can't visit me. If the numbers don't match, they'd get a man in the twenty-shilling class to cover the fifteen-shillings, not a ten-shilling to cover the fifteen-shillings.

Anyway, by the time your training is finished, you know what's expected of you. The director will say, 'Well, gentlemen, you know what your group is. Will you please go to the racks and get your cards.'

The campaign has started. But by this time, said the adviser, it was virtually over. What he objected to were the pressures at work within the committees, subtly employed to get the most out of people.

Other tensions are latent in the movement. Missionary contributions are already a sore point in the Church; there was the row, mentioned in Chapter 6, over the Statistical Board's missionary-giving figures; and one diocesan news-letter went so far, in 1961, as to print the names of 'forty-four parishes where missionary contributions are alarmingly low'. The figures will be scrutinized to see if the five per cent of income that English parishes give to missions will rise now that more money is coming in; preliminary figures from the Statistical Unit in 1962 suggested that the previous five per cent had risen only to six – so most of the new money was being spent within and on the Church itself, not on its work overseas.

There will be strong pressure to change this. The dioceses are likely to play a bigger part in stewardship generally. Given a generation or two, the companies will probably seem as unexceptional as bazaars. The Church might even come to feel easy in a prosperous society. But when this happens, it will be a very different Church.

CHAPTER TEN

PARTIES AND PARTISANS

SOME parts of the Church seem even more than usually remote from those who don't belong to it. Old battles and causes, long since abandoned and enshrined in biographies for many churchmen, still arouse fury, despair, and bouts of pamphleteering in others. The party organizations, though mellower than they were, still echo with dead causes. The Low Church ideal of 'personal salvation' (as seen at Oak Hill in Chapter 2), and the High Church ideal of a ritualistic and more corporate religion, still provide an explosive mixture for those who say it isn't a matter of preference, but that on his approach to words and gestures can depend the state of a man's soul and even his prospects in the hereafter. The patronage trusts, which choose about one twelfth of English incumbents, still make churchmanship – High or Low as the case may be – the first test of a vicar's suitability. If he goes to a strict Evangelical parish, he must, when taking Communion, stand on the north side of the altar – which he would call a table – and allow the movement of his hands to be visible. He wears cassock, surplice, and black scarf. The Anglo-Catholic, wearing vestments, would stand on the west side, facing east, his back to the congregation; he would mix the Communion wine with water, following the tradition that Christ did so – the Evangelical, lacking Biblical authority, would never do this. These things matter, and extremists will defend them fiercely. Or convictions may mean a life apart. There are many communities for Anglican monks and nuns. Their members teach, nurse, pray, contemplate, make incense, vestments, and wafers, and achieve, at least in the eyes of outsiders, who never tire of seeing glimpses of them on television, the status of experts.

These are the extremists – the parties and partisans who believe they are vital to the health of the Church, but who seem, to many people, a quite astonishing collection of survivals, living by technicalities. Concentration distinguishes the extremists. Eyes glitter. An official of one party organization, formed last century to fight for Protestantism when the Anglo-Catholics were on the move, said that if the Church went on drifting towards Rome, 'there will be a religious war in this country – I don't mean war in the sense of bloodshed, but trouble. The national Press has suppressed the Protestant voice. It doesn't think the Protestant voice is strong enough. Communists are allowed to state their point of view, to shout and to scream, but *Protestantism* isn't heard'. This feeling of being misunderstood, of having boundless ignorance to contend with from the uninformed public, and even from parts of the Church, is found among certain Low churchmen, but rarely among Anglo-Catholics, who are more sure of themselves. Someone connected with the Church Society, which, although commonly described as 'Low', insists that it is the norm from which others have departed, said:

We are not an Evangelical society – that may astound you. I know I'm an enigma to you – your mind, if I may say it with kindness, has come with preconceived ideas. In a sense your mind is guided by the wrong definition given by the official party in the Church of England. They call themselves the central party – the bishops. They're no more the central party than my foot. We are central, *they* have departed from the Prayer Book. This may be rather a blow to you, in that it upsets your former deductions, but I would say this is true of most bishops. If Prime Ministers had acted according to the Constitution and the Thirty-nine Articles, a lot of bishops wouldn't have been appointed – they don't accept the Prayer Book.

Anyone who joins the Church Society – membership is not disclosed – has to declare that 'I thank God for the Reformation and will maintain the Scriptural standards expressed in the Thirty-nine Articles and Book of Common Prayer', and that 'I am ready to help to drive away all erroneous doctrines contrary to God's Word'. Among the Society's other interests are a youth fellowship, a women's society, and a magazine, the *Church Gazette*. It runs two girls' public schools, and through the Church Society Trust has the patronage of 'between 150 and 200 livings', where, again, it is denied that 'party' enters into the matter: 'This is where bishops have been astounded. The Bishop of Oxford once asked, "What conditions do you lay down?" We said, "They're not our conditions, they're the Church's conditions."' Trusts of this kind claim, fairly, that they take pains both in finding incumbents and helping the parish – perhaps by persuading the parochial church council to pay more expenses, or by sending an expert to value church land before it's sold. Prospective incumbents are 'recommended' to the Church Society, and are discouraged from applying themselves: it is assumed that God would work through a recommendation but not through direct application. 'If a man tried to offer himself, we would say, "My dear man, get someone else to send your name in. Don't send it in yourself." We wouldn't see God's hand in that. It wouldn't be nice, would it? A man's not likely to run himself down, you see.' (Which is a rather different reason.) Patronage can be a wearisome task – bishops complain they spend more and more time exercising it. The Church Society produced a typewritten sheet with details of a vacant living. It was rural and hilly, had a scattered population of 1,200 over eight square miles, and a medieval church in good condition, with a silver cross of local workmanship for ornament, ten bells, electric light, and an oil-fired boiler. Both principal

H 225

bedrooms in the vicarage had been redecorated two years previously. There was a Methodist chapel, open on Sunday evenings, a home for seamen and another for babies, and one shop. The station was five miles away, and, a strong asset, two public schools were within eight miles. There was no resident squire. The net income was £819, plus £123 contribution towards expenses by the parochial church council. It had already been declined by eight men, and was now being considered by a ninth.

The Evangelical trusts as a whole possess more livings than the Anglo-Catholics. The Church Pastoral-Aid Society, founded in 1836, which aims to 'maintain home missions in the Church of England and in the Church in Wales', has about 180 livings: 'We never lay down any conditions to a man when we offer him a living, but we naturally try to find someone who will be in sympathy with the churchmen of the parish.' The C.P.A.S. is Conservative Evangelical, though a good many of its livings go to more moderate Evangelicals. All Souls' Church, in Langham Place, opposite the B.B.C., is the spiritual headquarters of the Conservatives, and the name of J. R. W. Stott, the Rector of All Souls', recurs in conversations. As at Oak Hill Theological College, there are few doubts. Before lunch at the C.P.A.S. offices, everyone goes to the chapel for prayers. If you are not saved, the blindness is yours. It's no good saying 'I can't believe' to a Conservative Evangelical, since he merely replies: 'You're refusing to obey.' Stott, who has the Evangelical's crisp yet placid conviction, said that 'with my preconceived views of God as a God who wants to be known – who is light, and wants to shine – it's difficult to believe it's God fault. The more I talk to people, especially to students, the more I think that genuine intellectual doubt is rare. It's almost always an unwillingness to face up to the challenge of Christ. I'm astonished to find how many people there are who say they are honest agnostics, who've never made any attempt – who've not read the Gospels since they were children.'

The Conservative Evangelical wing is sufficiently small and cohesive for the C.P.A.S. to feel itself in touch with every corner: perhaps a thousand parishes, which with incumbents and curates means about 1,500 clergymen, half of them thoroughgoing .fundamentalists and the rest more moderate. Grants for curates and other parish workers are made on a large scale – about £50,000 a year. The Society's income has been rising, and is now above £100,000 a year, from legacies, parishes, and interest on investments. There is an old-fashioned vigour about it all: belief is to be stated, not examined: the purpose of the money is to help more men to give more people a better chance to realize what they've been missing. One C.P.A.S. annual report makes a typically straightforward statement, old-fashioned to outsiders but not to Evangelicals, of the wonderful things that may be just around the corner. There is spiritual malaise in many parishes, says the report, and goes on: 'The quickest and most desirable remedy would be a Divine intervention by the Holy Spirit arousing in our people such a hunger and longing for spiritual satisfaction that they would besiege our churches to obtain it. . . . We must not rule out such a miracle but rather pray expectantly for it.'

The flow of books and pamphlets from this end of the Church is especially strong, written bluntly and sincerely, thickly sprinkled with Biblical references. *Your Suffering*, by the Rev. Maurice Wood, principal of Oak Hill, refers to twenty-six texts in the first chapter of eighteen pages. The Protestant Reformation Society, a small organization with basement offices off Piccadilly, has an income from all sources of only £4,500 a year, yet manages to publish and have in stock a great variety of polemical literature. An annual meeting was told a few years ago that 'the need for the Society's quiet, though none-the-less effective, opposition to the claims of Rome is in many respects more urgent today than it was in 1827, when it was founded'. A dark picture in a committee room showed 'The First Reformers presenting their famous protest at the Diet of Spires on the 19th April 1529'. In the general office were quantities of books and stationery, desks, a big radiator, a bathroom cabinet, and an enormous feather duster. Literature available included such titles as *Millions Accept a Dubious Dogma*, *The Faith of a Protestant*, *Roman Catholics and School History Books* (*An Attempted Censorship Described*), *Can We Cooperate with Rome?*, *Rome & Mixed Marriages* and *Eighteen Reasons why I am not a Roman Catholic*. *Whose Church? Conversations: Anglican and Roman*, written by an Anglican clergyman, probably a good many years ago, contains such dialogue as:

Roman Catholic: I don't want to pain you – but your Church lost her priesthood when Henry VIII made himself Head of your Church and claimed the appointment of Bishops. We can only look upon your Church not as a religious but a secular society.

Vicar: Not at all, what pains me is your ignorance and the stubborn way in which uninstructed Roman Catholics cling to fabricated stories.

There is also a pamphlet, marked '62nd thousand', headed 'A Religion of Despair. The following pitiful letter shows how a poor Romanist dreaded death, for he knew only a religion of despair – nothing of "peace with God through our Lord Jesus Christ".' The letter is written to the Rev. Thomas Connellan, a Roman Catholic priest who became a Protestant, and is signed 'An Unhappy Catholic. Limerick, November 7th, 1905'.

The central organization for Anglo-Catholics is the Church

Union, with about 14,000 members, including 2 or 3,000 clergy. It's a sizeable organization, producing several magazines; its secretary is also secretary of the patronage board of the Society for the Maintenance of the Faith, a trust which holds about eighty livings. This is the world where, in the more extreme cases, the ritual is close to that of Roman Catholics; Evangelicals are disgusted but High churchmen talk of 'Catholic glories', and point proudly to occasions like the annual Whitsun pilgrimage to the Anglican shrine at Walsingham.

Walsingham, 'England's Nazareth' to some Anglo-Catholics, is an untidy Norfolk village a few miles from the coast, once one of the great shrines of Catholic Europe. The Virgin Mary is supposed to have appeared to the lady of the manor of Walsingham Parva, Richeldis de Faverches, some time in the eleventh century, and to have shown her the house in Nazareth where the Annunciation took place – the announcement to Mary by the angel Gabriel that she would 'bring forth a son, and . . . call his name Jesus'. According to the legend, Richeldis was given the measurements, and told to build a replica at Walsingham. One of the Walsingham booklets, *England's Nazareth. A History of the Holy Shrine of our Lady of Walsingham*, recounts the legend as fact, adding that 'The historical evidence has been carefully investigated, and there can be no doubt as to the main outline of these events'. One of the assistant priests at the shrine said, in conversation a few years ago, that he assumed the truth was that 'as pilgrimages became more difficult to the Holy Land, shrines were set up in various places, including Britain. Probably a pious old lady here built the chapel, then locals came, and then they came from farther afield.' Various miracles are recorded. A succession of kings of England, from Richard the Lionheart to Henry VIII, went to Walsingham, where the Holy House, enclosed by a chapel, was in the keeping of Augustinian monks. The shrine was destroyed at the Reformation. The site was forgotten, and what had been a holy place became, in the nineteenth-century guide-books, 'quaint old Walsingham', with the holy wells turned into 'wishing wells'. In the early 1920s a High churchman called Hope Patten went to Walsingham as the village incumbent; it was then a rather down-and-out parish, said to have been declined by sixteen clergymen before he took it. Hope Patten determined to restore the shrine, was at cross purposes with the bishop for years, but raised enough money to build a replica of Holy House and chapel on a disused builder's yard in the middle of the village. Later this was extended to provide a pilgrims' church, and the foundations found beneath are, according to one school of argument, the remains of the original; others place this across the road. The re-foundation of Walsingham seems to have started off as a fairly eccentric enterprise. Hope Patten was fond of mystique and medieval dimness, as shown in the interior of the pilgrims' church. He planned to establish an order of Anglican Augustinians. Fervent young men came and went. Some of the building around the shrine, facing the village street, had their windows blocked up as part of the attempt to re-create a walled-in atmosphere. At one time the shrine had to be, technically, the 'private chapel' of one of the 'College of Guardians' who govern it, and Hope Patten was his 'private chaplain', so as to evade the bishop's jurisdiction. But the shrine came to be taken seriously by an inceasing number of Anglo-Catholics, and nowadays, although many would regard it as unorthodox, several thousand may arrive at such times as Whitsun. People staying on the coast at Cromer call in on their way to see the grounds of Sandringham. Parties from northern parishes come in Wakes Week and stay four or five days. The bishop is friendly, and licenses the priest in charge. Governing the shrine is a 'College of Guardians', made up of about eight priests and a similar number of lay-men, with the priest in charge as 'Master of the College'. If the shrine was ever faced with an unfriendly bishop, it would fall back on its claim to be a 'peculiar', outside normal juris-diction; counsel's opinion was once taken on the matter, and suggested that the present shrine could claim the privileges and exemptions that attached to the original foundation. Donations and endowments pay the priest in charge and several assistant priests, so the shrine is financially independent.

At the entrance, the wall is lined with hundreds of small plaques – 'Our Lady of Walsingham. We thank you for financial help after prayer here. 1933.' 'Our Lady of Walsing-ham. A pilgrim returns thanks for relief from spinal neuralgia.' The assistant priest said that 'We should cough if someone wanted to put one up now', and that he thought they might eventually be taken down. But this was only because 'there are better ways of saying thank you to God than by a tawdry little plaque. It's a question of aesthetics, not theology'. The Holy Well, inside the church, with a worn mat for pilgrims to kneel, supplies more than 50,000 bottles of water each summer for people to take away and drink in time of illness: 'this is sacramental, it's something to get hold of.' Glass covers the pool – smooth water and a skin of dust. Relics are here, in-cluding, according to *England's Nazareth*, 'three fragments of the True Cross'. There is a relic of St Vincent the Martyr; the priest holds out the relic-case, the pilgrim kisses it, and the priest says: 'May the prayers of St Vincent aid you.' A white light shines where the Sacrament is reserved – a few wafers of bread which have been consecrated and put aside in case of urgent need, a practice detested by Evangelicals, who say that Reservation leads to improper adoration, and write some of their fiercest pamphlets against it. Candles can be purchased.

Pictures and statues shine in the half dark. In the garden out-side live two female hermits, probably the only ones in the Church of England. They occupy green shuttered wooden huts behind a wattle fence. Nuns from the small community attached to the shrine pass their food in through hatches, and they emerge only at night, when they may spend eight or ten hours praying in the Holy House – a chapel of great stillness, contained within a larger chapel, measuring twenty-three feet six inches by twelve feet ten inches, the size recorded of the original. 'You can feel their presence as you pass by,' said the priest. He added that 'We consider prayer is the main thing. It's like a telephone exchange: people put a call in and we plug it through'. Another phrase used at Walsingham is that 'prayers drive a hole up to Heaven'. There is a ferocity of belief, a cool way of talking about extremism as an intel-lectual weapon: 'We want it to stay extreme. We want it to scream at people because it's saying something extraordinary, that God took flesh. We would want it to be the Shrine of the Incarnation.' As for latter-day miracles – 'We would fight shy of the term "miracle". But we get a lot of intercessions for temporal things.'

Walsingham would have been unthinkable a hundred years ago, and so would the large number of religious communities within the Church of England which have developed from the common source of the Anglo-Catholic revival. There are about 250 men, mainly in seven or eight communities, and about 2,000 women, in fifty or sixty. ('In the nineteenth century,' said a monk, 'far too many women felt the need to be mothers superior.') A few other monks and nuns are in communities that the Church won't recognize. What a monk called 'a dribble' of religious go over to Rome – because, he suggested, of 'a sort of frustration that might get solved if there weren't this alternative of Rome'.

Psychologists suggest many non-religious reasons why people might choose chastity, poverty, and obedience, but in the kind of visits a journalists pays to communities, the impression is usually of calm activity, sometimes accompanied by a little vanity, rarely by any uneasiness or uncertainty. *The Call to the Religious Life*, a precisely written pamphlet published by the Community of the Resurrection at Mirfield, says that the religious life 'is a state, like the married state or the clerical state; some are called to it, others are not. But everyone is called to perfection. Perfection is doing what we were created to do. The perfect teapot pours well, the lid does not fall into the cup, and the handle is so arranged that it is possible to hold it without calamity. The perfect Christian loves God as God wants to be loved, does what God wants him to do, and knows God as God allows himself to be known. So if you want to be the perfect Christian, and God calls you to the religious life, you will have to go'.

No doubt for the wrong reasons, the lives of monks and nuns can appeal to outsiders who are alienated by the gimlet eyes of the Conservative Evangelicals. Bare rooms, scrubbed tables, the life marked out by bells and silence, coarse clothes, a sense of order, the unusualness of a printer and a doctor of philosophy sharing common tasks or arguing over a meal of bread and sugarless tea, all contribute to the image.

Women's communities have the strongest atmosphere. The odd tradesman or painter or journalist – any man unless he's a priest – seems to clear a space around him; steel-tipped shoes fade away down tiled passages, a door shuts as you go round a corner. But except in the few enclosed orders, where, if anyone is interviewable, it will be the Mother Superior in the parlour, the nuns, once encountered, turn out to be no more or less interesting than any other kind of professionals. In a convent outside Wakefield – where in the garden a solitary nun with heavy black shoes and grey socks showing under her habit was trying to tear up a privet root – the Mother said that in the past, it had been the obvious sinners who went there for help: now sin was more sophisticated and they had people from every walk of life. What was the object of it all? 'We are forming islands of peace in a sea of wickedness and vulgarity. One isn't withdrawing from the fight, one is fighting in another way. I think one of the things we are meant to be is a place to which people can turn.' A sister, next in rank to the Mother, said: 'People go to a psychiatrist who does things to them. When they come here they've got to do it themselves.' They said things were changing. The old type of sister was exemplified by the nun who, when she was dying, heard a pit disaster announced on the radio, and immediately asked the others to get their litanies so she could pray for the dead. There was still one sister who, if someone said 'There's a drunk come in!' would ask, 'Where is he?' and rush to the waiting room to battle for his soul. 'Personally,' said the sister primly, 'I'd run the other way, unless I had to go there under obedience.' She recoiled from the knock-about kind of evil: strong drink, foul language. 'I wither inside. But I do it because I ought.' The nuns here, and in most communities, are less anxious to spend their time in 'good works'. They look after girls in trouble and run a day school, but prayer is looked on increasingly as the focus of their lives; they quoted, with pleasure, a provost's phrase about them, 'A powerhouse of prayer', and said that nowadays when a girl had a vocation, it was more likely to be simply as 'a nun' rather than as any particular kind – a nurse or a teacher. The most usual, and acceptable, answer of an aspirant when asked why she was coming to a convent was that she didn't know.

Income is from the schools, the embroidery, and the altar

bakery. There is no endowment. Some of the outbuildings are decayed, but the larder and kitchen were newly decorated and equipped. The corridors were polished; there seemed to be more doors than usual, and one was labelled *It is courteous, to God and to man, to close this door quietly*; it was difficult to get one's bearing in the place, which rambled like an old farm-house. The altar bakery, reached by a wooden staircase, was like an attic converted into an elementary sort of kitchen. There was a faint smell of gas. Three ovens were used to make the wafers. A mixture of flour and water was used, 'as for York-shire pudding', and 720 churches were supplied. The nun in charge said it was 'lovely when people say that instead of five hundred wafers can they have a thousand. Communions are going up like that'. Crossing between buildings with the Mother Superior, the nun in grey socks suddenly ap-peared, trundling a barrow fiercely. It was loaded with privet, topped with the defeated root. 'I've done it, Mother!' she shouted.

Practical results are expected at a convent. 'Every day we get requests for prayer by telephone or by post. It's marvellous what results there are – we're amazed, though we shouldn't be, really.' Only with an enclosed order is this feeling muted: the world is a long way off. At a small community in Bucking-hamshire, a few miles north of A 4, the Bath Road, the Mother Superior, mildly alarmed, received me in the parlour: polished bare floor, crucifix, smell of varnish and cooking. On the mantelpiece were two railway timetables, a clock, a pair of photographs of bishops and some books – *The Liturgy of the Mass, The Meaning of the Monastic Life*. Outside the barred window were thick trees, high rhododendrons, and shrubs; a van was delivering church candles. Day at the convent begins with matins at 2 a.m., which last an hour or a little more on feast days, after which the nuns go back to bed for a few hours.

Then, through the day, there are the 'hours' that, with matins, make up the Divine Office, and are common to all communities: Prime, 6 a.m., when Christ was led out to be mocked. Terce, 9 a.m., when he came before Pilate. Sext, midday, when he was nailed to the cross. None, 3 p.m., when He died, then evensong, and finally compline. Besides this is the daily mass, and two hours of private prayer – half an hour spent in intercessions for others, the other one and a half in 'adoration of God' – the Mother Superior was astonished to be asked how this hour and a half was spent.

She had a small white face, and nodded a great deal. Her habit was light-coloured, with a girdle and a big cross. For years, she said, no one had gone out, but the Health Service spoiled this: instead of the doctor dealing with everything on the spot, he would send a sick sister off to hospital. But this was the only time they left the house; they did the shopping by post. Nineteen of the sisters were enclosed, and there were six oblates who made contact with the world – answered the door and took breakfast to the priest from the Cowley Fathers at Oxford, who came to stay once a fortnight in the guest-house. The community was founded in London at the end of the last century. Later it divided, and this part came under an Evangelical bishop, who wouldn't allow Reservation. So they had to move to Potters Bar, and came to Buckinghamshire in the 1920s, to this house with sixty-six rooms, where they lived on whatever dowries sisters brought with them, and occasional legacies. For six months the newcomer was a postulant, for three years a novice; then she took her first vows. And it was a happy life: 'Quietly happy'. She said they were 'more of a Cistercian order, because of the silence, but we're not absolutely silent, like the Trappists. We're allowed to talk and have corporate recreation on Sundays and Feasts. We sit around in a circle, bring our needlework, and talk about general things. Everyone addresses her remarks to Mother, otherwise you get little cliques.' What did they talk about? 'What we're interested in. For instance, the Queen wasn't very well yesterday. They would probably ask me about her. I look through the papers and cut out anything of interest – things happening in the world – and put those in the cloisters for the sisters to read. Things happening between nations and things like that. We're very interested in the Tibetans.'

They have no television, and the radio is used only for the Queen's message on Christmas Day. In the war they had listened to Churchill's speeches – 'I don't mean for our own safety, I mean for the prayer.' Besides prayer, a certain amount of time is spent in 'individual spiritual reading'. They cultivate a garden, and grow much of their own food. Meals begin with 'pittance' in the mornings – 'We don't sit down to bacon and eggs and things like that – we have bread and butter and something sweet. We don't have meat. All through the winter we have three vegetables from the kitchen garden, besides potatoes. The main meal is at a quarter to one. We have fish twice a week – or it might be a vegetable pie with grated cheese. We buy our milk. After vespers (evensong) a cup of tea. Then supper about seven – a cheese dish, milk pudding, and fruit.' The youngest nun is thirty, the oldest eighty-one. There was a girl of twenty-five they hoped would come in soon. But God kept them the same size: 'We wouldn't really want to be bigger, or it wouldn't be family life.'

The men's orders – generally larger, sometimes well known, sometimes (like the Community of the Resurrection in South Africa) involved in politics – are less susceptible to the quick visit. Of the sixty or seventy Franciscans whose friary is at Cerne Abbas, in Dorset, not more than twenty or thirty are there at once. Unlike Mirfield or Kelham, which are primarily priestly orders, about half the Franciscans are 'lay brothers'. They work with industrial missions, visit public schools, help in parishes, preach to hop-pickers and jazz festivals, take in the maladjusted, and regard their work as fundamentally social: 'We must be on the look-out for who is the social outcast of the age. It's not the leper. It may not be the coloured man for much longer.' Academic qualifications are less common here than at Mirfield. They included men who had been a draper, a male nurse, a lieutenant-colonel, a sailor, a carpenter, a printer, the son of a peer, the son of a former Cabinet Minister, an engine-driver, a postman, a dance-band leader, and a Communist youth organizer.

At Cerne Abbas they print, farm, keep bees and chickens, make their dark brown habits, run a laundry, look after maladjusted children and some older people, and live an open-air sort of life that seems strangely unmonklike. The friary was once a farmhouse. In the First World War a hopeful group set up a utopian community, and a small square with a block of bow-fronted shop windows, and a wall pillar box inscribed *Commonwealth*, survive. The chapel used to be a stable. Outbuildings are tiled, or roofed with green corrugated iron. The friary itself has well-kept lawns with hedges. You hear chickens, a donkey, and a saw. The Society of St Francis was founded about thirty years ago, with a rule (which is private) written for the purpose. As at all the Anglican communities, the situation is recognized by the Church without being an official part of it; there is an 'Advisory Council on the Relations of Bishops and Religious Communities', and a bishop acts as 'visitor' to every community, and represents the external Church. Each community makes up its own rule, sometimes taking it virtually unchanged from its medieval form, sometimes adapting or inventing in order to suit the times. For Franciscans, poverty is one of the chief ingredients.

A trust owns the land on which the friary stands, and allows so much money a year; the buildings are owned by the society, but one of the friars said they would be 'happier to rent it all, since *then* we might be turned out'. They like to be adaptable. A friar who had been to one of their outposts in a slum said that 'they live at rock bottom there. I got something to eat there the other day – goodness knows what it was. Oh yes, it was curried hearts – hearts in rice. All the West Indians there seemed to love it, but it was hard to take.' At Cambridge, where they also have a house, the food (and the conversation) are better; 'some of us', said the friar, 'are a bit dubious about that'. One of the problems with poverty, they say, is where to draw the line. The rule talks about poverty consistent with good health and the ability to work. A printer, who wasn't keen on the Press, said they didn't want articles in the newspapers declaring that they were making great sacrifices, because they weren't: 'In point of fact we're a darn sight better off than most people in the world today – no responsibilities, no worries about money. There's no question of loneliness. For a true Christian, to have all the Offices laid on is a great advantage.' He said he was practical about poverty. He had had a shaving rash, and dropped some hints to his family about electric razors. They gave him one for Christmas. People came along and said: 'Fancy you living in poverty and you've got an electric razor! *I* can't afford one.' But there was the saving in soap and blades, and the other friars could borrow it. A letter from a mother superior to her novices, bound into a typewritten history at a convent, had made a complementary point: 'The *whole* Community may make more and fresh traditions but not the individual. The Community may move from brush and dustpan to a "Cedar Mop" and from "Cedar Mop" to "Hoover", from a "Dolly Tub" to an "Electric Washer", but the manner and the doing is *fixed* Tradition and that which makes the Sacrament of the Daily Life is the surrender of the personality into the Tradition.' At Cerne Abbas, no one carries money unless he has to. If he travels, he asks the Father Guardian what to take; he might go with a second-class railway warrant, and half a crown to cross London and buy a cup of tea. A noticeboard in the friary said: 'All brethren travelling on holiday are urged to use the cheapest method of transport. Railway travel is cheaper on Tuesdays, bus seats may be booked through the office, and "hitch-hiking" is cheapest of all.'

The Franciscans are impressive, though not, for the outsider, as impressive as an inward-looking order like the Benedictines of Nashdom, whose chanting and praying in the chapel, that was once a ballroom, carries through the abbey, that was designed by Lutyens as a house for a Russian princess, and creates an atmosphere indistinguishable from Roman Catholicism, which is what they want. Nashdom Abbey is off a country road a few miles from Slough – behind white columns and a sweep of walls, the wide staircase smelling of incense, the windows looking out on lawns and trees. There is a certain eccentricity about Nashdom. They use the Roman Mass book, not the Prayer Book – 'We prefer something different to having the Book of Common Prayer manhandled in a funny sort of High Church way.' They say that 'If we became Roman Catholic tomorrow, we would only change one word in the service: the name of the bishop. This is the importance of the place. We are living the Benedictine life. Four to five hundred priests a year come here to make their retreat. They go home to their parishes without the least thought of introducing any fresh practices. We're a perfectly normal part of the Church of England. We're not High.' But these are just words; it would be hard to be higher than Nashdom. There are only twenty-five of them – seven lay brothers, six priests in temporary vows, and twelve 'choir monks' in solemn vows, addressed by the title 'Dom' (for 'dominus'). The head of the community is the Abbot – installed by the bishop and equipped with mitre, pastoral staff, and throne, and wooden mallet to 'knock us up and down': that is, to give instructions for kneeling and rising in chapel, where they spend several hours of every day. The Abbot is elected. As the head of a private society he has no legal standing in the Church, but a monk remarked hopefully that abbots took precedence over bishops, and that 'all other countries would recognize that the Abbot is senior – this is a bit of medieval history that's finding its feet'.

They do a certain amount of work outside – supervising retreats, speaking, even broadcasting. But Nashdom is what matters – cowled figures in the chapel, observed with awe or curiosity by visitors in the gallery above, which was built for musicians in the ballroom days. A monk said: 'A Belgian secular monk came here for vespers and tea. He sat on the sofa and almost wept – "Incroyable!" he said. He had been to Mirfield, he had been to Cowley. And here he had found something that was utterly familiar.' Nashdom is clever, extreme, and snobbish. 'We had a metropolitan of the Church of South India,' said a monk, 'and then in the afternoon the Bishop of Buckingham dropped in, and the Archbishop of Cape Town called. So we had these three here. It's quite normal for people to blow in – we're in continuous demand. The Benedictine life goes back to the patristic age. It's a very simple, hearty thing, not marked with the later divisions of Christendom.' Monks sometimes reveal their pleasure at being taken for Roman Catholics. (This happens at many communities. A nun said that Roman priests and religious sometimes mistook them, and, when the mistake was realized, turned and hurried away. But sometimes they stayed to talk, which was gratifying. She added that there was a joke about being able to tell Roman Catholic nuns because their shoes were dirty.)

The first Anglican Benedictine community, on Caldey Island, off the Pembrokeshire coast, defected to Rome in 1913, and the order had to be re-founded within the Church of England. They have great respect for the Pope, and a monk at Nashdom said they accepted that he 'has a special position – though not what Rome claims'. However, he added, 'at a conference in Belgium, no two Romans agreed what Papal infallibility meant. One Benedictine said the decree of 1870 was an attack of wind in the belly'. They make incense, and once sent some to the Pope – Glastonbury, the best grade, which sells at 18s. a pound. 'Ten years ago the whole of the Church of England bought its incense from Prinknash Abbey, but recently we've been undercutting them. A young monk from Prinknash came here, and said, "I don't think much of your incense." He didn't know we had a letter from the Holy Father, saying "Thank you for your gift of incense, which was charming". We'd sent some with an Italian abbot who blew in.'

Sacristy expenses are high at Nashdom. A pamphlet called *Nashdom Abbey Finance* points out, among other things, that 'The worship of Almighty God is our chief duty as Benedictine monks. This involves for us a daily High Mass and perhaps as many as twelve or fifteen Low Masses. For these vestments, missals, candles, wine, and linen must be adequately supplied and renewed'. A monk said that 'we used to make our own, but we no longer have the monk-power to do it'. There are cabinets of drawers with coloured vestments: white for 'Our Lord and Our Lady', red for martyrs, green for 'nothing special', purple for penitential occasions, black for funerals. Prayer is a professional activity. And on the intercession board are the slips of paper with the requests. One was 'For Rosalind, just finished an association with a married man, and tentatively rediscovering the Church'. Another was for the quality of religious programmes on television.

There is the curious feeling of urgency, found among most extremists in the Church. Beyond the trees, the cemetery has plain wooden crosses: 'St Benedict said we should have death continually before our eyes, so now and then we come down and have a look.' One monk referred to it as 'the parking place'. Another said, with an oddly unChristian touch of drama: 'That's where it all ends.' They had been, some of them, a cavalry officer, a 'lad about Soho', a bishop's nephew, a metal worker from New Zealand, a man from the electricity board at Hemel Hempstead. But under their cowls, shuffling into chapel, they seemed the remotest men in England.

CHAPTER ELEVEN

THE THEOLOGIANS' WORLD

A PHRASE of Hooker's, 'The science of things divine', is quoted by the *Shorter Oxford Dictionary* as part of its definition of theology; alternatively it is 'the study or science which treats of God, His nature and attributes, and His relations with man and the universe'. The subject is large and obscure; the private world of theology can be richly unrewarding unless you understand the vocabulary, care about the issues, and sympathize with the differences that separate theologians. Perhaps the only way to write about it in a book like this is to find those English theologians who seem to be talking to people outside the Church – who do not, in Archbishop William Temple's phrase, spend blameless lives giving correct answers to questions no one wants to ask.

Professional theologians, many of them intellectually in the front rank, have created an apparatus that outsiders would never dream existed. Writing in the *Church Times* in February 1962, Dr Richard Hanson, then lecturer in theology at Nottingham, called it a 'high-pressure subject'. Nowadays, scholars needed to examine periodicals written in Swedish, Dutch, and Italian, as well as German and French. 'If you want to be an expert,' he said, 'you must choose. You cannot be an expert just in theology. You can concentrate on the Old Testament, on the New Testament, on the Fathers (up to 461), on the Middle Ages, on the Reformation, on the Modern Period, on the Philosophy of Religion, on Comparative Religion, on Dogmatics, or on Liturgy.' Dr Hanson mentioned two further specialities, the Theology of Mission and Ecumenical Theology, before going on to specialities within specialities; for good measure he suggested four of these.

Distinguished though many of them are, English theologians don't seem to make international reputations. We have no Karl Barth (who is a German), no Reinhold Niebuhr (an American), no Rudolf Bultmann (another German). But native theologians, centred mainly on the universities, and especially Oxford and Cambridge, are enormously active. Historical scholarship – examining and explaining texts, studying the history of ideas – has been the chief Anglican contribution for a century or so. The Rev. David Edwards, of the S.C.M. Press – already quoted in Chapter 1 – gave this account in 1961 of some of the current concerns:

A key question for them is: What is the Christian significance of the Old Testament? That means really: How did Jesus himself interpret his work? Eschatology is a sort of blessed word in theology: the doctrine of the last things. Did Jesus expect the end of the world? What is the meaning of the announcement of the coming of the Kingdom of God? C. H. Dodd and others have been arguing that the Kingdom is inaugurated in the person of Jesus and his followers, so that the date when the world would end didn't matter to Jesus. That's in reaction against the views of Albert Schweitzer.

What's the nature of the Church in the New Testament? What is its creed? Well, they look at the Gospels. That's quite a lively subject today. It's had pins stuck in it by the discovery of the Dead Sea Scrolls and the heretical Gospel of Thomas, but the really interesting thing is this: within the theological world it's realized that the Gospels don't set out to be historical documents – they spring out of preaching rather than newspaper reporting. A lot of theologians take the view that you can't get at much of the history behind them. The Virgin Birth, for example, is reckoned poetry, not prose. People have investigated the Christmas narratives and found them full of Hebrew expressions which indicate their early origin, but one is quite able to interpret them as meditations.

In the nineteenth century the Bible was a history book. The great scholarly thing was to get at the history behind the Bible. Now, because people are forced to think more deeply about the nature of religious faith, the whole historical element has been pushed out of the centre, and historical questions have ceased to hold the same fascination. This is where Bultmann comes in, saying that the Virgin Birth and the Resurrection are myth, and that the thing to do is to abandon them and concentrate on what the myth is intended to express. The open-mindedness among the best theologians is marked, with the Germans, as always, in the lead. I'm not pretending that Anglicans as a whole are prominent in all this, but *someone* must soak up the flood of theological books being published.

From the outside, unfortunately, the debate doesn't seem to be on this level. Before *Honest to God* altered the climate in 1963, the theology that made news seemed to concern private disputes – technical matters, consuming the energy of clever men. The question of 'intercommunion', when it was raised dramatically in the autumn of 1961, came into this category. The men who raised it were, most of them, concerned to show that a technical point about the nature of the priesthood didn't matter, or mattered less than many people said it did. But since at least half the clergymen in the Church think this particular technicality is one of the most important things in their lives, a tortuous debate ensued.

The matter was raised chiefly on account of church unity – the 'ecumenical movement' which began fifty years ago, concerned with bringing together the Christian Churches. As far as Anglicans are concerned, ecumenicism looks both ways in Christendom – to the Roman Catholics (who officially take no part in the movement, though talks have gone on for years) and to the Free Churches, with whom there has been visible progress: notably in the formation in 1947 of the 'Church of South India', which brought together Anglicans, who have bishops, and Methodists, Congregationalists, and Presbyterians, who don't. During the late 1950s many Anglicans began to feel that progress with the Free Churches had stopped, and a small group of theologians discussed some kind of public statement that would clear the air on one of the matters of sharpest disagreement: what it is that happens when an Anglican priest is ordained, and the bearing of this on intercommunion, the practice of sharing Communion services between Anglicans and nonconformists.

The Church of England is divided on what happens at ordination. One school, which includes all High churchmen, says that when a bishop lays hands on a man, something happens to his soul that would not happen if the hands belonged to anyone but a bishop who carries on the Apostolic succession; it is the more 'official' line, since legally the Church believes in the 'indelible' nature of ordination. Roman Catholics don't concede this supernatural power to Anglican bishops, and by no means all Anglicans claim it for their own Church. It was to hammer home this point – that a sizeable slice of Anglicans think that clergymen in churches without bishops are just as good as clergymen in episcopal churches, like the C. of E. – that the theologians began, in 1959, to discuss their project.

They were not a formal group, but they included some of the liveliest English theologians. What they finally drafted was an 'Open Letter' to the Archbishops of Canterbury and York, headed 'Intercommunion'. The practice of attending one another's Communion services has long been an important point of contact between Anglicans and nonconformists. Considerable licence is given to Anglican priests to offer Communion to nonconformists, but Anglicans are not supposed to receive it from clergy ordained by anyone not 'standing in the historical succession'. The open-letter theologians, who finally numbered thirty-two, not all of them professionals, denied that a Methodist or a Baptist or a Presbyterian minister was any different in kind from an Anglican, or that differing views of the ministry were a barrier to intercommunion.

Among the originators were a Professor of Divinity at Cambridge, Canon G. W. H. Lampe, who is a distinguished scholar; and Canon Max Warren, then general secretary of the Church Missionary Society, a man of homely appearance, unremarkable in small doses, but highly regarded both as thinker and man of action, and credited with turning down a number of bishoprics; he thinks theology is more vigorous in Britain than at any time since the sixteenth century, 'more prepared to approach the kind of world we are going into than ever before'. Warren has an impressive set of overseas contacts, and in 1959 he circulated some friends with a letter about intercommunion that he had received from an Anglican bishop outside England. This began two years of unfeverish activity – it was, says Warren, 'a wonderfully disorganized business' – before a letter was ready with its signatures. Nearly half the signatories were clergymen connected with Cambridge, and five of them were linked by a common interest in a radical kind of theology, mentioned later. These five were Dr Vidler of King's; Lampe; Hugh Montefiore, Dean of Gonville and Caius; H. E. Root, Dean of Emmanuel, and G. F. Woods, Dean of Downing. One of the Cambridge giants, Canon Charles Raven, formerly Regius Professor of Divinity and Master of Christ's College, signed. He was among seven 'liberal' signatories prominently connected with the Modern Churchmen's Union: W. R. Matthews, the Dean of St Paul's; J. S. Bezzant, Dean of St John's College, Cambridge; W. C. Frend, Fellow of Gonville and Caius; D. E. H. Whiteley, Fellow and Chaplain of Jesus College, Oxford; W. G. Fallows, principal of Ripon Hall, the theological college, which is at Oxford, and A. C. Bouquet, lecturer in theology

at Cambridge. Modern Churchmen had their heyday in the
1920s – doubting the Resurrection and Virgin Birth, trying to
liberalize Christianity but finding Christians weren't ready for
it. The movement as such has declined, probably because it
concentrated too much on doctrinal details, but there are
many distinguished liberal churchmen. In the 1920s there had
been talk, behind the scenes, of heresy trials, and nothing raises
the hackles of extreme Anglo-Catholics more than a suspicion
of liberalism. What made the Open Letter even more dis-
agreeable was the fact that a couple of Anglo-Catholics had
signed it: Professor Donald MacKinnon (a favourite subject
for anecdotes with theologians) and the principal of Ely
Theological College, once a calm Anglo-Catholic backwater.

After the letter was out – published on 1 November, All
Saints' Day – Warren remarked (to me) that it wouldn't be
judged by correspondence in newspapers, or by the attention
it drew from those outside the Church: 'They'll say, "A
plague on all your houses". It will work out in other ways. It
will get the attention of those we want to notice it' – that is,
the Free churchmen. But the correspondence and editorializ-
ing that went on for months was a sign of how much partisan
feeling surrounds the nature of a clergyman. 'Faulty theology,'
declared an Anglo-Catholic, 'dictated by generous but mis-
leading yearnings of the heart.' The *Church Times* said that a
'vast body of opinion within the Church, often inarticulate but
perfectly firm in faith', had not the 'slightest intention of
being stampeded into a blithe acceptance of non-episcopal
ministries as in all ways the indistinguishable equal of the
Church's own duly ordained ministry'. In public, most
bishops kept quiet – to avoid embarrassing them, none had
been asked to sign the letter. In private, one bishop said coldly
that 'receiving Holy Communion together, one gets a pleasant feeling of fellowship. But that is not the idea of Holy

Communion. I'm afraid that isolated acts of intercommunion could lead to a confederation of isolated Churches that occasionally come together, as they have in Wales – they have intercommunion between the Free Churches there, but they aren't any closer.' Dr E. L. Mascall, of Christ Church, Oxford, a leading Anglo-Catholic theologian, wrote to *The Times* quoting the former archbishop Dr Fisher, in turn quoting 'the highest legal authorities,' who had said that 'it was against the law of the land to admit to Communion in the Church of England any person who was neither confirmed nor ready and desirous to be confirmed, whether a member of that Church or not'. Others pointed out that only clergymen ordained by bishops could hold benefices in the Church, adding thankfully: 'That is the law of the land.' But if *they* are the same as *us*, wrote one parson – if a Methodist layman could, as he understood the letter allowed, fulfil a priestly ministry – then 'ordination is no more than a pompous farce'. Fifty-three non-theologians wrote a second open letter refuting the first.

On the Evangelical side, there was a rousing welcome for, as the *Church of England Newspaper* put it, the statement that our Lord is not tied to any particular form of ministry and that a non-episcopally ordained ministry may be real and efficacious within the Body of Christ's Church'. The need to be episcopally ordained before becoming an Anglican clergyman was described as 'an innovation in 1662 [i.e. the date of the Prayer Book] . . . purely a domestic regulation to restore some sort of order after the upheavals of the Commonwealth'. From this point of view, the stampede was in the other direction: clergymen were being 'stampeded into agreeing with [the Anglo-Catholic] position not from conviction but from fear'. The air thickened with charges and counter-charges, and at the height of the argument the *Church of England Newspaper*

scooped everyone with a 'poll on intercommunion'. Cards
went to all incumbents in England for them to indicate whether
they supported or opposed the Open Letter. Many clergymen
said they were disgusted at this brash attempt to answer a
question that never had been answered before, but 4,244
clergy, or an estimated forty per cent of incumbents, replied.
Of completed cards forty-three per cent (1,835 clergy) were
for the Open Letter and intercommunion, forty-eight per
cent (2,061) were against; another 348 didn't know or spoiled
the cards, with comments ranging from 'All popular polls
are dangerously fatuous' and 'I regret to say I'm not *quite* sure
which letter you mean. Sorry' to 'Some of the signatories
have no right to the word theologian. I have a degree in
theology'. The poll clobbered the confident Anglo-Catholic
objection that the thirty-two theologians were academics out
of touch with reality, far removed from the parish priests of
England. The debate goes on, and unity is a long way off.

Even when theological intricacies are set aside and the conversation reduced to simple terms, outsiders fail to be com-
municated to. Talking to a clergyman – not a professional
theologian, but an amateur one of some reputation – he said
that what the Church most needed was to allow the spirit of
God freer course. I asked what the phrase, 'the spirit of God',
meant. 'Exactly,' he said. 'It doesn't mean anything to you
because you're a twentieth-century man. You're interested in
a subjective kind of religion. If you can't make the assumptions on which the whole of the New Testament is based,
that one day justice will be done, then the phrase is only pious
jargon, disguising half-baked psychology. But if you find it
intolerable that dishonesty is got away with, that men fiddle
jobs – in the Church and out of it – then you *must* believe.'
I said one could find it pretty intolerable and still not believe.
'Then you're disguising in your soul a fundamental despair –

because in that case it's a mere accident at best that truth triumphs,' he said. 'What I am really asking is what your concern is worth, what you're prepared to stake upon it. It's an historical fact that Christ didn't ask for intellectual approval. He demanded people's worship. And if you don't want to worship something, then I say you're not a man – or you're a very self-centred man.'

Not all theologians are so arrogant as to expect phrases like 'the spirit of God' to mean something to outsiders. The idea of a communicable theology, which takes in matters that people discuss without being aware that they would count as theology, has been widely canvassed in recent years, but without much result until recently. Bultmann's demythologizing somehow went on in another world. The books of Paul Tillich and Dietrich Bonhoeffer were known to a minority of clergymen, but their ideas stayed bottled up in the minds of these few as far as the Church of England was concerned. In such conditions, liberals have tended to be voices in the wilderness. Canon Raven, who signed the Open Letter, is an example. Raven is in the rare category of scientist-theologian – a member of the Linnean Society, with a high reputation as a biologist, and one of the few theologians ever to have been a member of the Natural Science Faculty at Cambridge. Married several times, and now an old man, with a fine head and long jaw, and an air both of power and frailty, Raven has been a controversial figure, sometimes battling for pacifism and toleration and half a dozen other causes at once. When he talked to me in 1961 he sounded more unorthodox, perhaps, than he would have done eighteen months later.

In the twenties we had the emergent evolution of a philosophy that was trying to relate the traditional Christian cosmology to the whole creative process. Then there was the business of trying to establish unity by getting a new missionary spirit – instead of talking about the 'heathen in darkness', recognizing that Buddhists and Muslims are trying to find the truth about the human soul.

This coloured things till 1932 or 1933, when came the economic crash and political failure: when we discovered our attempts to avoid a second world war were too late. We had started from the conviction that another world war in this generation was unthinkable. We got our time-sequence wrong. We encountered the fascist movement, and we found the whole world falling to pieces again. It meant that the whole liberal Christian movement – whether on the social side or on the intellectual side, the doctrine – was swept away by a flood of neo-orthodoxy. Barth, ably supplemented by people like Niebuhr in the U.S., strongly influenced first the Church of Scotland and then the Church of England, to say that liberalism leaves God out of account: that you can't expect any progress in this world, you can only wait for the fulfilment of God's purpose.

It meant the icebox for my sort of folk, of whom there are quite a lot in the Church of England. Those of us in academic posts were all right, but it did mean that the sort of thing for which the best minds in the previous generation had stood was completely abandoned.

Raven is immensely respected but right outside the ortho-dox circles of Church authority. He isn't part of the ecclesi-astical Them. He observes, with resignation, that the fact that science and religion have drawn closer together is due to the scientists and not the Churches.

The tone and temper of science have changed astonishingly in the last fifteen years. In a very small section of scientific humanists, the feeling has become bitter – a phobia, a sort of hysterical bitterness about religion. But physicists and chemists – who used to be the most difficult – and biologists are taking a more friendly attitude. It's not that they have become convinced Christians, but they realize they can't stay within narrow frontiers. There's a feeling that the world is one, and that knowledge must be unified at whatever cost in pulling down barriers. This doesn't presuppose a religious solution, but it means recognizing that the influences that make man a religious

THE CHURCH OF ENGLAND

animal can't be ignored – that they arise from his power to stand apart
from his background and contemplate it. The maddening thing is that
this didn't happen twenty-five years ago, before the great blight – the
cold wind of bitterness and despair.

This is Raven's view of a theological revival:

If there's to be one, I think it will come about from the accommodation of three things. First, the feeling that we must have an interpretation of one universe, not two. Scientists agree that the universe is a
whole, but the theologians hang on to the idea of a 'Second Coming'.
It's appropriate enough to say that the heavens will be rent asunder.
But the universe has got another hundred million years of sustaining
life – and even if you eliminated the human race by an atomic bomb,
it would only be a question of another million years or so before it
reappeared. Most of the hymn books have nothing except this
mythology. And the theologians have used it literally – or they use it
in a sense in which any ordinary person realizes that unless it's meant
to be taken literally, it means nothing.

The second thing is a change in psychology. The criticism of
psychology has always been that it gives us no psychology of community – in spite of the fact that the world is controlled by composite
bodies with huge resources, that the evils from which we suffer,
whether they start with the Stock Market, the advertising market or
the war market, are evils that no one person starts. Psychologists have
never tried to do more than understand the individual. I think we shall
get a more expanded and intensified study of what integration means
– how we can weld together the elements in the individual so that we
can release the power that is at present wasted in conflict. The third
thing is how could we review the whole cultural-credal moral apparatus of the world's religions so as to make them effective in integrating
the world itself.

But Raven, in 1961, was not optimistic about the Church's
mood.

Ordinary people have not been encouraged to meddle in
theology; they are given glimpses of learned men at work on

matters of which they can know nothing, or they are encouraged to use theology in special ways that don't question the basic assumptions. An attempt to use theology as a kind of palliative is the much-talked-about experiment in 'clinical theology' which began a few years ago, and attracted a good deal of attention from clergymen who felt that here was a way to bring the divine science to bear on the common life of the parish. For years a few clergymen in Britain, compared with thousands in the United States, have experimented with psychotherapy as a means of helping worried or deranged parishioners. On a more modest level, the Church's Council for Social Work has organized courses to teach marriage preparation and counselling: how to listen to other people's troubles without laying down the law, or even using such loaded phrases as 'If I were you'. But the idea of elementary psychotherapy, backed by the Christian faith, being used daily by parish clergy who have attended a course of lectures, wasn't introduced until 1958. In that year a former medical missionary, Dr Frank Lake, who had returned from India and qualified as a psychiatrist, wrote to the Archbishop of York (then Dr Ramsey) and fourteen diocesan bishops in the Midlands and North, offering to run 'clergy seminars in pastoral psychiatry'. Lake later changed the name to 'clinical theology', which he defined as the pastoral care of 'persons suffering from spiritual and emotional distress, from psychoneurotic and psychotic illness, from personality disorders and the like'. His idea was, and is, to give clergymen some basic psychiatric knowledge, teach them how to listen to patient-parishioners in distress and identify, if possible, their clinical condition; and finally to present Christ and Christ's suffering to them as offering the ultimate consolation. In one of his book-length typescripts prepared for the clergy courses, Lake writes that 'The Cross of Jesus Christ is in itself our central resource, able to deal with those buried experiences of mental pain, experienced in infancy at the hands of adult humans, which are the stones of offence leading to the loss of good relationships and the substitution of fixed patterns of rage, envy, jealousy, hatred, pride, lust, and all the besetting sins'. Lake suggests to bishops that the clergyman in a diocese who looks after clinical theology should not be a 'psychological specialist', since the course is 'genuinely theology, and tends not always to appeal to those who have already ingrained opinions of a Jungian or Freudian kind'.

Clinical theology has the blessing of many bishops, and a centre was opened in Nottingham in 1963. (Inevitably there is no 'official' Church view, and the Council for Social Work in London carries on with its own counselling courses.) Lake, who looks unassuming but speaks and writes with great conviction, is not satisfied with any of the schools of analysis. He was one of the first doctors in Britain to use the drug known as lysergic acid, which produces hallucinations of childhood, and, it is said, very early infancy, even back to the moment of birth. According to Lake and others, patients injected with lysergic acid re-live the 'buried experiences of mental pain' that they underwent as babies; having done this, they are better able to understand and deal with their adult condition. Talking in the consulting room of his house, where a desk-lamp is weighted by the chamber of a revolver – presented by a former gun-carrying psychopath, who, after long treatment with lysergic acid, was cured, and confirmed in the Church of England – Lake described how, as a Christian, he had come to speculate on the nature of man as seen by the three schools of analysis. The Freudian model of man said people were out for pleasure; trouble arose when the super-ego ruled that they shouldn't have it. 'If this is true,' said Lake, 'it was true of Jesus. He wanted to get pleasure out of his skin surfaces, he wanted a good sex act – which is absurd. Adler says people are motivated by the drive for power – so Jesus was out for power, which again is absurd. The Jungian view is that I'm not concerned with the ordering of human affairs, but with a gnostic ideal – Christ, of all people, isn't this. When one looks at the three basic models, one finds, in Pascal's terms, the three lusts: for feeling, to dominate, and to escape through knowledge. In the Christian sense we couldn't admit these as satisfactory models. Query: what model do you use? Answer: Christ himself. If we want to look at what is normal, we must look at the unspoiled specimen.'

Lake says he isn't in love with his own system, and is quite content if the clergy accept only the counselling part. Clergymen, he suggests, are often unskilful in presenting the comforts of Christ to those in need of them: 'Those who train marriage guidance counsellors,' he writes in one set of notes, 'find that doctors and clergy are, of all categories of persons, those liable to be most useless . . . because they can only give advice and cannot listen.'* When a clinical-theology class is

---

* At one session with young clergy – nothing to do with Lake – held in a diocesan retreat house, a marriage guidance counsellor, a laywoman, gave an example of 'non-directive counselling'. A woman was pregnant by her husband, who wanted her to have an abortion. Distressed because she couldn't make up her mind, she visited the counsellor, who let her talk, and suggested she come back the following week. She returned happy, having decided to have the baby, and credited the counsellor with solving the problem: but she had really done it herself. The clergy discussed this easily until someone (not a clergyman) asked what would have happened if the girl had decided on an abortion. The counsellor said it would have been her duty to concur. 'This must be your attitude,' she said – 'respect for other people's integrity. I was once told by a vicar that I respected people too much. This is the point: do you really respect people enough?' In quick succession, one clergyman agreed with her, and three disagreed. The first of the three said: 'What the priest meant was that you could respect people so much you could cease to

practising interviews with parishioners, a 'senior and highly respected vicar' may be 'stilted, formal, uneasy, clueless, frivolous, and insensitive' (while a curate with no reputation may be 'pleasantly direct, unaffected, understanding, serious, and perceptive'). These classes – entitled 'clinical theology seminars' – are held in various centres, so that clergy, in groups of about twenty, attend twelve three-hour sessions a year. They are addressed alternately by Lake, one of his qualified assistants, and one of a panel of twenty or thirty trained clergy; there were twenty-six of these in the autumn of 1961 – seven of them from one theological college, Westcott House, which endorses its reputation for intellectual boldness. At the opening class for one group, held in York, the clergymen sat on rows of chairs in a smallish room, with bookcases and gas fire, to hear an address from one of the assistant psychiatrists. The literature, which caused some of the class to murmur and point out to one another how much there was, included a couple of thick typescripts and seven sheets of stout paper, eighteen inches by fourteen, each packed with panels of text joined by arrows and dotted lines, with such titles as 'Schizoid Personality Disorder' and 'Phobic Reactions'. One of the clergymen moved his finger slowly along the words in one of the two panels on the 'Phobic Reactions' sheet: '8. Fear of being afraid. Phobias related to the risk of the

---

love them.' The second: 'I'd have said, "I'm sorry, you have decided to do wrong. Change your mind. I'll pray for you".' The third: 'Surely you can't accept non-directive counselling as a Christian? The girl would have to face up to the lack of any moral right to take a life.' The counsellor shrugged her shoulders, and the conversation lapsed. An Anglican moral theologian in London said he agreed the girl should solve her own dilemma, but not simply as a matter for her own convenience: 'The priest shouldn't say, "Carry on", nor should he let loose the thunder of Sinai. He should try to get her to see it was wrong to have an abortion: but get her to see it herself.'

sudden emergence of Panic or Dread into consciousness; of
being STARTLED; of LIGHTNING; sudden flash; THUNDER;
of loud noises; THE ATOMIC BOMB; EXPLOSIONS; bursts;
PLANETARY COLLISION; of being in an ACCIDENT; The
END of the WORLD . . .' But the psychiatrist led them easily
into the subject: 'It may seem quite a mouthful . . . we hope to
go down into the depths and emerge again . . . there's no idea
that we should steal one another's profession: I hope we can
help one another.' He soon had the class relaxed: 'A neurotic
is someone who builds castles in the air, a psychotic is someone
who lives in one, a psychiatrist is the one who comes along and
collects the rent.' He suggested that the three main types of
reaction – hysterical, depressive, and schizoid – were laid down
in the first year of life. To the psychiatrist, the depressive might
say: I feel very low, especially in the morning, I can't sleep,
I've got no drive. To his doctor: I'm not enjoying my food,
I'm losing weight, I'm constipated, I get headaches. To the
vicar: Life's getting me down, I can't pray, I can't get to Communion, my thoughts wander. The psychiatrist might pre-
scribe electrical treatment in vain, the doctor pills. The vicar
might suggest more prayer or give him a job to do in the
community: 'and that would make the burden worse'. A lot
of people were ticking over; the clergyman, if he could spare
more time than many psychiatrists managed nowadays,
could 'let them ventilate their rage, or could cope with
hysterical behaviour so that the patient learns to trust and
wait'. Men in the ministry were often distressed by the woman
in the parish who was always seeking the vicar's advice:
'You're the only one who can help me, Vicar.' Several of the
clergymen nodded and said 'Yes'. 'Folk of this kind,' said the
psychiatrist, 'have an uncanny ability to penetrate to your
needs.' There was laughter. 'This is the person one shies
from. You look at your watch. When they say, "Nobody

understands me", they're quite right: nobody does. You mustn't look at your watch. You must make a definite appointment – say, six – and be adamant when the hour's up at seven.'

It was their first lecture, and the psychiatrist gave a general introduction. He talked about unconscious preferences for the different church services. The schizoid type was inclined to like the 8 a.m. Communion: 'Nobody bothers him at all. He has a little isolated session on his own. It's unlikely that anyone'll slap him on the back.' Depressives favoured eleven o'clock matins, when everything was orderly, including the sermon. Those with hysteric tendencies liked evensong – 'soft lights, catering for the sentimentalists'. The psychiatrist smiled and added: 'That's just banter. But it's a fact that some people aren't able to face some services.'

A clergyman cleared his throat and said: 'I always feel sceptical about the effects of outside experience. It isn't due so much to what happens to them as children but what they are when they arrive.'

'But what *are* they when they arrive?' asked the psychiatrist. 'Bear with it as we go along, will you?'

'What about the old groupings?' said a second clergyman. 'You're born a sanguine type, say.'

'I would challenge that,' said the psychiatrist.

'Oh, you would.'

'Yes.'

But the interruptions had broken the ice, and other clergy leaned forward with particular questions. A parishioner had a child of eight who was jealous of his sister, aged two. A parishioner suffered from claustrophobia in church. A woman wouldn't go to church on her own, only with her husband. The psychiatrist suggested brief answers, and was presently describing how a woman who had lost her faith wrote a

Kafka-like story involving an endless search in a tunnel. 'One must not speak,' said the psychiatrist, 'in terms of a God who is outside looking in, but in terms of a God who is in the tunnel with you. We can relate people to the lengths to which God went on the Cross. Their longing can only be met on the level of someone who – well, in technical terms, gives one status as a child of God. Does this seem to make some sort of sense?'

A clergyman said: 'Very much so.'

'Forgive me asking as a sort of prodder,' said another, 'But where is the point of communication? If we were to try to present to a girl such as this the fact of Christ – the fact of his love – would we be in danger of providing her with personal affection?'

'These are real hazards,' said the psychiatrist. 'Transference comes in . . . they may lean for a time, yes. You may have to bear with this.'

'So we needn't be alarmed if there's a great expression of personal affection? If someone should throw her arms round your neck?'

'No,' said the psychiatrist. 'I know of a clergyman who encountered a fifteen-year-old who was labelled an hysterical psychopath. Here be dragons, brother.'

The results in parishes are said to be promising. But much of this must be due to clergymen as more efficient counsellors rather than as 'clinical theologians'. It's an interesting experiment, but it seems a long way from the really important questions of theology.

*

These questions have come into the open in Britain in typical contemporary fashion. They are the questions that people who are not Christians, or only shallow Christians, or perhaps profoundly doubting Christians, have come to raise with themselves and their friends. If God is not an old man in the sky, then what is he? Is he a 'He' at all? What do words like 'Heaven' and 'Hell' mean? What do 'sin' and 'free will' mean in the light of psychiatry and analysis? Why was the revelation of Christ in that place, at that time, and what is one required to believe about the events of two thousand years ago? What has the massive, ingrown structure of the Church got to do with love in the Christian sense? What have the Thirty-nine Articles got to do with the lives that people lead, or ought to lead, or the intricacies of space and time that the astro-physicists are indicating? It is this kind of questioning, so easily and glibly dismissed by professional theologians as 'undergraduate' or 'uninformed,' which was made a public and more respectable activity by the Bishop of Woolwich's *Honest to God* – published as a paperback, preceded by a summary of the bishop's views in the *Observer*, followed by the usual inquiries, gossip-columns, and interviews. Like Walter Boulton with his book on marriage (Chapter 3), Woolwich was attacked not only for what he said, but for saying it to a large audience; the Church is full of people saying 'Sh-h-h!' A major-general wrote furiously to the *Church Times* about the 'junior bishop' who had written a 'cheap paperback', and you can see what he meant. If the bishop had been seventy-five years old and of a retiring disposition, instead of in his forties and well aware of the merits of publicity; if the book had cost two guineas instead of five shillings – it would have been somehow more palatable. But the bishop used direct, popular methods to spill the beans, and there are many people in the Church who will never forgive him for it.

The situation in the churches was summed up in the fifth volume of the 'Pelican History of the Church' – *The Church in an Age of Revolution*, by the Rev. Dr Alec Vidler, published in 1961. Many Christians, said Vidler, have assimilated 'the fruits of science and of humanism', yet the churches have 'not yet candidly acknowledged their duty to recast their teaching and their *mores* accordingly, or gone nearly far enough towards incarnating in the contemporary world the traditional faith which they represent. By the middle of the twentieth century, when Christian thinkers were by no means up to date with their homework, it was becoming clear that far reaching and largely new questions were being put to them by linguistic philosophers and Freudian psychologists.'

Vidler, who was later to be seen, against his protests, as a central figure in a 'Cambridge school of theology', is one of those slightly mysterious churchmen who is obscured by a cloud of small eccentricities. When he goes on television he insists on wearing a black shirt and white tie. Outside his rooms in King's College, where he's the Dean, a notice on the bare landing says: 'If a knock on this door evokes no answer, please enter and knock on the door in the far corner of the room.' Beyond the second door is a room crowded with books, arm-chairs, and little ornaments. Here Vidler – small beard, thick eyebrows, curly pipe – edits *Theology*, a journal that can be surprisingly readable, and sees many visitors. When I was there, at the end of 1961, he remarked, over tea and cakes, that he didn't regard the Open Letter on inter-communion as an important operation. 'If its effect was to concentrate everyone's attention on Church order,' he said, 'I'd regard it as deplorable. But the Open Letter, after all, was saying that those matters weren't all that important. Unity isn't the most important thing. In parts of Asia where the Christian Church is in quite a different situation, the need for unity is much more manifest. In this country the different churches are so deeply entrenched, they're not going to be shifted easily. One reason why people got so worked up about it is that they want to evade having to address their minds to the much more difficult questions.' And he went on to list them: linguistic philosophy – did the word 'God' mean anything? The relation between science and theology. 'The whole new perspective arising out of psychological insights.' Comparative religion. How the Bible was to be understood. 'Our view,' he said, 'is that there is a deplorable complacency in the Church about these very profound and grave matters, which they more or less close their eyes to.'

I had been advised to see Vidler by someone at the B.B.C., where there was also enthusiasm for another Cambridge clergyman, the Rev. H. A. Williams, the Dean of Trinity College. The B.B.C. has brought down fury on its head from conservative churchpeople because it has put radicals on the screen. Journalistically it scooped everyone, and was the first of the mass media to get hold of the fact that pressures inside the Church were beginning to distort its structure. I was told that Vidler was connected with these pressures, that he was editing an important collection of essays that would be published towards the end of 1962, and that Williams would be one of the contributors.

It was Williams who wrote to *The Times*, when the argument about the intercommunion letter was going on, to say that it was obvious that 'theological investigation has nothing more to offer on the Church's ministry. Distinguished scholars have long studied the New Testament and come to different conclusions'. He suggested that what might help was to consider the need of people to 'belong to what is felt to be exclusive. That this need is very deep in human nature is shown by the most important of all human relations, that of husband and wife, which is absolutely exclusive in its most vital aspects. It may well be the same need for exclusiveness which leads to the conviction that only certain people are eligible to receive or celebrate the Holy Communion, while others are not.' In a second letter a week later, Williams put his case broadly: the future for theology lay in 'the attempt to relate theological opinion, or if you prefer, Christian doctrine, to what is being discovered about the profound needs and complex workings of human personality. This method arouses fear in many Christians as the historical method did a hundred years ago. That is a sign of its vitality.'

Williams, formerly the chaplain at Westcott House, is a bachelor in early middle age. His especial interest is psychology, and he has been through the mill of analysis himself. He first reached a large audience with some interesting but orthodox radio talks at the end of 1959, and caused eyebrows to be raised in 1960 and 1961 with two Sunday-evening television broadcasts. In both he was interviewed by Ludovic Kennedy. The first, in April 1960, was about the Resurrection. Faith, said Williams, was not 'believing what you know isn't true and so on, it's that you have such confidence in this personal God that you can't believe that death – your death, my death – is the end'. But he also spoke about 'a kind of mythology'. People wrote to protest because Williams had described the Ressurrection as a vision: 'The force of his presence upon his disciples was so terrific that they did in fact project it into a vision of himself. . . . Yet I wouldn't like to say that in, let us say, the room where the disciples were sitting they saw the same physical particles which they had seen on the Cross.' But others wrote to thank him. In October 1961, Williams was interviewed about sin. He spoke of free will as something he believed existed, but severely circumscribed by 'compulsions within us of which we are unaware'. Sin he defined as 'treating another person not as a person but as a means to give me gratification or power or pleasure or anything'. He mentioned in passing that although fornication would generally be a sin ('I think probably that in fornicating they are exploiting themselves and each other') it didn't necessarily follow: if there was no exploitation there was no sin. This piece of moral theology was more than the *Church Times* and some of its readers could stand, and there was angry correspondence. Again people wrote to thank him – more than half the ninety who sent letters. Williams talked of more than fornication. From a Christian point of view, he suggested, you could believe in God without knowing that you did: 'If God is infinite, it's absurd to say that you can only believe in him if you use the trade name for him. . . . Belief is concerned with a superficial level of our personality, or consciousness. Below that is something much more vital, our subconscious, and we may serve God with our subconscious and deny him with our conscious mind. And, mind you, many good Christians do the opposite: serve him with their conscious mind, deny him with their subconscious.'

Talking to me at his college in 1961, Williams gave this example of psychology applied to belief – in this case the doctrine of the Trinity:

Why does the doctrine of the Holy Trinity have such a hold on Christendom? There's no dispute about this. The Church may be divided but it's not divided on this. Now, it's a terribly abstruse doctrine. No doubt it arose from historical reasons. People believed in God, and then they thought Jesus Christ was God, and they were conscious of a power indwelling which they called the Holy Spirit, which they believed was also God. But in its working out it's immensely complicated, and in fact it can't be stated – not even in the so-called Athanasian Creed. So I've asked myself: what is there behind it? And it seems to me this, that the two fundamental threats that we have to face as human beings are, first, the threat of complete isolation, and second, the threat of complete absorption – being drawn into a society or being dominated by someone else. If either of these threats is carried to its ultimate extent, it means destruction.

The doctrine of the Trinity says that although God is vast, there are three eternally distinct persons. Now, theologically God is also considered as the ground of being – he's not an object up there, he's the ground of all being. This is orthodox, everyone would agree with that* – sorry, this sounds like a supervision, you must forgive me, it's just my idiom. The doctrine of the Trinity seems to me to assert that in that very ground of our being in God, the threat of absorption and the threat of isolation are eternally met and eternally overcome: the threat of absorption because the three persons remain eternally distinct; the threat of isolation because of the assertion that it is nevertheless one God.

The collection of essays edited by Vidler was published in September 1962 as *Soundings*. Among the contributors were a number who had signed the Intercommunion letter: Root, Woods, Montefiore, Lampe, and of course Vidler himself. In title and general tone the collection had a tentative air. Vidler wrote sympathetically about the idea of 'religionless Christianity' put forward by Dietrich Bonhoeffer, the German theologian who was killed by the Nazis. Root wrote about 'the disengagement of theology from imagination ... from the deepest sources of intellectual and artistic creativity.' And H. A. Williams pursued his theme: the need to include Freud in theology. He made his accustomed suggestion that there was an 'enormous amount of double-think' about sexual ethics; because this touched people on the raw, there was a particular venom about conservative reviews and comments on his essays.

* The idea of God as 'the ground of all being' may have seemed orthodox to Williams, but it is the kind of idea that caused dismay when the Bishop of Woolwich wrote about it. Everyone *wouldn't* agree with it.

A few months after *Soundings* came out, word got around that the Bishop of Woolwich, Dr John A. Robinson, would soon produce another book that would cause a stir. Robinson, however, wasn't thought to be theologically radical, and for this reason had not been invited to contribute to *Soundings*; he was an extremely newsworthy suffragan bishop, willing to defend a principle in public, but radical only in a socio-political sense. He was a modern-type bishop, of the kind that many people find displeasing. Glyn Simon remarks in *Bishops* (quoted in Chapter 4) that the public largely approved of Dr Ramsey's appointment as Archbishop of Canterbury because of his venerable appearance, and largely disapproved of the way Robinson gave evidence in favour of publishing D. H. Lawrence's novel, *Lady Chatterley's Lover*, 'on the ground that this was not the sort of book a bishop should have supported'.

Dr Robinson is a slightly nervous-looking, round-faced man with brushed-down black hair, who lives with his family in a comfortable suburban house in Blackheath and is a long way from the traditional idea of a prelate. With a First in Theology and a Cambridge Ph.D., he had a successful spell as dean of a Cambridge college, and went to Woolwich in 1959. He came to the notice of the public in October 1960, as one of the witnesses for Penguin Books Ltd, when they were charged with publishing an 'obscene article' – *Lady Chatterley's Lover*. Robinson said he thought that Lawrence was trying to portray 'the sex relation' as 'in a real sense something sacred, as in a real sense an act of holy communion'. The fact that he had one son and three daughters was elicited; he was told rudely, as all painstaking witnesses are liable to be told, that 'you're not here to make speeches'; and he gave the newspapers a powerful headline. Asked by counsel for the defence, Gerald Gardiner: 'Is this a book which in your view

Christians ought to read?' the bishop answered: 'Yes, I think it is.' 'A Book All Christians Should Read' was the result. Robinson was referred to in headlines as 'The Chatterley Bishop', until *Honest to God* proved a better label. 'Chatterley Bishop Hits Trouble in Back Street' announced the *Daily Mail* in 1961, when he had a car crash in Westminster (earlier, Robinson had advertised in the personal column of *The Times*: 'Bishop in urgent temporary need of car'). He had a heavy mail after the Chatterley case, much of it critical, and was censured in public by the Archbishop of Canterbury, Dr Fisher, who said Robinson was 'mistaken to think that he could take part in this trial without being a stumbling block and a cause of offence to many ordinary Christians'. But Robinson has continued to offend where he finds it necessary.

He once preached against capital punishment in Canterbury Cathedral, taking a text from Genesis: 'And the Lord put a mark on Cain lest any who come upon him should kill him.' It was an outspoken sermon. 'Make no mistake,' said the bishop, 'capital punishment is on the way out in every civilized country. There will be attempts to put the clock back, as in the motions at the Conservative Party conference this week actually to extend the death penalty and other forms of legalized violence – and I hope that every Conservative who is a Christian will resist any such move. Yes, hanging will go . . . the only issue is whether the Church will be in the van of reform, or as so often in the past be found dragging its feet.' As the 'final Christian objection' he gave the Christian faith, which 'says there is no man, no social situation, which is unredeemable'. He ended by describing how, a couple of years before, he 'stood at the Communion table and began at 8 a.m. on Ascension morning to celebrate the lifting up of all our manhood in Christ. But throughout the service I could not get out of my mind the fact that at 8 a.m. that same

Thursday morning another young man was being hung till he died from the gallows of one of our gaols. At that moment the obscenity of this contrast – between what I was doing as a Christian and what I was doing as a British citizen – burned itself in upon me in a resolve not to rest till this blot was removed from our national life.'

The sermon was widely reported – Robinson took the precaution of advising the Press, and had copies of the sermon, covering three and a quarter sides of closely typed foolscap, mimeographed. Then came the letters; a week after the sermon they were piled on chairs and the floor in his study, a tide of sour disagreement, often incoherent with fury or nasty with the peculiar nastiness of the illiterate letter-writer. 'Well, you bloody fool,' one began. A woman from Hampstead wrote briefly to say that 'There *are* evil men who are unredeemable'. 'This is all rot,' said an anonymous writer. 'Just HANG 'em. I say dam the church and such talk.' 'Rev. Sir,' said a lettercard from Worthing, 'You are again playing with fire re hanging. Young Terry deserved what he got and *you helped to make him* what he was. His morals were so loose he spent his life depraving the teenage girls whenever he met them. Your mind and his were very similar. "The Lady Chatterley Idea" in fact.' Many, perhaps the majority, of the letters were from avowed Christians. 'If you have a daughter,' wrote one man, 'and she was raped and strangled by one of the filthy things, you would think very differently. My father, uncle, brother, and brother-in-law were all priests in the Church of England.' The bishop's attention was drawn to useful texts, generally in the Old Testament, by people who knew their Bibles; verses like 'The murderer shall surely be put to death' were flung at his head from Genesis, Deuteronomy, and Numbers. 'There is a dangerous tendency in the Church these days,' wrote a churchman, 'to chip away the granite glory of the moral law and put in its place a sloppy milk-pudding sort of sentiment that has no scriptural authority. So desperately anxious are some of the clergy to keep up with the moderns that religion is misrepresented and Christ dishonoured.'

Robinson remained at a distance from many churchmen. Not only the social conscience but the intellectual enthusiasm of a bishop like this can drive him on to a point where many laymen lose sight of him. Before 1963 he was known, theologically, as a New Testament scholar and an advocate of the 'liturgical movement' – a movement which is difficult to describe in secular terms, yet is often spoken of as the most significant thing in the life of the Church (though this is a phrase which is used indiscriminately, a sort of ecclesiastical shrapnel). The liturgical movement seeks to involve congregations more thoroughly in church services, mainly by concentrating on Communion – or the Eucharist, as High churchmen call it. The altar is at the head of the nave, where it's closer to the congregation; people take a greater part in services, perhaps reading lessons from the pew where they happen to be sitting; the services as laid down in the Prayer Book are experimented with; sometimes one family a week bakes a loaf and brings it to be consecrated and used for Communion; most noticeable to the outsider, the traditional English pattern of early Communion followed by matins at 11 a.m. is replaced by a main service at about 9.30, often called the 'parish Communion' or 'family Communion', where children are welcomed along with their parents, and where, in some cases, the service is followed by a 'parish breakfast' in the church hall. In its fiercer and more technical aspects, the liturgical movement tends to be 'High' rather than 'Low,' since in the Communion it treats Christ's sacrifice not as a reminder to men (the 'Low' interpretation) but rather as a reminder to God. An anti-movement writer in *Church and People*, an

Evangelical magazine, explained it by saying that the movement 'puts forward the novel idea that the whole congregation unite together with Jesus Christ in presenting to the Father and pleading before Him our Lord's sacrifice together with their own'. Extremists on the Evangelical wing can be very sharp about it, deploring the way 'undiscerning Evangelicals' are 'taken in' by the liturgical movement, which, say these extremists, implies that Christ's death wasn't enough, and that people must themselves contribute something towards salvation.

Talking to me in his study at the end of 1961, Robinson said that the Communion was 'the pattern, the germ of all society renewed in Christ, the classless community, if you like. The true society renewed around the altar is the sort of pattern which the Church ought to show in all its relationships.'

He went to be Dean of Clare College without giving liturgy much thought, but found himself asking: 'How does one be the Church in a college?' He decided that 'the instrument of evangelism in our day, in any way that's going to be relevant, is not the high-powered mission of the Billy Graham type, or the individual buttonholing you and asking, "Are you saved?" – but the witness of the Christian fellowship itself, the Christian community saying, "Here is the Gospel in action". . . . This is to direct people's eyes to what has always been the centre and focus of everything – Holy Communion – and to invite men to look at the quality of their own lives. This really brought me up with a bang.'

But Robinson said he realized with dismay that anyone looking at the 8 a.m. Communion service of the Anglican tradition might suppose that this embodied his understanding of the Gospel. Such a service would strike people as 'individualistic, pietistic, remote from the world we're supposed to be serving'. A new kind of service was needed. One way of relating the Church to the 'common life in the college' was to have 'a loaf that was baked in the college kitchen and a bottle of wine from the college cellar'. Such details, he had no doubt, 'did transform the whole feel of things', and 'made people realize the implications of what they're doing'.

Early in 1962, Robinson was ill for three months with a slipped disc. It was now time for something else to bring him up with a bang. Unable to do his ordinary work, he wrote a book in which he set down his thoughts about theology. Like other intellectuals in the Church, he had read books by American and German theologians which contained ideas far more radical than any that were abroad in Britain; but unlike anyone else, he wrote his conclusions into a book for the mass market.

Robinson's book is easiest to follow where he's being negative; just after it was published, a bishop remarked in private that he understood the first part well enough, but that the positive conclusions escaped him. They escaped, and still do escape, a lot of people. From Bultmann, Robinson took the idea that much of the New Testament is myth, which must be translated into contemporary terms. From Bonhoeffer came the idea that Christianity should be freed, in Robinson's phrase, 'from any necessary dependence upon "the religious premise"'. And from Paul Tillich, the German-born theologian in America, came the metaphysical assertion that 'God' means 'the depth of life': if the word 'God' is meaningless, says Tillich, 'translate it, and speak of the depths of your life, of the source of your being, of your ultimate concern, of what you take seriously without any reservation'.

In Robinson's hands all this became an assertion that only a revolution in Christian thinking could save Christianity from being abandoned. To speak of God was to speak of 'ultimate reality'. God was not a Being. Christianity was full of myths – Christmas and the Virgin Birth might be valuable stories, but essentially they must be seen as myths. And 'the whole scheme of a supernatural Being coming down from heaven to "save" mankind from sin, in the way that a man might put his finger into a glass of water to rescue a struggling insect, is frankly incredible to man "come of age", who no longer believes in such a *deus ex machina*'.

When it comes to positive statements about Christianity, Robinson might seem to depend on parts of the very structure that he has been demolishing. To the outsider, Robinson's faith is as incomprehensible as the faith of an orthodox Christian. Christ, he said in the *Observer* article that summarized his book, is 'a window through the surface of things into the very ground of our being'. The ultimate Christian conviction was that 'at the heart of things' there was 'nothing in death or life . . . that can separate us from the love of God in Christ Jesus our Lord'.*

But if there is no ready-made theology to be seized by the hopeful agnostic, this was hardly Robinson's purpose. A dialogue has begun between Christians and non-Christians at a comparatively popular level. Some ecclesiastical reviewers of *Honest to God* patronized Robinson, trying to draw the sting from his book by saying that it was all very pleasant and commendable, but not really new. Christians, it became fashionable to say, had always known that God wasn't up in the air. If Dr Robinson wanted to use a new set of images involving 'depth', that was fine – but why the fuss? These commentators viewed Robinson's book from within the framework of traditional Christianity. But this was the very framework that so many outside the Church were, and are,

* Romans viii, 38. New English Bible.

unwilling to accept. *Honest to God* was the first indication, for many people, that there are some in the Church who are also unwilling to accept it.

The row was enormous; the bewilderment painful; the tempers frayed. The fact that the book was by a bishop gave the affair a peculiar fascination for those who were shocked by it. 'It is not every day,' wrote the *Church Times*, 'that a bishop goes on public record as apparently denying almost every fundamental doctrine of the Church in which he holds office.' Some future anthologist of invective could find rich pickings in the correspondence columns of Church newspapers in 1963. Other things happened – supplementing one another in the curious way of 'movements', denied by many of those involved to be connected with one another, yet all forming part of an apparent whole. *Objections to Christian Belief,* a series of open lectures given at Cambridge, was published, with Vidler and Williams among the contributors. Unorthodox sounds came from the diocese of Southwark – a public protest against the Thirty-nine Articles, a series of sermons on sexual ethics.

Sex, in fact, was the front on which much of the interest became concentrated: it was bad enough to upset people's ideas of God, but absolutely unforgivable to upset their ideas of sex. The Bishop of Woolwich, who devoted a chapter of his book to 'The New Morality', found himself, like H. A. Williams, the subject of bitter attacks for suggesting that divorce and sex before marriage weren't sinful in themselves. He was called soft and dangerous for saying that 'the only intrinsic evil is lack of love', and presently the Church Press was ablaze with letters suggesting that the Profumo affair – which happened to come into the news, with its tarts and liaisons, forcing the War Minister to resign – was somehow connected with the wicked liberalism of this 'new morality'.

One letter from a leading Anglican layman made the extraordinary suggestion that 'an influential section of the teaching clergy have by the spoken and written word actually undermined the will of the community to resist evil'. 'Mr Profumo,' he wrote, 'can hardly be blamed if it should be found that he has taken the Bishop's [of Woolwich] advice.'

The letters about the 'new morality' might also be worth anthologizing one day. They would matter less if they weren't a sign of the way the Church of England reacts when faced with new ideas. It's an alarming reaction; religious conservatives never realize that the prime objects of attack – Robinson, Vidler, Stockwood, Rhymes, and the rest – are the men whose voices mean something outside the Church, in the secular world that has all but despaired of the mumbo-jumbo that goes on within.

This is H. A. Williams on sin and love – a long way from home for many Christians, and others:

When I see someone who has sinned, what I think is simply: you haven't been loved. I cannot conceive of generous, self-giving love not being responded to. It's all very well saying people are told about it and they don't respond. Of course they don't. The very terms in which it's delivered are so shop-soiled. If my experience of love has been of a very possessive kind, it's all very well to say, 'God loves you'. I may know this intellectually, but there are large areas of my being not subject to the control of my critical reason. Hence my rejection – which is, paradoxically, an assertion of real love. People's rejection of unlove when it comes to them in religious disguises seems to me one of the best witnesses to God who *is* love that there can be. . . .

When a man is a gangster, society has got to protect itself – that's a different question altogether. I'm talking about ultimately. And it seems to me that he wouldn't be a gangster unless he were complaining about a state of affairs which is absolutely wrong. This is his reaction to not being loved, not being accepted. And inasmuch as he has not found love and acceptance, his protest against this is right.

Whether Williams and the others are right or wrong, about love, sin, sex, God, and everything else, theirs is the kind of talk that has a resonance in the world as it is. Of all the varieties of shouts and whispers within the Church of England, this is the kind that carries outside.

APPENDIX

This list of questions (answers in italics) was sent to 120 clergymen, thirty of whom replied:

(1) An Anglican layman has written to me: 'In the long run, the poverty which . . . makes ordination a much severer challenge to a young man than it used to be will be seen to have had a very healthy effect. The disappearance, in the parishes if not in Westminster Abbey, of any social snob value in churchgoing, has also done good.' Would you agree with these statements? (*19 agreed, 9 disagreed, 2 were non-committal.*)

(2) Another layman says that parsons should no longer regard themselves as 'masters in their houses', but as members of the community. Would you agree? (*23 agreed, 4 disagreed, 3 n.c.*)

(3) Would you agree with these statements by an Anglican writer,* and have you any comments?

(a) 'The Diocesan Conference . . . is both too large and too brief for any effective consultation. Its real purpose is to provide an audience for the bishop and speakers invited by him, and to be a rubber stamp.' (*17 agreed, 10 disagreed, 3 n.c.*)

(b) 'The C. of E. is no longer "the Conservative Party at prayer" if one judges it by the composition of its congregations or by the nature of its leaders' teaching. It is a pity that its legislature does not reflect this social revolution.' (*13 agreed, 5 disagreed, 12 n.c.*)

(c) 'It would probably be sensible to call [the rural dean] a "chairman" and his area a "district"; there are at present too many fancy names in the Anglican vocabulary.' (*3 agreed, 24 disagreed, 3 n.c.*)

* Not identified. It was the Rev. David Edwards, in *Not Angels but Anglicans.*

(d) 'The whole ethos of the ordained [Anglican] ministry has become bourgeois.' (*10 agreed, 9 disagreed, 11 had no views or said they didn't know what the question meant.*)

(e) 'It is an indisputable fact that most parish churches in England have no strategy whatever.' (*10 agreed, 12 disagreed, 8 n.c.*)

(4) Is there a case for a Central Appointments Board? (*Yes, 15. No, 9. No view, 6.*) Would you say that patronage vested in party trusts is abused to any significant degree? (*Yes, 1. No, 14. n.c., 15.*) Is any other kind of contemporary Anglican patronage abused? (*Yes, nil. No, 14. n.c., 16. No one thought much of this question.*)

(5) Would you agree that it is in the urban, not the rural, areas that reputations are made in the Church, and if so does it bother you? (*17 agreed, 3 disagreed. 6 were explicitly concerned, 12 were explicitly unworried.*)

(6) Would you say you have a social standing in your parish? (*Yes, 21. No, 4. n.c., 5.*) Do you play a part in civic life? (*Yes, 17. No, 4. n.c., 9.*) Have you ever intervened in, or commented from the pulpit on, any local secular dispute or controversy? (*Yes, 8. No, 13. n.c., 9.*)

(7) Why did you enter the ministry? Was it an easy decision to make? (*Yes, 9. No, 11. n.c., 10. 'Family opposition' was frequently blamed for difficulties.*) Were you brought up against a clerical background? (*Yes, 6. No, 21. No answer, 3.*)

(8) Do you consider your training at theological college was adequate preparation for work in a parish? (*Yes, 16. No, 9. No answer, 5.*)

(9) How closely do you adhere to the Prayer Book? (*Answers too varied to be tabulated.*) Do you consider liturgical experiment is important? (*Unqualified Yes, 13. Qualified Yes, 11. No, 4. n.c., 2.*)

(10) What do you think of Christian Stewardship and Planned Giving? (*13 gave unqualified approval. 11 gave qualified approval. 3 were against. 3 n.c.*)

(11) Have you any views on the advisability or otherwise of unilateral nuclear disarmament by Britain? (*3 favoured unilateral disarmament by Britain. 2 favoured multilateral disarmament. 19 were opposed to nuclear disarmament at the moment. 6 n.c.*)

(12) A woman writes to me to complain bitterly that no Anglican clergymen would marry her daughter to a man who had been

divorced (not for adultery). To her, 'the Church has whored my daughter and bastardized my grandson'. I know that an Act of Convocation forbids remarriage in church, but does it trouble you that in matters such as this, church folk may turn away from what they regard as excessive strictness by the standards of the rest of Christianity? (*11 were troubled, 18 were not, 1 n.c. Among the comments were 'prejudiced ignorance', 'nonsense', 'rubbish', and 'hysterical'.*)

(13) Are the members of your congregations drawn from more or less the same social/financial class; could you describe a typical congregation?

(14) What is your view on disestablishment? (*9 for, 17 against, 4 n.c.*)

*

These books are referred to:

Chapter 1
Honest to God, The Bishop of Woolwich (S.C.M.).
What's Wrong with the Church? Nick Earle (Penguin Special).
Safe Lodging, Merfyn Turner (Hutchinson).
The Uses of Literacy, Richard Hoggart (Pelican).
Britain Revisited, Tom Harrisson (Gollancz).
English Life and Leisure, Seebohm Rowntree and G. R. Lavers (Longman).
The Tiger in the Smoke, Margery Allingham (Chatto & Windus).
The Humbler Creation, Pamela Hansford Johnson (Macmillan).
Christianity and History, Herbert Butterfield (Bell).
Facts and Figures about the Church of England (Church Information Office).
Not Angels but Anglicans, David Edwards (S.C.M. Press).
Soundings (Cambridge).

Chapter 2
Anglicanism, Stephen Neill (Pelican).
William Temple, Archbishop of Canterbury. His Life and Letters, F. A. Iremonger (Oxford).

APPENDIX

Chapter 3
Marriage, Walter Boulton (the Mothers' Union).

Chapter 4
Bishops, edited by Glyn Simon (Faith Press).
God and the Rich Society. A Study of Christians in a World of Abundance,
   D. L. Munby (Oxford).

Chapter 5
The Country Parish Today and Tomorrow, Frank West (S.P.C.K.).
The South Ormsby Experiment, A. C. Smith (S.P.C.K.).
   The remark by Dr Barry, Bishop of Southwell (p. 119), is taken
from his book *Vocation and Ministry* (Nisbet).

Chapter 7
Christianity and the Social Order, William Temple (Pelican).
Church and People in an Industrial City, E. R. Wickham (Lutterworth).

Chapter 10
Your Suffering, Maurice Wood (Hodder & Stoughton).

Chapter 11
The Church in an Age of Revolution, Alec R. Vidler (Pelican).
Objections to Christian Belief, A. R. Vidler and others (Constable).

★

   Although not directly quoted, I have found *The Church of England.
Its Members and Its Business* (Oxford), by the Archdeacon of Hastings,
Guy Mayfield, invaluable.

*Some other books published by
Penguins are described on the
following pages*

PENGUIN NO. 2000

THE NEW ENGLISH BIBLE
THE NEW TESTAMENT

This New Testament in current English is the first part of The New English Bible to be published. The New English Bible is a translation of the whole Bible undertaken by the principal Christian bodies, other than the Roman Catholic, of the British Isles.

The New English Bible is a completely new translation from the Greek and Hebrew texts. It draws on the best available biblical scholarship and tries to present the true meaning of the text in language which is as clear and natural to the modern reader as the subject matter allows. It aims, in short, at accuracy and clarity without affectation, ancient or modern. It expresses no personal or doctrinal leaning. It is offered to all who care to read it whether or not they know other versions.

Work began on The New English Bible in 1947; the New Testament was published in 1960. It became a best-seller at once and in three years nearly five million copies were distributed throughout the world. This Penguin edition, published by arrangement with the University Presses of Oxford and Cambridge, represents a further step in accomplishing the wish of the sponsoring bodies that it should be readily accessible to the widest possible audience.

WHAT'S WRONG WITH HOSPITALS?

Gerda L. Cohen

It is generally recognized that our hospitals offer a fine medical service. But patients are human beings, as well as 'cases'. Does consideration for the individual in hospitals match the medical treatment?

Gerda Cohen set out to find the answer to this question. She toured the country, talking to administrators, doctors, matrons, nurses, and patients in both medical hospitals and mental institutions. Her book is a highly personal account of what she discovered. In addition to the many impressive advances she noted, there were many things that shocked her. She reveals a world of hierarchies, humiliations, rules, and condescension: but these are increasingly mitigated by a new recognition that patients are human, that they pay the piper, and ought more often to be allowed to call the tune.

Much has been achieved in the last ten years by individuals and on the advice of the Ministry of Health. But only widespread knowledge and insistence on change can produce the revolution we are entitled to expect in the 1960s.

THIS ISLAND NOW

G. M. Carstairs

The significance of the 1962 Reith Lectures – 'the most important series of lay sermons in our culture', as Cyril Connolly has described them – was that they allowed the State of the Nation to be interpreted in psychological, rather than economic, political, or moral, terms.

We may profess to know that 'the proper study of mankind is man': but we tend to forget it. It required an authority with the standing (both in the social and the psychiatric field) of G. M. Carstairs, the Edinburgh Professor of Psychological Medicine, to make a deep survey of Britain today from an entirely human stand-point. His observations on the changing pattern of child rearing, of adolescent problems, of the role of women, and of our national character are delivered in these lectures with a humility which is frequently more persuasive than the scepticism of exact scientists.

'All who missed them should get them at once, for they tell us persuasively, but not dogmatically, what has been happening to ourselves and our community and also relate the changes to each other' – Cyril Connolly in the *Sunday Times*

ANOTHER PENGUIN BY PAUL FERRIS

THE CITY

In a style reminiscent of John Gunther's *Inside Europe*, Paul Ferris closely scrutinizes the City of London, which, in a very real sense, is still the master of most and the servant of few. Ferris describes just how this mastership is exercised and interviews some of the patrician few who exercise it.

Trained as a journalist to ask questions, Ferris probes into a world where even the terms are obscure. How many people, for instance, know what contango is, or what it means to be caught short in a bull market, or could explain the difference between a lead and a lag? In terms which are intelligible the author explains the functions of such city men as the stock-jobber, the bill-broker, the underwriter, and the powerful banker, and comments on the efficiency of what – they pride themselves – is the gentleman's way of doing things. He also examines the extent to which the merchant-banker has been forced to loosen his legendary control over world events. As for the Bank of England itself, he shows how, despite its archaic traditions and inordinate love of mystery, it still calls the tune wherever sterling is king. The chapters on the Harrods take-over bid, the Indonesian crisis at Lloyds, and the London gold-market are as exciting as thrillers yet at the same time are thorough and informative.

For a complete list of books available please write to Penguin Books whose address can be found on the back of the title page